D0915898

WITNESS TO EVIL

WITNESS TO EVIL

by
George Bishop

**Illustrated
by Bill Lignante**

NASH PUBLISHING
Los Angeles

COPYRIGHT © 1971 BY GEORGE BISHOP
ILLUSTRATIONS COPYRIGHT © 1970 BY BILL LIGNANTE

ALL RIGHTS RESERVED. NO PART OF THIS BOOK
MAY BE REPRODUCED IN ANY FORM OR BY ANY MEANS
WITHOUT PERMISSION IN WRITING FROM THE PUBLISHER.

LIBRARY OF CONGRESS CATALOG CARD NUMBER: 72-127477
STANDARD BOOK NUMBER: 8402-1155-4

PUBLISHED SIMULTANEOUSLY IN THE UNITED STATES AND
CANADA BY NASH PUBLISHING, 9255 SUNSET BOULEVARD,
LOS ANGELES, CALIFORNIA 90069.

PRINTED IN THE UNITED STATES OF AMERICA

FIRST PRINTING

FOR PATSY

CONTENTS

I   Pretrial — Day One   1

II   Pretrial — Day Two   12

III   Pretrial — Day Three   30

IV   The Trial   39

V   Day One   49

VI   Day Five   60

VII   Day Thirty-five   73

VIII   Day Thirty-eight   91

IX   Day Forty-one   117

X   Day Forty-two   132

XI   Day Forty-three   152

XII   Day Forty-four   169

XIII   A Fashion Note   190

XIV   Day Forty-five   201

XV   Day Forty-eight   212

XVI | Day Forty-nine   235

XVII | Day Fifty   253

XVIII | Day Fifty-six   270

XIX | Day Fifty-seven   286

XX | Day Sixty-three   300

XXI | Day Sixty-five   311

XXII | Day Seventy-nine   322

XXIII | Day Ninety-nine   334

XXIV | Day One hundred and twelve   345

XXV | Day One hundred and twenty   357

XXVI | Day One hundred and twenty-eight   364

XXVII | Day One hundred and fifty-eight   381

XXVIII | Day One hundred and sixty-nine   390

XXIX | Day One hundred and ninety   395

XXX | Day Two hundred and eleven   408

XXXI | A Summation   417

XXXII | Index   427

A REFLECTION

People afford me pleasure every day of my professional life. Especially young people.

It is very easy, as I know only too well, when talking with thousands of well-adjusted, ambitious, *practicing* Americans, to forget how easily outside influences can upset that happy balance. What is even more difficult for the reader and myself to comprehend is that this abrupt "turning off" from the values that most of us hold to be basic to our way of life can occur under our very noses, to those who are closest to us physically and emotionally.

Something shocking, truly shocking, must happen to bring the terrible immediacy of the problem home to us.

The events described in this book convey to me a sense of shock similar to the private grief I experienced when my daughter died after being exposed to drugs.

Society, as we understand it, has witnessed the aftermath of what one of the trial attorneys characterized as "the first of the acid murders." The chilling implications of both the crimes and responsible citizens' reactions to them have motivated the publication of this volume.

The "evil" described in the following pages is twofold: the unspeakable physical acts connected with the crimes, and, of much greater importance, the states of mind that gave rise to those acts. Expose the poison that made it possible for one man to turn his followers, young men and girls, into seemingly unrepentant killers and we go a long way toward making the *first* of the LSD murders the *last* as well.

There is no simple solution, no magical panacea that will halt this frightening acceptance of perverted moral values. It is too easy, too much of a "cop-out," for us to bow our heads in self-condemnation and to treat the problem as a temporary aberration that will be solved by the normal social regenerative process.

We must confront the drug problem in its most heinous forms, then if necessary, act to strengthen our laws to prevent the recurrence of the shameful deeds recorded within these pages.

But more stringent laws are meaningless without the supportive will of the people. Here is an opportunity to show that our system works, a chance for all concerned citizens to use the tools already available to us — existing statutes and provisions for rehabilitation — to combat the insidious growth of illegal drug usage among our young.

Every individual in every community, no matter of what age or calling, must be made aware that this problem will, sooner or later, *affect him or her personally* either through tragic contact with inflicted relatives or friends or through a spreading lawlessness that the promiscuous use of illegal drugs promotes.

What follows is not always pleasant reading. It may be a "bad trip" to some who would ignore the emotional depravity described, hoping that it will simply go away. But the journey through this real-life story is well worthwhile if only for the increased awareness that its very telling inspires.

— Art Linkletter

ACKNOWLEDGMENTS

This book would have been impossible to write in its present form without the cooperation of Los Angeles County District Attorney Evelle J. Younger.

It would have been a great deal more difficult to write without the freely departed knowledge and hospitality of J. Miller Leavy, Director of Central Operations of that office.

It would never have been written at all without the inspiration and guidance of my friend, Clyde M. Vandeburg.

Many others helped along the way. I am indebted to James J. Shea, Head, Complaints Division of the Los Angeles County District Attorney's office, for his interminable patience in answering a layman's question about the law, and to Frank Fowles, District Attorney of Inyo County, for making possible much of the original pretrial research reported in these pages.

G.B.

Illustrations broadcast by ABC News on *ABC Evening News with Howard K. Smith and Harry Reasoner.*

The assistance of Av Westin, Executive Producer of ABC Network News and William P. McSherry, Director ABC-TV News, West Coast, is also gratefully acknowledged.

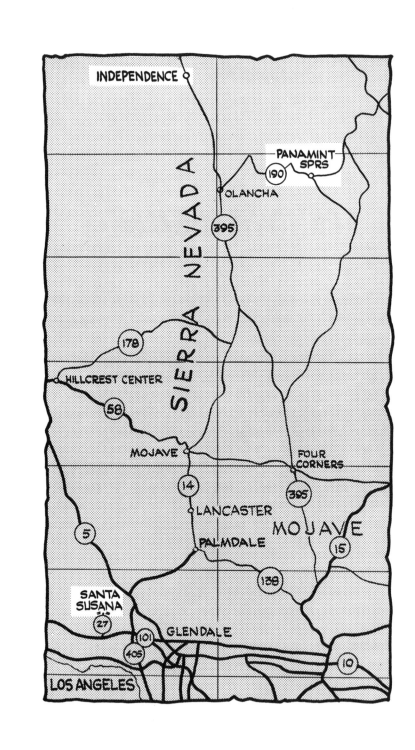

Chapter

1

PRETRIAL
DAY ONE

There was fire on the desert.

Ranger Richard Powell stood beside his four-wheel drive patrol jeep staring intently through field glasses at the rising smoke. It was not the light greyish wispy smoke that follows flame leaping through the dry spiny hop sage dotting the desert floor, rolling like tumbleweed through heat shimmering up from the sand; this was dense, billowing black smoke, oil and rubber burning in a depression obscured from his view by the broken ridges of the Panamint Range.

Powell, his radio silenced by the mountains boxing him in, altered his patrol route and turned onto a barely discernible set of tracks leading eastward toward Death Valley on the range's far side.

Several tortuous miles later — it is impossible to measure distance accurately in the boulder-strewn badlands of the Panamint — the National Park Ranger set his brakes and descended in front of the smouldering remains of a county owned Michigan Articulated loader valued in excess of $30,000.

1

The fire puzzled Powell. The loader, being used by an Inyo County crew to shape mounds that would act as watershed when the spring runoff turned the dry creek beds into rushing torrents, had been left while its crew trucked back down into Independence for the weekend.

An electrical malfunction was possible but highly unlikely in that type of vehicle.

He walked slowly around the loader, his eyes scanning the chips of ore-bearing rock that dotted the sand and gave the desert surface a gravelly texture. He stopped to pick up a partially full matchbook from Ralphs, a prominent California supermarket chain, walked a few steps farther then squatted down on his haunches, reading signs in the uneven ground.

Tiny hoof prints, about half the size of a horse's, told him that a small herd of about fifteen wild burros that he had been observing earlier in the day had passed this way after the Michigan loader had been parked; sections of its massive treads were marked with their prints. But another set of tire tracks had arrived after the fleet little animals had departed. This set crossed over their prints, circled the loader once, stopped, then drove off up an unused dry wash, heading into the virtually inaccessible reaches of the inhospitable range. Powell identified the tracks as belonging to a four-wheel drive Toyota and prudently turned back to make his report dated that day, September 19, 1969, and to enlist help for a deeper penetration of the plateau.

Rumors had been filtering down to Independence, Lone Pine and Bishop that hippie style individuals had been seen with increasing frequency traveling in dune buggies in the area; the Ranger guessed that some of them might be responsible for the loader being set on fire. What he could not know as he maneuvered his patrol jeep slowly down the treacherous rock falls was that he was about to touch off a manhunt destined to net one of the most improbable groups of accused murderers in the annals of premeditated homicide.

Six months later in Los Angeles, a dark stocky man of medium height stood in front of a lectern in Department 107 of the Superior Court of Los Angeles County and read with seriousness but without histrionics: "That on or about the 9th day of August, 1969, at and in the County of Los Angeles, State of California, the said defendants Charles Watson, Charles Manson, Patricia Krenwinkel, Susan Atkins and Linda Kasabian did wilfully, unlawfully, feloniously and with malice aforethought murder Abigail Anne Folger, a human being."

Deputy District Attorney Aaron Stovitz went down the list of victims, reading the formal indictment in its entirety each time, betraying no emotion, revealing only to those who knew him very well, in the slight pause that invariably preceded the words "a human being," his strong feelings about the case.

Stovitz was, and is, an uncomplicated man with a personal philosophy as simple as the "Do your own thing" aspired to by the pale, unbeautiful people who stood facing him across the courtroom. He believes, deeply and with a conviction that transcends the legal, that murdering people is wrong. In the furtherance of this simple credo he commands the lightning mental reflexes of a top trial lawyer and the dogged persistence of a homicide detective. These attributes have brought him, at forty-five, to his present post as Head of the Trial Division of the nation's largest juridical district.

"Aaron is a good man," a female attorney who once served in his division, remarked earnestly. "And a good lawyer."

"He's a bulldog," one of his fledgling crop of Assistant

D.A.'s volunteered. "He just won't let go."

What does Aaron Stovitz see when, at the end of each carefully enunciated "a human being," he lifts his deceptively mild gray eyes and glances across the courtroom? He sees Charles Miller Manson; for it is obvious that the prosecutor's gaze invariably falls first on the head of the Family before flicking quickly over the giggling acolytes.

Charles Manson. A sly, smirking predator finally brought to bay.

"I lived in a ditch," Manson will later defiantly tell the court. "You live on a street."

His presence is the proof of his declamation. He looks as though he recently has been lifted by the scruff from some brackish place, shaken by a provident hand until the grimy excess has spattered free, then laid aside to dry. The enforced regular bathing of routine prison life during the months of pretrial ritual have had little apparent effect on Charlie; he manages, despite some attempt at trimming long hair and the periodic shaving off of his beard, to look unclean, to uphold the tribal tradition of the clan living in communal filth and freedom.

"We moved in up wind of 'em," Sergeant Ray Hailey of the California Highway Patrol, one of the officers who led the original raids on the Barker and Myers ranches near Death Valley, recalled. "Those little gals were sure giving off a powerful scent."

What Sergeant Hailey took to be the result of a reluctance to bathe may have had more sinister overtones. As detective Clyde Watson, a veteran Los Angeles Police Department narcotics officer, explained at the time of the trial: "Repeated use of narcotics tends to make the human body give out a characteristic odor, much like body odor, that washing will not eliminate."

What is Aaron Stovitz thinking as he stands before Judge William B. Keene's bench watching Charlie and his girls plead not guilty, then exchange ressuring grins? Perhaps, for the moment, his gaze rests on Susan Denice Atkins, pale from her long confinement, her skin breaking out in blotches, her eyes staring vacantly at the courtroom; a bump-and-grind Ophelia making, while standing at the prisoner's dock, the little buttock motions of her former specialty as a topless dancer; choosing, instead of a watery grave, the self-immolation of public confession.

"I went over and got Sharon and put her in a headlock. She didn't fight me. I just held her. At times it seemed so easy. 'Woman, I have no mercy for you,' I told her. And that was myself, talking only to me."

Or perhaps Aaron Stovitz is thinking of the official Los Angeles Police Department pictures of the bodies of Rosemary and Leno La Bianca. Rosemary, a slim, youthful woman lying nude, face down on her bedroom floor with the ugly brownish stab wounds dotting her skin like burst pustules; and her husband, also nude, lying on his back with a bloody towel thrown across his face, a carving fork handle protruding obscenely from his fleshy abdomen.

Once again, Susan: "Katie (Patricia Krenwinkel) said she saw the fork. She said she saw it and she flashed, who-ee, that will scare somebody. And she picked up the fork and stuck the fork in the man's stomach. She sat and watched it wobble, and she said she was fascinated by it."

Who-ee. Talk like that fairly blows the mind and sends one reeling emotionally, hoping to find some stable point of reference to restore a sense of values.

"How," I later asked Paul Fitzgerald, Patricia Krenwinkel's

attorney, "could all this have happened?"

"She thinks that Charlie is Jesus Christ," he told me. "They all do."

I expressed my incredulity.

"Really," his sympathetic grin recalls a tousle-haired Boy Scout improbably defending an accused multiple murderess. But a super-smart Scout who, as we shall see, with every other principal in this case, generates his own private mystique.

"I mean that literally," he continued. "They actually think that Charles Manson is the second coming; they are absolutely convinced that he is Jesus Christ."

CHARLES MANSON, ALSO KNOWN AS JESUS CHRIST

Do all the Family feel this way?

"It depends on what you mean by the Family. These girls do."

I asked if they felt any sense of remorse for anything they might have done.

"No guilt feelings at all," Fitzgerald replied. "They've been conditioned away from society's generally accepted mores." I suggested that committing murder would seem to involve quite a bit of conditioning.

"There's nothing unique about that," the attorney said. "You take a boy from a middle class family, brought up to respect God and the flag, put him into the army and he's soon sighting down that barrel, pulling the trigger and murdering people without any sense of guilt. A few of them never become accustomed to it, but most do."

But surely what has happened to the Family is different. The army is an accepted institution and its function has become a part of civilization itself. How can he compare thousands of years of traditional behavior with one man setting up a group of teen-age men and girls as his personal assassins?

"What the military system and tradition does for those young men, LSD might well do for the young girls of the Family," Fitzgerald said. "First of all they are alienated from their normal social base; there is no family love and understanding; none of the usual safety valves. Then they are introduced to the acid trip, the LSD experience. Enough of this and they attain a different level of reality; the citizen becomes the soldier and killing is all right, the tripper loses all contact with learned upbringing and becomes ripe for conscious manipulation by the right person.

"The girls manifest no sense of guilt in prison. They laugh and sing and are generally happy; they drive the matrons crazy. People up on murder charges, especially if they have seven counts like Patricia has, tend to be morose and filled with remorse or foreboding. These girls are not like that. It's no put-on. They genuinely do not feel a sense of guilt.

"And they won't get a fair trial. They can't. What kind of jurors are we going to have? People who are willing and can afford to sit for perhaps six months, who won't mind being locked up in hotel rooms for that time. What does that leave us? People who can afford to do it are usually retired people or older men and women who have succeeded in their own business; or employees whose bosses will pay their salaries for that time. Since most employers will only pay for thirty days, if they'll pay for that, we are reduced to fifteen per cent of the population. And that fifteen per cent are older, self-made, and not given to understanding the acid world that young, long haired, bearded people have gotten caught up in." Fitzgerald shook his head. "I don't think there's a hope in hell that justice will be done.

"On December the 11th (1969), the day after Manson was arraigned, I sensed instinctively that this would be what (Deputy District Attorney) Vince Bugliosi would call 'The case of the century.' I would be less than candid if I didn't say that I welcome the recognition that this trial is bringing me. This will be remembered as the first of the acid murders; our changing social structure is making more people turn on and we're on the brink of a whole new concept of violence . . . violence perpetrated against society by people who have reached a different plateau of reality through LSD.

"You know," he said earnestly, "this acid thing has been around for a long time. I've taken acid, back when it was fashionable for so-called intellectuals to try it. It really works. It moves you onto another level of awareness. I became intensely aware of sights and sounds around me that I had scarcely noticed before. It really does turn you on."

To the point of committing guiltless murder?

"That's pretty far out," Fitzgerald acknowledged, "for you or I. But maybe not for someone who had nothing much going for them with the old values."

Like his client?

"Whatever she may have done," he said, "she'll never get a fair trial. None of them will."

I asked him if Patricia Krenwinkel was guilty.

"She's guilty of love, of finding love in the Family," he replied. "I guess you could say she's guilty of that."

"Charlie's M.O. is very simple," Aaron Stovitz explained to me in his sixth floor office in the Hall of Justice, after the preliminary hearing. "He says to a new girl, 'You want to feel good? Here, take one of these.' He gives her acid and takes one himself. Pretty soon she's feeling *great.*" Stovitz furrowed his brow in a characteristic gesture indicating emphasis. "Then," he continued, "Charlie says: 'You want to feel even better? Here.'" The D.A. hands an imaginary offering across his desk. "'Take another one.' Only this time Charlie *pretends* to drop some acid with the girl. After he's done this three or four times she's so far out that he can get her to do anything. Especially if he repeats the treatment a number of times."

Then it was a deliberate process, a cold, calculating act on Manson's part?

"Think of it this way," Stovitz said. "Here's a small-time ex-con, a punk who never even made good as a criminal. Suddenly he's surrounded by girls. Not only can he have all he wants but here are people who are willing to do what he tells them. For the first time in his life he, Charlie Manson, can give orders and have them obeyed."

Stovitz stood up, crossed the room, closed his office door then sat back down at his desk, pulling a cigar from his breast pocket. He has an agreement with his secretary: whenever he smokes a cigar he closes the door. Some people, he confided to me, think that cigars smell bad.

"So," he resumed, lighting up, "he tests them. First it was little different things with sex. Then maybe it was stealing something. Finally," the D.A. stared reflectively through the thickening smoke, "it was killing people."

I remarked about the news media's references to Charlie's "hypnotic stare," and "charismatic personality." Must not someone possess these qualities in order to direct people to commit murder?

"That's all baloney," the D.A. replied. "Charlie was cunning enough to pick only girls and young fellows who were already dropping out. You fill people with enough acid on a regular basis and it doesn't take a great mind to move them around. He made them dependent on him. He told them that as long as they did what he wanted, they didn't have to get up in the morning, they didn't have to do anything they didn't want to do, they could have all the sex they liked and that there was nothing wrong with any of this. He gave them drugs to help them see it his way; pretty soon *anything* Charlie wanted was what they wanted and anything they wanted was right."

The real significance of the crimes begins to dawn on the observer, and its impact is chilling. The vicious acts that led to this incredible trial; the convoluted personalities that we meet along the way; the dubious motives to be examined as society strains to dispense justice; all these separate parts, fascinating though they may be, tend to obscure the whole. The significance here is not that a man has reduced a group of young men and girls to a condition of moral debauchery and emotional vacuity that found a final fulfillment in remorseless murder, the significance lies in the fact that a *weak* man has done all this.

Rejected by society, rejecting it in turn, Charles Manson is not the only man to be born out of wedlock but he is the only one to successfully manipulate other human beings to strike back, seemingly at random, at that society as an instrument of his revenge. And, if both the defense and prosecution are to be believed, he did it through the use of LSD. What other psychopaths, nurturing real or imagined wrongs, are following this case, perhaps tentatively experimenting with Charlie's *modus operandi?* The term "drug abuse" takes on frightening new implications in this context.

But Aaron Stovitz is prosecuting a case, not formulating a plan for social survival. He listens with interest to a projection of the crimes and nods in agreement.

"And you know the funny thing about Charlie," the D.A. says, carefully tapping cigar ash into a tray on his desk, "is that if he hadn't set that loader on fire up near the Barker place he might still be there, maybe sending out more people to do those terrible things."

What *did* happen in the desert wilderness in mid-September, 1969, that led to Manson's capture? Let's take a look.

Chapter II

PRETRIAL DAY TWO

First of all, Ranger Powell found a Toyota. After turning in a report suggesting possible arson, he decided to take one more look on his own. Sure enough, three days later, on September 22nd, not far from the burned out loader in a place called Hail and Hall Canyon, he stopped a red four-wheel drive Toyota occupied by four scantily dressed girls and a "hippie type" male.

Normal procedure would have had Powell ask for a radio check on the Toyota license plate, California 36309 A, but the natural barriers of the Panamint blacked out his transmitter; lacking any reason for holding the group he chatted with them briefly and resumed his patrol.

Back at the Death Valley National Monument Park Headquarters the report on the Toyota plate caused Powell sufficient concern to have him telephone Deputy Dennis Cox of the Inyo County Sheriff's office and suggest a joint trip back to the Hail and Hall. The Toyota plate was registered to Gayle Beausoleil, wife of Robert Beausoleil then in custody in Los Angeles County in connection with the slaying of Gary Hinman.

After hearing the charge against Beausoleil — 185 P.C.: Murder — Cox agreed that a combined investigation was called for and two days later, on September 24th, he and Powell entered a circular depression called the Racetrack and headed for the point of last contact with the red Toyota.

They found nothing. An elderly miner, one of the scattered loners patiently working silver claims long since abandoned by the big companies, told them that the Toyota had pulled out of the Hail and Hall about four hours after Powell had spoken with its occupants. The venerable sourdough was emphatic, however, in his denunciation of a larger group of hippies who had "taken over" a couple of previously abandoned claim shacks in the area and were intimidating local inhabitants.

Powell was anything but satisfied. Although the sheriff's office was reluctant to commit manpower to what seemed, at most, a possible arson and auto theft investigation of an itinerant band, the ranger saw it differently.

In defense of the sheriff's position, it should be understood that there is no such thing as a "routine investigation" in the Panamint. Customarily, patrol units involved in anything more than a cursory inspection set out with not less than two four-wheel drive vehicles, in the often realized expectation that one will break down before the day is over. So rugged is the terrain bordering Death Valley that, of four vehicles involved in a subsequent armed police sweep in which this writer participated, two broke down on the way in and one of the remaining trucks had its heavy duty tire tread sliced through by slate rock as effortlessly as a razor blade cutting through butter.

INTO THE DEATH VALLEY BADLANDS

It isn't necessary to mount an armed expedition against potentially dangerous criminals over all but impassable terrain to come to grief in the Panamint. Recently three Los Angeles businessmen purchased a speculative mining claim in nearby Saline Valley and drove up one weekend to inspect their property. An improved dirt road, normally more than adequate for a large passenger sedan traveling circumspectly, led from Highway 190 to their claim. Ignoring warnings to register their departure and estimated return times with the local authorities, the men set out from Lone Pine on what appeared on the map to be a two or three hour trip.

A waterhose burst in the intense heat, draining their engine cooling system. When, two days later, all three were found dead, it was obvious from their scattered locations that each had tried to walk out in a different direction. The ultimate irony was that, had they registered with the police, they would have been told the location of special water caches maintained by the Park Service for just such emergencies, one of which stood, undiscovered, a scant fifty yards from their abandoned car.

Ranger Powell acquired a new ally in California Highway Patrol Officer James Pursell who, on September 29th, accompanied him on a patrol that, for the first time in the investigation, included the Goler Wash, a series of dry rock falls some of whose angles of ascent were capable of causing a heavy patrol truck to flip over on its back should an inexperienced driver challenge them too cavalierly.

This time Powell hit pay dirt. At the Barker Ranch (a misnomer; the "ranches" in the area actually comprise forty acre mining claims usually staked out on a spring fed small plot of level ground surrounded, hopefully, by ore-bearing hills) he and Pursell found two teen-age girls who would tell them only that the person who lived there had gone down to Ballarat, a one store crossroads at the base of the range, and would soon return.

More importantly, the two officers stopped Paul Crockett, a long time local fixture, and Brooks Poston, a younger man who had been vacillating between full hippiedom and a more conventional existence, in a truck full of automotive equipment. Crockett said that the supplies belonged to a hippie group and that he was delivering them because he feared for his life. He told of "sex orgies" and repeated drug use by the hippie group as well as seemingly far-fetched tales of armed dune buggies, hidden bunkers with telephone communication and overlapping fields of fire, and a leader who called himself Jesus Christ and whose very presence Crockett found to be intimidating. Although the significance of the conversation was necessarily lost to both Powell and Pursell it represented the law's first knowledge of the existence of Charles Manson and his unorthodox Family.

The patrol yielded even greater results when, halfway between the Barker place and another claim called the Myers Ranch, they flushed seven young women in their late teens hiding in the brush. A hippie male was also questioned and a second male, thought later to be Manson, was seen running away down a dry wash. The officers also found a red Toyota with a different license plate from that seen originally by Powell, and a dune buggy carefully camouflaged by sleeping bags and desert scrub.

A check with the Los Angeles Police Department revealed that both vehicles were stolen; after one more fruitless search through the Goler during which, it was learned later, the Family had either hidden out in the surrounding hills or escaped down an equally rough back trail into Death Valley, it was decided that a full scale raid was called for on what was now believed to be a highly organized and possibly heavily armed hippie stolen car ring.

On October 10th, 1969, California Highway Patrol officers led by Lieutenant Howard M. Hurlbut, Commander of the Bishop, California station and accompanied by Inyo County District Attorney Frank H. Fowles, set out from Lone Pine to enter the Panamint through the Goler Wash; a second group including C.H.P. officer James Pursell and Fowles's assistant, Deputy District Attorney Buck Gibbons, had left the night before, camped out on the Death Valley side, and were to head up into the Panamint in a pincer movement that same morning.

Alerted to the possible connection between their quarry

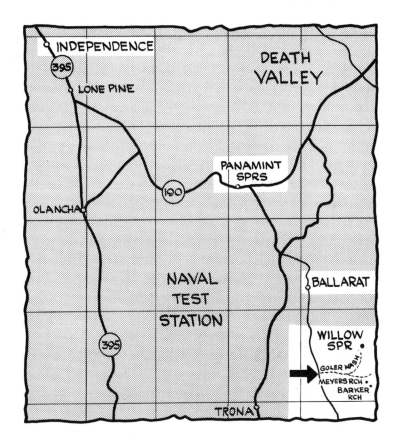

DESERT LOCATION OF FAMILY CAPTURE

and a gun oriented hippie group recently flushed from the Spahn Ranch near Los Angeles, the expedition was armed with high powered rifles and would attempt to keep the two converging groups in contact through the use of walkie-talkies; communications, however, were to prove intermittent at best, forcing the two raiding parties to feel their way up the dry washes with little knowledge of each other's positions.

Under more pleasant circumstances, merely getting to the

base of the Panamint, approximately ninety miles from Lone Pine, would be half the fun. Leaving the lush greenness of the Owens Valley, sitting on the slopes of the Sierras, the convoy first skirts the Owens Lake Bed, a now dry, bleached white table of residual potash, reflecting even the post-dawn sun into the viewers eyes with uncomfortable brightness. A sense of isolation, enhanced by the abandoned metal processing tanks of once bustling soda ash surface mines, is abruptly shattered by the ear-splitting shriek of jet engines. Before the unprepared stranger can duck, a navy fighter, less than fifty feet off the deck, has announced its passing with a trail of unburned fuel, clouds of white ash sucked up from the lake bed, and an unpleasant ringing in the ears. The news that the China Lake Naval Ordnance Test Station abuts Owens Lake does little to assuage the sense of embarrassment implicit in getting up from where one has somehow become wedged between the dash and the floorboards.

Whatever secondary sense of comfort the comparative nearness of jet-age civilization suggests is soon dispelled by the seemingly boundless dimensions of the high desert. The convoy winds its tortuous way up the precipitous sides of the Argus Range, past unworked silver and dolomite mines gaping from apparently inaccessible rock faces, cresting finally six thousand feet up at Padre Crowley Point, and affording a spectacular view of the valley beyond.

"Death Valley," the visitor gasps, gazing in undisguised awe at a panorama too vast for his eyes to fully encompass.

"Hell, no," Sergeant Ray Hailey echoes the rest of the group's laughter, "that's just a little dried-up wash. Death Valley's on the other side of that mountain range over there."

So, after a respectful reading of a bronze plaque proclaiming Father Crowley, 1891-1940, the padre of the desert, we begin the trip downward into Panamint Valley. (The padre's diocese at the height of the mining boom was most impressive. Nearby Darwin, now best described as a living ghost town, at one stage of the two cities' development is said to have surpassed Los Angeles in population.)

Cautiously, in low gear, we follow Charlie's trail to the valley floor. For this is the way he and the Family drove their cumbersome bus as they fled in their drive north from the consequences of their violent acts. But if visions of pioneer women and sunbronzed, steely-eyed men braving the unknown begin creepy-crawling into your thoughts, forget it.

"You say, Paul, that they think of Charlie as Jesus Christ. How?"

"What do you mean?"

"What overt manifestations did they have? Or was it just an idea?"

"Some of them say he performed miracles."

"Can you give me a specific case?"

"Well," Fitzgerald pushed his glasses up on the bridge of his nose, and gave me a knowing smile. "They say he floated that bus up to the place near Death Valley."

Bumping across the Panamint Valley in a sweltering preview of the crossing that charitably we would not have to make on the range's other side, I reflected on my conversation with the defense attorney. As one of the Los Angeles Police Department officers who flew up to interrogate the Family when they were first captured remarked: "Man, if we were at three thousand feet, they were at six. They were flying." Claims of levitation, it would seem, must be taken in context.

A turn from the valley floor toward the Panamint Mountains and we were at Ballarat, a general store surrounded by creosote brush, that remarkably adaptive desert plant that grows evenly spaced, allowing just enough distance between shrubs to sustain itself. A look toward the ridgeline, three thousand feet over our heads, and one could only observe that the creosote, stopping at the foot of the rocky wall, was displaying better sense than the humans about to drive in.

In where? A dirt trail, heavily pitted by spring runoff, snaked along the Panamint watershed, parallel to the towering cliffs, maintaining a distance of about fifty yards.

Abruptly, without comment, Sergeant Hailey turned the lead jeep off the road and drove straight toward the mountain. As the distance shortened the cliff face seemed more and more impenetrable. We were now riding over virgin desert, following no path except an occasional trace of a dry wash, left after the spring streams pouring from the mountain had finally trickled to a stop and dried up.

Twenty-five feet from the sheer rock face Lieutenant Hurlbut ordered a stop, waved his hand in the direction of the range and said; "There she is, the Ronald Reagan memorial highway!"

A foot reconnaissance revealed that what, from a mere ten feet away, appeared to be a series of jagged scars was, in fact, the beginning of a narrow rock fall, literally a dry waterfall that turned almost at right angles from the cliff face and began a steep, rambling ascent into the mountain.

The first vehicle went in, tilted its nose up, appeared to rear back and, with all four tires on different levels and its drive in four-wheel compound, incredibly began inching its way up the fall.

Charlie Manson drove up this in a bus?

"Not this exact wash," Lt. Hurlbut said. "But one almost like it from the Death Valley side."

How?

"We don't know." Sergeant Hailey, who had led the original raiding party, was fighting the wheel of the jeep, his back and neck muscles straining to prevent the tires from skidding sideways and slamming us into the rock wall. "One thing I know," he shouted over the revving motor, "that bus is up there to stay. No one will ever drive that thing out."

We stopped as the first fall leveled off briefly.

"Now here," Hailey pointed out as we walked ahead a few yards, "is where we found the first of 'em. Clem Tufts and another guy lying on the outcropping," he indicated a flatish piece of slate jutting out about twenty feet from the ground, "with a sawed-off shotgun and twenty-five rounds of ammunition." Hailey hitched his thumb down over the handle of his holstered revolver. "We went mighty careful after that," he said. "Mighty careful."

The slate outcropping was a perfect ambush point; it presented a direct field of fire down a jeep-width defile whose walls rose several hundred feet on both sides. A determined man could have held off an attack indefinitely.

"We know it," Hailey admitted. "The only thing that saved us was that Tufts and the other guy were sound asleep. Seems as though they'd had a little pot party the night before."

The second of many absurdities. Here was badland all around, a natural redoubt from which to operate, comfortably remote from busy U.S. Highway 395. The Family, hopefully to multiply perhaps a hundred fold ("Charlie wanted to settle ten thousand people up here," Lt. Hurlbut said), safe from detection yet capable of inflicting heavy casualties when cornered ("We'd of lost two, three men just getting out of the trucks if Clem had been shooting," a C.H.P. officer calculated), had, instead, inexplicably compromised its position with a futile, play-acting gesture of defiance.

The first absurdity was, of course, the burnt Michigan Articulated loader.

"Charlie just got mad at it," Frank Fowles, the affable, Shakespeare quoting Inyo County D.A. explained. "In setting up water diversion runs and fire breaks the loader had cut off one of his private trails. He had plotted the whole area with his dune buggies and knew where to move around. When he came across the loader he lost his temper, stripped it of anything valuable, and set it afire."

It was not the first time that Charlie had given vent to anger.

Juan Flynn, twenty-four year old Spahn Ranch employee, told how Manson was subject to irrational outbursts of temper. "I've seen him take girls," the wrangler, real name, John Lee Flynn, said, "and bash their heads against the road and car doors and they hadn't done anything. It was because Charlie got mad at somebody and took it out on the girls."

A successfully executed hegira north to a safe haven negated by a rash act; a careful positioning of sentries rendered ineffective, presumably, at their leader's whim; are these random inconsistencies or could they reveal a basic pattern that, at very least, indicates an erratic pre-psychotic personality?

The painstaking, cautious move up the Goler Wash with scouts ahead now on foot probing each new outcropping and crevice, accumulates evidence of Manson's emotional instability. The first man-made barrier to the posse's advance, a sturdy, boarded-up shack marking the bottom of the Lotus Mine, a now unworked silver lode whose main shaft several

JUAN FLYNN TOLD OF CHARLIE'S STRANGE "LOVE"

hundred feet up the mountain face was reached by a cable car whose rusted tracks still remain, was approached by the lawmen with thoughts about Clem Tufts (real name, Stephen Dennis Grogan) and his shotgun fresh in their minds.

"We circled it," Sergeant Hailey recalled with a wry smile, "and kicked in the front and back doors. We couldn't take any chances."

The shack was unoccupied but, it was learned later, had been stripped of all its cooking utensils by the Family.

"Charlie sent one of the girls up there," Fowles said, pointing to the mine opening, looking like a small black dot in the sun-baked rock of the nearly vertical cliff. "He told her that if she could stay up there for three days and nights alone, it would prove her loyalty to the Family and he would then do it to prove his."

The girl, later identified as Kathleen Lutesinger, accepted the challenge but when she descended, seventy-two hours later, exhausted and unnerved by her experience, Charlie merely smiled and said that since she had done it there was no point in himself, an obviously superior individual, going to the trouble. Miss Lutesinger, understandably disillusioned, became a Family drop-out and subsequently provided the authorities with a considerable amount of information about their activities. The incident provides another example of Manson's unpredictable, priggish behavior, essentially self-destructive in nature and tending to confirm a growing suspicion that the Jesus Christ of the Panamint harbored within himself more than a trace of the recognized symptoms of paranoid schizophrenia.

The possibility that they might be seeking a potential madman rather than the calculating chief of an auto theft ring would have been of small comfort to Lieutenant Hurlbut's expedition as they inched their way up to the plateau that afforded level, if uneven, ground and considerably speeded up their advance.

The plateau, running along the top of the Panamint Range, also gave the Goler Wash party their first voice contact with officer James Pursell coming up the back way. Pursell, approaching the Mengel Pass, a narrow defile that gave access to the plateau from the Death Valley side, had already flushed two young girls and a baby at Willow Springs, another unworked mining claim; it was soon established that both sections of the raiding party would converge almost simultaneously on the Barker Ranch, thought to be the suspected hippie band's headquarters.

Sergeant Hailey recalls coming up to the main Barker Ranch house, a cement and stone structure, much more substantial than the average claim building, and surrounded by several smaller wooden and tin shacks. "We had just stopped," the C.H.P. officer recounted, "when a voice on the radio coming from the other side shouted that we were being observed by someone in a bunker way up there in the hillside." He indicated what was now an obvious dugout in one of the hills hemming in the Barker place; a camouflaged tin roof had been peeled back against the spiny hop sage and mattresses that had been dragged out by the posse lay scattered below the bunker's lip. At the time, however, it represented a potential threat and the officers reacted with dispatch.

"We all took cover," the sergeant continued. "I had one man lay down right there," — he indicated a large tire of the type used on heavy duty earth moving equipment, laying on its side on the ground — "with his telescopic site zeroed in on that spot; he had orders to shoot anything that moved."

Another posse member circled through a small ravine and came up directly behind and above the suspected bunker; he picked up a large rock and sent it crashing down on the tin roof, ordering everyone inside to come out with their hands in the air. After a brief pause three of the Family girls clambered out of the bunker, all dressed skimpily, two with knives strapped to their naked thighs. The raid eventually netted eleven young girls and three men, one of whom, identified as Charles Miller Manson, was found hiding in a small commode under the main ranchhouse bathroom sink. Hailey, who flushed Manson with the business end of his rifle, recalled that the Family leader looked up at him, smiled and said "Hi!" Not exactly the posture of blazing defiance that he attempted to instill into the girls should they ever be confronted by the law.

One of his indoctrination lectures was later recounted by Stephanie Schram, a sometime acolyte who first met him at Big Sur, when he was traveling south from the Haight-Ashbury district of San Francisco. "Charlie had held classes for the girls on how to kill people," Miss Schram recalled. "And had asked different girls if they could kill the 'pigs' from the city. Then Charlie showed them how to stab people in the neck and stated that if they were going to stab someone, they should try to cut the person from ear to ear, also to stab them in either ear or eyes and then wiggle the knife around to get as many of the vital organs as possible."

Manson, according to Miss Schram, also told them if they killed anyone that they would have to learn to cut the person up and get rid of the parts so no one could find them; that if the girls didn't obey him, he threatened to cut one of their breasts off.

During the Barker ranch raid (which also included a side trip to the nearby Myers Ranch, another unworked mining claim), while the officers were uncovering skillfully camouflaged stolen dune buggies and caches of emergency dried food buried in holes dug in the ground and covered with sand and rocks, the Family girls, obviously not up to taking on a group of armed men with their sheath knives, did, however, indicate their defiance in less violent, if no less explicit ways. Quoting from the official report filed on the incident:

"When the initial group of female prisoners was arrested, several of the females disrobed. Several of them urinated on the ground in the presence of officers. They also undressed and changed clothes in the presence of the officers."

Absurdities abound. An unlikely sentinel, Clem Tufts, whose previous record includes time served at Camarillo, a mental facility, for indecent exposure, lay stoned on picket duty. A defense bunker carpeted with mattresses and manned by half naked teen-age girls with sheathed knives and full bladders. A communications system of war surplus army field telephone wire not connected to any instruments. (This writer followed one length of wire that began in the middle of a hillside and led, literally, to nowhere in the middle of another hillside.)

To crown the unlikely melodrama, the leader who led by preaching love but threatening mutilation, crouched smirkingly beside a toilet bowl, his charisma dissipated in the dank shadows of a moldering commode. And, of course, that first absurdity, the Michigan Articulated loader, set afire in a moment of childish pique.

Was it all a bizarre game with the rules changed at the leader's whim, the outcome subject to a child's undisciplined thought or a paranoid's unpredictable mental quirks? Was it all play-acting for real? Had some outside agent, perhaps lysergic acid diathylamide, reduced a group of people to a level of reality from which telephone lines running helter-skelter over the desert and knives plunging repeatedly into human flesh both made sense? Is it possible that Charles Manson, uneducated petty thief and sodomist, has unwittingly conducted the first controlled experiment exploring the relationship between LSD and crimes of violence? Is this the ultimate absurdity?

Patricia Krenwinkel, a Family member accused of seven counts of murder, spoke freely to two police officers who were returning her for trial from Mobile, Alabama. She "acknowledged frequent usage of marijuana and LSD. (She

PATRICIA KRENWINKEL, ACCUSED OF SEVEN COUNTS OF MURDER

said): 'You do not lose any of your senses when high on pot or acid, but become more sensitive. You can see better, hear better, and think more clearly. Music and dancing are so much more beautiful and appreciative (sic).' She always remembered each and every thing that happened after smoking pot or taking acid."

A testimonial from one of the bearded clinician's most willing subjects. But the world must bear witness, and to do that, it must first know the nature of the experiment. So back to the first absurdity in the Panamint Mountains that led, on October 22nd, 1969, to the people of Inyo County of the State of California holding one Charles Miller Manson, also-known-as Jesus Christ, to answer on charges of violation of section 449a of the California Penal Code: Arson. A comparative small, pointless crime when viewed in the context of its consequences.

Chapter III

PRETRIAL DAY THREE

If, as he was to frequently imply later during his trial, Charles Manson had some private compact with the Fates, some Platonic belief — without, of course, being aware of that belief's genesis — in the concept of universals that relegated life and death to the role of inconsequential way stations on the journey to the achievement of the absolute, those esoteric thoughts were not borne out by his behavior prior to his indictment for murder.

His life style is best characterized by a convicted forger, now on parole, who served time with Manson in the State of Washington at McNeil Island Penitentiary. "Charlie," the ex-con reminisced when pressed by this writer for a capsule description of the Family leader years before he acquired a supposed charisma, "took it up the ass."

Now it is anything but inconsistent with the later expressed philosophy of universal love to have its proponent manifest that love in a somewhat unorthodox manner. What is important here, as Attorney Irving Kanarek repeatedly tried to get across to the prospective jury during the *voir dire,* or pretrial examination, proceedings, over equally repeatedly sustained objections by the prosecution, is ascertaining Manson's state of mind.

"Charlie was a punk," the forger continued.

Punk? Aaron Stovitz had used the same word.

"Yes. A guy who goes to the big prison jocks for their protection and does them favors in return."

"Jocks" are the reigning prison inmate homosexuals. I inquired further as to Charlie's behavior.

"It's fairly common," I was told. "Charlie is a little guy and the only way he could avoid being shoved around was to trade his ass for protection. I don't have that clear a picture of him; he was nobody in the joint. But I remember him as an operator; he was always willing to trade to stay ahead."

It was from McNeil Island, fresh from the last of twenty-two intermittent years spent behind bars, that Manson journeyed, in 1967, to the Haight-Ashbury district of San Francisco. A thirty-five year old man with thirty-seven separate counts recorded on his arrest "rap sheet" has to play it cool on the outside in his first months as a free man. The law knows that he has to live and the police evince an uncommon interest in a newly freed ex-con's method of survival; especially if he grows a beard and drifts from place to place.

In his wanderings Charlie was looking for something to trade; something that would give him the edge in the square world and enable him to survive without returning to his only profession: thievery, with the almost inevitable result of his being busted and returned to prison.

Not, incidentally, that he was all that averse to prison life.

"Manson said that he does easy time," Charles Hollopeter,

the respected Pasadena court appointed criminal lawyer whom Charlie dismissed early in the pretrial proceedings because Hollopeter wanted to have him take a psychiatric test, told me, "and I believe him. He says that his world is on the inside and that he experiences a sense of security there."

Ironically, ten months before Manson arrived in Haight-Ashbury, the State of California gave him the lever that he would use to accumulate his vagrant Family. In 1966 the state legislature enacted a law making possession of lysergic acid diethylamide illegal.

It didn't take the now hirsute Manson long to blend into the hippie scene and to locate a source of the difficult-to-acquire LSD. During that period the Haight was becoming less a haven for the indolent hedonism of relatively inoffensive flower children than a stagnant backwater into which drifted rejected, often bitter young people actively seeking redress from society for real or imagined wrongs.

Charles Manson told these alienated people that they were right and the world was wrong, set himself up as a combination of satyr and oracle — most of the girls didn't know that he had been in prison until his arraignment in Independence — and gave them a glimpse of another, hopefully Utopian, world through the use of the now outlawed LSD.

Many more prospective disciples kept moving than stayed but the few who did, beginning with Susan Denice Atkins, latched on to Charlie's developing philosophy.

Most people have a philosophy of life but few are aware that they possess it. Manson seems to have arrived at his "All is love, I know no guilt," pattern by practicing an instinctive pragmatism. If something worked, he pursued it; if it didn't, he dropped it. He soon found that the kind of girl who had lost all normal emotional attachments and who, in part because of her disengagement from society, retained almost none of the conventional moral scruples, would accept a God image properly presented. He moved cautiously, flattering here, threatening there and rewarding obedience with carefully doled out portions of LSD. Some, like Kathleen Lutesinger, stayed at least partially because of fear. "He made me have sex and he gave me drugs," she later complained.

Others, like Sandra Good (Family name, Sandy Pugh), one of the small hard core to stay on right through the trial, professed to reciprocate, if not completely to understand, the theory of universal love. "Charlie is us and we are him," she told me in the Los Angeles Hall of Justice. "He never wanted anything for himself; he always gave away what he had if someone wanted it."

The fact that almost everything Charlie possessed and gave away belonged to someone-else fails to sway the faithful. (The fabled bus is the one exception; registered to Charles Manson it sits up at the Barker Ranch, windows shot out by itinerant hunters, sand whipping through its stripped interior and desert brush pressing importunely against its sides, at once an extension of and hollow monument to its absent driver.)

The image of a leader's selflessness toward his flock, the already noted irrational behavior aside, simply does not hold up in the light of known facts. When the Inyo County law officers accomplished the considerable task of transporting their prisoners down from the Panamint to the jail in Independence everyone was hungry and tired. Manson wolfed down his prison meal of hamburger and beans while in adjoining cells the Family, fearful of the master's wrath should they break a loyalty-proving vegetarian oath, sat nervously picking at their plates.

"Charlie ate meat," a sheriff's deputy at the jail said, "and the girls wouldn't. They were afraid of him."

Frank Fowles recalls his first Family questioning session with rueful amusement. "All we had them for was suspected arson and suspected grand theft, auto," he told me later. "I picked this one kid who seemed out of place with some of the rest of them. I decided to give her a break so that she wouldn't have a record following her around."

Fowles took the Family member aside and gave her a fatherly talking to; he explained that she was traveling with a rough crowd and that she was too nice a kid to get involved over her head.

"She listened very respectfully," Fowles recalls. "Answered 'Yes, sir,' and 'No, sir,' and thanked me most sincerely for letting her go."

The girl was Patricia Krenwinkel, later charged with seven counts of murder and extradited from Alabama to stand trial in Los Angeles.

One would have a difficult time convincing Frank Fowles and his fellow citizens of Charlie Manson's implied concept of universal love. Independence, whose one thousand permanent population nestles contendedly at the base of the High Sierras, looks and acts like its District Attorney's proud description of "A truly nineteenth century town."

Its courthouse, a graceful, colonnaded structure set back from the main road and surrounded by broad green lawns and stately pine trees, typifies the serene self-reliance of the people. Born to packing into the lofty peaks behind them or living for days on the inhospitable desert to their east, the people of the

Owens Valley do not frighten easily; most men own a rifle and know how to use it.

In October, 1969, however, the inhabitants of Independence knew the meaning of fear, in a collective sense, for the first time. Somewhat quizzical and even mildly amused by the ragtag group of prisoners brought down out of the Panamint and lodged in the sheriff's lockup, the local citizens gradually became aware, as did the authorities, that something far more ominous than a band of half-naked hippie car thieves had descended into their midst.

Homicide detectives, grim, unsmiling men who appeared not to notice the magnificent scenery, let alone be impressed by it, began arriving from Los Angeles and were quickly followed by newspaper and wire service reporters and television camera crews.

"It looked for a while like there were more T.V. cameras in town than television sets," a waitress at the Pines, Independence's only restaurant and the unofficial press headquarters during the days preceding the Family's arraignment, told me. "It was real exciting."

Most of the press and police officers put up at the Winnedumah Hotel, a once elegant hostelry directly across from the courthouse. The "Dumah" as she's known locally, is peeling a little here and there and, notwithstanding her name (*Winnedumah* is Waucoba Indian for "Stay right where you are") is accustomed to having traffic speed by on U.S. 395 heading for somewhere else. Not so during that fateful October; the "No vacancy" sign flashed an unusual admonition. Things were definitely not normal in Independence and the Dumah's bustling occupants, by the very nature of their callings, caused ripples of speculation to diffuse through the town.

The local people felt the first emotional tremor triggered by the unaccustomed activity soon after the true nature of the Family's alleged crimes became known.

Rumors spread quickly and multiplied as they spread. In a place where, as Buck Gibbons observed, "Everyone knows what everyone else is doing, all the time," the first nagging apprehension of one soon became the near terror of many. A heavily armed band of drug crazed hippies, word had it, were preparing to take the town by force in order to liberate their satanic leader and his followers. So great was the pervading sense of impending violence that Fowles, an intelligent, worldly individual not given to fleeing from demons, packed his attractive wife Cathy and their five children off to a safe haven in Northern California until the Family presence was resolved. "Murder most foul," was very much in the air, hanging over the verdant freshness of the valley like a threatening invisible shroud.

Stark tragedy, unleavened by humor, hangs heavy indeed, and the minds of Independence officialdom were diverted for a brief time by what quickly became known as the "Locust letter."

Inyo County Sheriff Merrill H. Curtis found himself surfeit of an embarrassment of riches. As the official Independence jailer he was suddenly in great demand. Wire service reporters camped on his doorstep, television lenses poked through his cell doors, other law enforcement agencies, notably the crack homicide team of Sergeants Charles C. Guenther and Paul J. Whiteley of the Los Angeles County Sheriff department, who first arrested convicted murderer Robert K. Beausoleil (Family name, Cupid) in the Gary Hinman slaying, arrived to question his prisoners.

Sheriff Curtis had been, at best, a reluctant pursuer, at one time telling his men to stop wasting their time chasing a bunch of hippies all over the desert; he was more than a little annoyed that the hippies, in addition to being famous, were currently in his charge largely through the efforts of his chief law enforcement rival, the California Highway Patrol. Beseiged in his private domain, reduced to the role of turnkey, Curtis, a man of some spirit, issued an edict, copies of which immediately became prize collector's items, to the Bishop office of the California Highway Patrol. It read, in part:

> Gentlemen:
>
> The front office of the Inyo County Sheriff's Department is not the proper location for bull sessions or social meetings of the Highway Patrol, or any other law enforcement agency. During this last week, this Department has felt that it had been converged upon by a pack of locust. (sic)
>
> In the future, anything pertaining to the Highway Patrol will be given to a member of your department through the glass partition in the foyer. We will appreciate it if your officers can find another location in which to conduct their business.

Such are the jurisdictional disputes that plague even the most celebrated criminal investigations.

As the Los Angeles County Sheriff's office and the Los Angeles Police Department took custody of the Tate/La Bianca murder suspects (arrests made possible by Susan Atkins, in jail in Los Angeles as a suspect in the Hinman murder, telling her cellmate about the other slayings), the atmosphere around Independence gradually assumed a near normal tranquility. The Family, however, had left an indelible impression on the citizens of the Inyo County seat, a suggestion of potential violence that causes lawmen, more than a year after the original raids, to make surveillance sweeps of the Panamint and the surrounding valleys, keeping tabs on and, at times, closely interrogating, strangers who arouse their suspicions.

In Los Angeles, much later during the trial, Charlie was asked what he would like to do if he was given a choice. "I'd like to go live on the desert," he replied. "I'd like to go back to the desert." It would be safe to assume, in the unlikely event that he is afforded a choice, that he will have to find himself another desert.

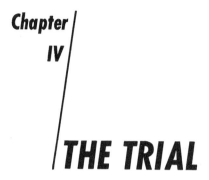

Chapter IV

THE TRIAL

The Principals

The Court:
> Hon. Charles H. Older, Judge

For the people:
> Aaron H. Stovitz, Esq., Deputy District Attorney
> Head, Trials Division, County of Los Angeles
> Vincent T. Bugliosi, Esq., Deputy District Attorney
> Donald A. Musich, Esq., Deputy District Attorney
> Stephen R. Kay, Esq., Deputy District Attorney

For the defense:
> Irving A. Kanarek, Esq. for Defendant
> Charles Manson
> Daye Shinn, Esq. for Defendant
> Susan Atkins
> Ira K. Reiner, Esq.
> Ronald Hughes, Esq.
> Maxwell Keith, Esq. for Defendant
> Leslie Van Houten
> Paul Fitzgerald, Esq. for Defendant
> Patricia Krenwinkel

Pretrial motions, like premarital courtships, exist principally in anticipation of the main event. The very fact that the motions are pretrial presupposes a trial.

True, motions to dismiss are sometimes granted on technical grounds such as the improper wording of an indictment (at which time it is reworded and promptly refiled), and sometimes, in cases involving less serious crimes, for lack of evidence; rarely, however, does the motion to dismiss, in terms of immediate relief the one truly significant defense motion, achieve the desired result in a capital case as carefully prepared as was Tate/La Bianca.

Pretrial motions then, in essence, become posttrial motions, aimed at appellate courts beyond the final verdict. It might be argued that the more apprehensive the defense is about the outcome of their case, the more vigorous will be their pretrial activity; if that criterion is adopted in Tate/La Bianca, the courtroom observer is forced to conclude that seldom in the history of criminal law have four defendants gone to trial represented by attorneys of a more pessimistic turn of mind.

On Thursday, December 11, 1969, Paul J. Fitzgerald, then Assistant Chief Trial Deputy of the Los Angeles County Public Defender's office and the first attorney to represent Charles Manson in the multiple murder case, asked Judge Keene for a delay until December 22 to enter a plea on behalf of his client. The request was granted. Six months later, on June 15, 1970, Charles Manson was finally brought to trial.

Much that happened in the intervening time taxes the understanding of even the most law-oriented layman.

Some of the legal maneuvering took on an aura of pure chicanery. Irving Kanarek, Manson's final attorney of record after a long list of lawyers had been found wanting by the defendant, regularly undertook, during the jury selection phase of the trial, to have the entire case dismissed because of supposedly improper wording of specific questions addressed to prospective jurors by Deputy District Attorneys Aaron Stovitz and Vincent Bugliosi.

Motions for a mistrial based on newspaper, radio or television interviews allegedly granted by the prosecution or defense became commonplace. Most of these exchanges took place in the judge's chambers out of the hearing of the press, public and jury; some are most instructive.

Before going behind the scenes ourselves to better understand what happened in open court we must grapple with another of the many ironies that make Tate/La Bianca a legal experience of near hallucinogenic proportions.

First of all, Paul Fitzgerald, who began as attorney for Charles Manson and ended up defending Patricia Krenwinkel, was in large measure responsible for the case finally being tried in Department 104 of the Superior Court of the County of Los Angeles, the Honorable Charles H. Older presiding. The only reason that Fitzgerald was not *totally* responsible was that Judge Older was assigned the case by accident, due to a difference of opinion among the defense counsel.

It all began with the fact that Los Angeles County District Attorney Evelle J. Younger was running for election as Attorney General for the State of California. Rumor had it that Judge Keene who was hearing the Manson pretrial motions was very interested in the District Attorney's post should Younger win his election.

The rumors were not without substance. Cases are assigned to trial courts in Los Angeles County by the judge presiding over the master calendar in Department 100. The assigning judge, elected by his peers, serves one year then returns to his regular courtroom duties. This arrangement made it possible for Judge William B. Keene, presiding judge in Department 100 whose term there was soon to expire, to assign the important Tate/La Bianca murder case to trial Judge William B. Keene in Department 107 who would soon be presiding over a regular calendar. Taken by themselves these events are not particularly sinister; Judge Keene may have simply felt that he was the best man for the job, that he was familiar with the case and that it would be a disservice to the public to have another jurist come in at that time.

JUDGE WILLIAM B. KEENE BADLY WANTED THE CASE

Other, less charitable opinion had it that Judge Keene saw the favorable public image that would attend the man who heard a case that had aroused international interest and that the image would, inevitably, influence Californians voting for district attorney.

Paul Fitzgerald, now representing Patricia Krenwinkel because of a conflict of interest in the public defender's office arising from their defense of Robert Beausoleil in the Hinman case in which Manson was implicated, leaned toward the more cynical appraisal of Judge Keene's motives. Dramatically, he resigned from the public defender's office, cutting himself loose from a most promising career, to represent Miss Krenwinkel.

I asked him why.

"I was caught in a political squeeze," he told me. "Keene wanted this case very badly. He even assigned it to himself. When he applied the gag order on December 10, 1969 (an order severely restricting public comment by the trial principals) I have reason to believe that he knew that Richard Caballero, who was Susan Atkins' attorney at the time, was selling the rights to her story of the murders, yet he did nothing about it. I believe that he wanted that story to stir up public interest. Since the alleged confession implicated my client I filed an affidavit of prejudice to get Keene to disqualify himself."

Fitzgerald pushed his glasses back up to the bridge of his nose. "Pressure was exerted to get me to withdraw the affidavit," he continued. "I wouldn't do it. I suddenly realized that the only way I could honorably keep my commitments to my client was to quit and represent her privately. So I did."

This is the stuff of heroes. From twenty-six thousand dollars a year to zero, overnight. Not only that; he promptly refiled the affidavit of prejudice and Judge Keene, forced to accept it, left the case, sending it back to Department 100, now presided over by Judge George H. Dell, for reassignment.

According to Miss Bijou Nolan, an attorney and former co-worker of Fitzgerald's in the public defender's office who possesses, in addition to a good legal mind, what surely must rank as one of the finest pairs of legs in the history of public defense, the young lawyer was motivated by a simple desire to see justice done.

"Paul is like that," she told me. "He's an idealist. He was always going out of his way to help the younger attorneys in the office. I know he would often take a lot of his time to go over a case with me, make suggestions, and help me out."

Aside from the fact that a male in Miss Nolan's company for any length of time experiences a not completely unselfish urge to help her in some way, Paul Fitzgerald did appear to be running true to form in his public gesture of defiance.

I asked Aaron Stovitz for his opinion. "He thinks that he'll make his reputation on this capital case," Stovitz said. "And that everyone will come to him with their big retainers." He shrugged. "It doesn't work that way. I've seen this same thing happen too many times before. Maybe some old lady with a hernia who is suing her insurance company will see him on television and say, 'There's a fine, idealistic young man,' and she'll ask him to take her case on contingency. Famous he won't be two months after the trial."

Nevertheless, on Friday, April 17, the four defense attorneys, their clients and two prosecutors were back in Department 100, appearing in Judge Dell's master calendar court. It was widely assumed that as Dell reassigned the case, each of the three remaining defense attorneys in turn would emulate Fitzgerald and file an affidavit of prejudice which, if "presented in a timely manner" is usually granted and supposedly looks good on appeal. Each counsel is permitted one such challenge and it was with genuine surprise that Judge Dell, after having his first two judicial candidates cast aside, found his third, Charles H. Older, unchallenged.

Later viewed either as clever defense strategy to foil a prosecution-court conspiracy to have the fourth name on the list assigned, or as the result of simple cussedness on the part of one of the defense attorneys, the failure to challenge placed the Tate/La Bianca murder case in Department 104 with Judge Older, a Ronald Reagan appointee, former member of the Flying Tigers and World War II fighter pilot, presiding.

The first day of the trial began, prophetically, in the judge's chambers with a private admonition to the attorneys and the defendants.

"I don't need to tell you that this has attracted publicity," Judge Older began. "We are all aware of that. I don't have to tell you that the case will undoubtedly make law in various areas, because of novel problems.

"And I don't have to tell you that the eyes of lawyers and judges and of the public generally throughout the country, and possibly various parts of the world, will be on this case, and specifically on you people during the trial, and I would earnestly beseech all of you to at all times, notwithstanding in the heat of the trial it is easy to say and do things that you might not do on reflection at other times, that you conduct yourselves in a professional and ethical and responsible and dignified manner at all times."

Judge Older, if he harbored any illusions that he was about to fly a straight course through cloudless judicial skies by keeping a firm hand on the controls, had them quickly dispelled by turbulence in the person of the younger, more volatile member of the prosecution team, Deputy District Attorney Vincent Bugliosi. While the press, public and prospective jurors waited impatiently (as they would do many times during the course of the trial) outside in the jammed courtroom, the deputy took the floor.

DEPUTY DISTRICT ATTORNEY VINCENT T. BUGLIOSI

BUGLIOSI: I have just one brief point that I would like to raise. With respect to the pronunciation of my name, which doesn't bother me because it is so extremely difficult to pronounce, it has been mispronounced throughout my personal history and it doesn't bother me, but what does bother me is that I have information from two sources, that an individual came up to Mr. Kanarek (Irving Kanarek, representing Charles Manson) — and I can produce this person — and told Mr.

Kanarek that the way to get to me — and it is wrong, it is not the way to get to me — Kanarek's personality might, per se, but not this particular way — is to pronounce my name, say, BUGliosi.

I am raising the issue because the court beseeched everyone, all the lawyers, to act in a professional manner in court.

Mr. Stovitz also heard Mr. Kanarek in court practicing, as it were, practicing the mispronunciation of my name. And I want to state, on the record and ask the court to tell Mr. Kanarek to make an effort — and that goes for Mr. Shinn (Daye Shinn, representing Susan Atkins) also — to make an effort to pronounce my name correctly.

OLDER: Let me say this: I'm not going to do anything about it. Maybe Mr. Kanarek has a speech defect.

KANAREK: I ask for sworn testimony on this. I ask to be sworn.

BUGLIOSI: If the court does not instruct Mr. Kanarek on this point, I will say this for the record, I intend to tell the jury — I intend to tell Mr. Kanarek in front of the jury — how to pronounce my name.

OLDER: I think you have a right to tell him how to pronounce your name.

BUGLIOSI: I am telling him right now for his benefit, or else it will come out before the jury. My name is pronounced Bugliosi (Boo-lee-oh-see),. You can forget about the "G." "G" before "L" in Italian is silent. And that is for you, Mr. Shinn, although I am sure it was in good faith on your part.

As to Mr. Kanarek, it was not in good faith and I have evidence.

KANAREK: I would like to know the evidence.

OLDER: I think I mispronounced your name.

BUGLIOSI: It is an extremely difficult name to pronounce. It doesn't bother me, but when counsel is making a deliberate attempt to mispronounce it, that is another matter. It annoys me.

KANAREK: I ask for sworn testimony.

OLDER: As to what?

KANAREK: As to my intent in connection with his name.

Mr. Kanarek's request was denied. Minutes later the attorneys and the defendants solemnly took their places in open court, the clerk called the room to order and Judge Older assumed the bench. Amid whispered speculation by the press as to the profundities exchanged in chambers, the trial of Charles Manson, Susan Atkins, Patricia Krenwinkel and Leslie Van Houten for murder officially resumed.

Chapter V

DAY ONE

If pretrial motions may be compared to premarital courtship then jury selection must surely correspond to the gropings that precede the nuptial consummation.

The wooers, defense and prosecution counsel, disport themselves before the wooed, the prospective jurors. Aggressive, patronizing, sympathetic, threatening, depending on the relationship established with an individual juror, the attorneys ask questions and draw conclusions that determine whether or not that juror will be retained or excused. The selection process was made more difficult in Tate/La Bianca because of Judge Older's decision to sequester the jury in the Ambassador Hotel from the time it was sworn until it arrived at a verdict and, should that verdict be first degree murder, until it decided on a life sentence or death in the gas chamber for each defendant.

First there was the prospect of spending six months away from their families: "Your spouses may visit you at the hotel on weekends," Judge Older would tell them, invariably adding, with the suggestion of a commiserative smile, "at their own expense." Then they would receive only $5.00 per day from the state; most employers would guarantee only 30 days regular salary to an employee serving on a jury and many not even that. An excuse for hardship became almost mandatory in the majority of cases. By the time the first twelve members were sworn 141 had been called and of these 67 had been excused for hardship.

Sharply criticized by the district attorney's office for "wasting the peoples' money" by unnecessarily dragging out the trial because of his sequestering decision, Judge Older, in a private meeting in chambers attended only by the attorneys, addressed himself to the situation.

OLDER: I may have stressed, and I am sure I did, to you that my feeling is, as a matter of fact I put it even more bluntly than that, that I don't intend to let any juror sit on the jury who has been exposed to a confession. (Susan Atkins's recounting of the murders that received wide national and international attention.)

I don't change that opinion. I still think just that.

I realize the problem, Mr. Stovitz. Let me say one other thing, now, if I read tomorrow morning in the newspaper or some day soon that the court has now ruled that no juror will sit on the jury who has been exposed to a confession, we may be here six months picking a jury.

So I hope you and your employer, and I am not singling out anybody, I hope you all have the good sense not to go out and make statements like that, apart from any violation of the publicity order.

STOVITZ: If you read about it today, your Honor, it would not come from our side because we are not having our meeting until tomorrow morning.

OLDER: You are not having your press conference today?

STOVITZ: (Dryly) Tomorrow morning I will discuss it with
   Mr. Younger.

Potential jurors' exposure to pretrial publicity became more
and more of a concern to Judge Older as the *voir dire* made
it increasingly obvious that almost everyone in Los Angeles
County had some prior knowledge of the case. Soon each
juror was being taken individually into chambers to be questioned by Older and the attorneys, a laborious and, for both
the participants and the excluded press, nerve wracking procedure. Inevitably, bits and pieces of the chamber proceedings
leaked to the news-starved reporters (some days the judge
appeared in open court for less than a minute, to officially
adjourn for the day), and each dribble of information that
appeared in print fell on Older's strained sensibilities with the
cumulative effect of a Chinese water torture.

In early July matters came to a head when articles appeared
in two prominent Los Angeles dailies substantially revealing
the proceedings in chambers the day before, including
an accurate account of how defendant Manson had told
his attorney, Irving Kanarek, to remain silent and not ask
the jurors any more questions. (What Manson actually said
was "Shut up and sit down," a command that Kanarek
meekly obeyed.)

Older again called a private meeting of counsel.

"I am going to admonish all of you," he said, "that any of
the proceedings in this case that occur in chambers, or any
of the proceedings that occur out of the presence of the jury,
whether at the bench or anywhere else, are confidential and
they are not to be disclosed to the press.

"So the record will be absolutely clear, if that publicity
order (Judge Keene's original order) does not now cover

matters which are conducted in chambers or out of the presence of the jury, I will now amend that order to add the express proviso that any session of this trial which is conducted in chambers or out of the presence of the jury, and not in open court, are not to be disclosed to anybody."

Since Judge Keene's order had expressly forbidden the attorneys to discuss the case under any circumstances with anyone not directly party to the proceedings, this additional proviso put an almost unprecedented gag on every aspect of the trial.

The day following Judge Older's unequivocal declaration, the Los Angeles Herald-Examiner carried a front page reproduction of a drawing by Leslie Van Houten of the prospective (and painstakingly interrogated) jury panel with their names clearly marked and a caption, "All the lonely people judgement." Whereupon, in the words of one of the court bailiffs charged with maintaining security, "The shit really hit the fan."

THE JURY AS SEEN BY THE ACCUSED

Once again fifty reporters and nearly sixty veniremen and women waiting to be called, filled the spectator section of the courtroom and gazed in restless boredom at the vacant bench while Judge Older confronted the attorneys in chambers.

OLDER: I'm really appalled. I am absolutely appalled at the conduct of some of the counsel in this case from time to time.

Now that (referring to the printed sketch) to me is an irresponsible act. I think that if counsel know their clients are passing notes around and drawing pictures in close proximity to the media, there is a danger you are going to have to anticipate, that is all.

REINER: (Ira Reiner, at the time representing Leslie Van Houten) Is your Honor suggesting that this is one of the normal dangers one encounters during a trial? That some other attorney at the table would pass off confidential information to reporters? I don't agree with that. (Reiner had earlier accused Daye Shinn, representing Susan Atkins, of taking the drawing and giving it to a reporter).

OLDER: You don't agree with what?

REINER: This is just a normal danger that counsel should anticipate.

OLDER: I am saying you are aware of what is happening out there and you should anticipate the obvious, is what I am saying.

REINER: I don't consider it obvious that some other attorney may pass confidential matter to a reporter.

OLDER: That's not what I said. What I said was, the passing around, the making of those diagrams and drawings and the passing around of notes. I can see that from the bench.

Now, it must be clear to you that there is a risk that some or all of that material may fall into someone else's hands.

I think you have a responsibility, too, Mr. Reiner, as well as the other counsel to prevent that.

REINER: Is your Honor suggesting that I cannot communicate with my client with notes? That is absurd.

OLDER: Your statement is absurd because that is not my intimation at all, and you know it.

REINER: I do not know that, your Honor. And I did believe and I do believe that to be your intimation.

OLDER: That is ridiculous, Mr. Reiner.

REINER: Then I cannot find any other possible explanation.

OLDER: I am suggesting that if you are irresponsible yourself, you may find that these things find their way into other hands, that is what I am saying.

REINER: Are you suggesting that I have done anything irresponsible?

OLDER: I am suggesting that you better keep your eyes open or this may happen again.

REINER: I know of no way to respond to your Honor's comments.

OLDER: Then don't.

"This trial could result in some basic changes in the law," Aaron Stovitz, who had been present in chambers but who would not tell me what occurred there, remarked later. "I think that we're going to have much closer supervision of what police officers and attorneys can say to the press right from the moment of arrest. I think there is going to be a much tighter clamp-down."

I asked if he agreed with that possibility.

"Well," he said, "I personally think that when someone commits a crime, especially a serious and bizarre crime, there has to be an assumption of risk, an understanding that the crime is going to be discussed in the press. I think that the protection of the defendant's rights can go too far."

To someone who sat through the seemingly interminable pretrial hearings and now daily faced an empty courtroom where the trial was supposedly in progress, a new law, possibly termed Manson's Law, suggested itself: *The more heinous the crime the more due the process.*

Months before, when he was first appearing in Judge George H. Dell's court on pretrial motions, Manson was experiencing his first contact with due process in the big time and was, characteristically, feeling his way, finding out how far he could go. Prior to his present bust Charlie had been a run-of-the-mill crook and had been treated as such; now, with attorneys flocking to represent him — Judge Dell, reading down a formidable list of attorneys who had visited Charlie during a single week was given to remark "Well, I see that there are some members of the bar not represented here." — the Family head began to savor his new role as a defendant of some moment.

First of all, Manson tried to use his courtroom appearances to communicate with the press. He wanted, from the beginning, to represent himself, to appear *in propria persona,* and he repeatedly rebuffed the court's attempts to provide him with qualified counsel. Sample exchange between the defendant and Judge Dell, early in the pretrial proceedings:

DELL: I would be privileged, Mr. Manson, to appoint the best counsel I can for your defense.

MANSON: I'll bet you would.

DELL: Yes, I would.

MANSON: (Looking at the courtroom) That's how you'll
send me to the gas chamber.

But the slight, 140 pound, 5'7" defendant, soon found that
the press were not championing his cause. Later, during *voir
dire,* a favorite defense question of a prospective juror as
regards pretrial publicity, was: "Have you ever read or heard
anything good about the defendant?" The answer, inevitably,
was in the negative. ("No wonder," Stovitz remarked after one
such exchange, "he never *did* anything good.")

As the trial drew nearer, Charlie, in large part displeased
with the press — the "magnetic, hypnotic eyes" of the first
stories were gradually giving way to less flattering adjectives
such as "little" and "sallow" — attempted to communicate
with the Family, to reassert his dominance, to show them that
he could cross the boundary between their world and that of
the establishment and could, in effect, look after them all by
surviving himself.

Once again, pretrial in Judge Keene's court, on the subject
of a defense attorney:

KEENE: Please consider again, Mr. Manson, the matter of
defense counsel.

MANSON: I don't see how I can.

KEENE: Think of what you're up against. The District Attorney's office will put their very best in court.

MANSON: (Smiling and nodding his acknowledgment of that
fact to the courtroom) I have the truth, you know. I
have fifty witnesses. I live in the desert and I think a
court of law is where you should come back to earth,

you know. Lawyers and judges talk over people's heads. The judge is a father figure and is really on the side of the prosecution. I have love on my side.

Manson then glanced toward the spectators' section where three giggling Family members squirmed excitedly. A closer look at these girls, most still in their teens, affords us another glimpse into their leader's personality.

How a small time loser can transform himself into a guru, no matter how suspect, is partially explained by the quality of his acolytes. On the whole the girls appear to be very moderately endowed both intellectually and physically. It is easy for the middle-aged observer to mistake vacuity for cuteness and nubility for sensuality; the fact emerges as the case proceeds into the trial stage and the girls come under more intensive scrutiny that, despite the well publicized family backgrounds of a few (Sandra Pugh's mother, for example, is a minor San Diego social figure), no big brains or even very attractive bodies surround Charlie. He knew better than to expect the best or, in many instances, the second best. He made do with what he had and exploited them as fully as is humanly possible.

As he stood at the prisoner's microphone during the protracted pretrial hearings Manson, using his own terms of reference, had accomplished quite a lot. The judge's joking aside to the press at the conclusion of one hearing that they probably would not want to stay for the remaining court calendar now that the "special guest" is leaving pleased that guest tremendously; it represented a grudging acknowledgement that he, Charles Manson, had made master calendar Judge George H. Dell's court momentarily an important place.

To understand just how important, let's disregard the judge's chiding suggestion and sit through part of that calendar to watch an assortment of felons and lesser miscreants being afforded due process.

Six men now sit on a long bench occupying the space allotted to Charles Manson. Each, when his name is called, rises in turn, stands in front of the microphone and hears the charge read auctioneer style by an assistant district attorney much junior to Aaron Stovitz or Vincent Bugliosi. The question "Doyouwaiveyourrighttoajurytrialoftwelveindividualsto-unanimouslydetermineyourguiltorinnocence?" spews unintelligibly forth; the suspect, taking his cue from the public defender, replies "Yes."

"Doyouwantatrialbyjudge?"

The defendant looks on numbly and the public defender points impatiently to the bench and nods.

"Yes," the defendant says.

Six up, six gone and before the last one has disappeared through the jail door, another six are seated in their places. Occasionally the public defender, who is probably seeing the facts of the case in the file before him for the first time as the defendant stands to the microphone, interjects a request for a continuance or a plea for leniency, but these are quickly heard and ruled on so that six, twelve, eighteen men are processed in the time it took to hear Charles Manson's first pretrial motion. These prisoners make no motions, exchange no humorous banter with the court.

In the Manson Family trial the presumption of innocence is being confused with the protection of rights. Both the accused petty thief and the accused murderer are presumed to be innocent; if the layman were to suggest that by all standards of common sense one is more innocent than the other he would be told to fall silent and wallow in his ignorance of judicial procedure. Yet the same legalistic minds who perform ritualistic mental genuflection before the concept of "Justice" regularly assign degrees of protection to different criminals that, by extension, assume degrees of guilt or innocence.

Now, however, the stretched-out version of equal protection that has comprised the Tate/La Bianca pretrial proceedings are at an end; the first twelve potential jurors are seated in the courtroom, and the stage, for the moment, is the property of that fascinating breed of legal practitioner: the trial lawyer.

Chapter VI

DAY FIVE

"The whole machinery of the state, all the apparatus of the system, and its varied workings, end in simply bringing twelve good men into a box," wrote Henry Brougham commenting on a nineteenth century jury.

In twentieth century California the twelve good men (and women) get into that box by means of a keyed number system. The state voter registration list is programmed into a selector in alphabetical order together with a random number that is changed monthly; every name that comes up at that number (in the Tate/La Bianca selection the number was forty-one) is notified by mail that he or she has been chosen as a potential juror. Every citizen who responds (the names of those who simply ignore the notice are fed back into the machine for another try) is given a language comprehension and word meaning test; if the prospective juror passes the test with the required sixty per cent score he or she is assembled in a central pool that may vary in size from 650 to 800 people at any one time.

When a court indicates the need of a panel, sixty names are

drawn at random from a wire mesh wheel at the assembly point, the people selected are taken to the court and seated in the courtroom and twelve names are drawn, once again at random, from the sixty yellow slips that accompanied the panel. These veniremen and women, as unsworn jurors are called, are then interrogated by both the judge and the defense and prosecution lawyers — when one is excused for whatever cause another yellow slip is drawn and another member of the original sixty moves to the box — until twelve prospective jurors and six alternates are found who are acceptable to all parties. In Tate/La Bianca it took four panels to accomplish this task.

Judge Older, after explaining that they will be sitting in judgment on two trials, the first to decide guilt or innocence and the second, if the guilt is murder in the first degree, to decide on a penalty of life imprisonment or death, asked each prospective juror these two questions:

"Do you entertain such conscientious opinions regarding the death penalty that you would be unable to make an impartial decision as to any defendant's guilt regardless of the evidence that develops during the trial?"

and,

"Do you entertain such conscientious opinions regarding the death penalty that you would automatically refuse to impose it without regard to the evidence developed during the trial?"

When the answer to the second question was "Yes," Older pursued the implications of that particular response to a degree that some of the waiting veniremen and women found irritating. What they failed to grasp was that the judge was establishing the pertinence of the word "automatically" in the two questions; on the basis of the Witherspoon decision a juror must be excluded from duty in a capital case if he or she under no circumstances would impose the death penalty. "I don't think I could," or "I'm certain that I couldn't," or "My conscience wouldn't let me," were simply not good enough answers. Older had to fish out the "automatically" or its equivalent and, in doing so, he set both the pace and style of the *voir dire*.

The slow pace, variously described in the press as "turtle-like," "lethargic," and "snail-paced," especially when judge, attorneys and defendants began disappearing into chambers with increasing frequency to question individual jurors, was relieved somewhat by a second trial being heard before a kangaroo court of attorneys and the press; the defendant: Irving A. Kanarek.

Kanarek, whose appointment as Charles Manson's final attorney of record was described by Aaron Stovitz as "A disaster of major proportions," entered the case as an enigma in search of an identity. Before the trial even started Vincent Bugliosi presented a fifty minute, carefully documented, impassioned plea in open court to have him kicked out. Portents of doom spread through the District Attorney's office as Bugliosi, in a television interview following the denial of his motion, estimated conservatively that the trial might now run from two to five years.

When asked by Judge Older if he really wanted Kanarek to represent him, Manson, in chambers, replied: "If I can't defend myself I want whoever gives you the worst time. He gives you the worst time. I want him." It would appear, from the dust kicked up in the staid old Hall of Justice, that the defendant had made, from his viewpoint at least, a wise decision.

The main charge against Irving Kanarek appeared to be

IRVING A. KANAREK, " . . . A DISASTER OF MAJOR PROPORTIONS?"

that he was an obstructionist, that he did not adhere to the rules of the legal game. It seemed that everyone had at least one Kanarek story to offer in support of the charge.

"You know what he did once?" Burton Katz, successful prosecutor of Robert Beausoleil in the Gary Hinman murder, asked me. "He objected to a prosecution witness stating his name. Said it was hearsay evidence. He asked the guy how he knew his name and the guy said his mother told him." Katz, an ebullient young man, threw up his hands in despair. "Hearsay," he explained. "Not something he knew of his own knowledge."

John Miner, the District Attorney's office's medico-legal expert, once tried a statutory rape case with Kanarek. "All you had to prove in those days was that the victim was under age and that sexual intercourse had taken place," Miner recalls. "That's all. There were no mitigating circumstances. A stat-rape case took one day at the most to select a jury and another day at the most to present the case. Never more than two days. One asked the victim's name, her age, whether intercourse had taken place and who the assailant was. That was it. Nothing else had to be proved."

Miner, obviously becoming irritated at the mere recollection of the occurrence, continued. "Kanarek cross examined," he said. "He'd sidle up to the witness, leer at the jury and ask something like: 'Now do you recall having an orgasm as a result of this alleged act?' We objected, of course, and it was sustained. But that didn't bother Kanarek. He'd leer again at the jury and ask: 'At the time the penis was allegedly entering you, were you in pain at that time?' Objection. Sustained."

Miner shook his head in disbelief. "Nine trial days he kept that up," he reminisced. "He lost, of course. And he irritated a hell of a lot of people, including the judge. Finally the judge called us to the bench and said, 'Mr. Kanarek, you can go on asking these questions as long as you like but, if you persist, when you are finished I want you to know that you are going to jail for five days for contempt. Let's proceed, gentlemen.' Kanarek," Miner recalled with a smile, "rested his case."

Kanarek's abrasiveness was not limited to judges and opposing counsel. "He's a strange one," Charles Hollopeter told me. "I remember him on the Jimmy Lee Smith case." Smith, who had received the death sentence for the kidnap-murder of a Los Angeles detective, had been granted a new trial. "The second trial was dragging on for months and Smith repeatedly asked the court to dismiss Kanarek and appoint a new attorney. It got so bad that Smith wouldn't talk to Kanarek. Finally Smith lost his temper, picked up a chair in open court and tried to attack him. The judge finally agreed to relieve Kanarek." Hollopeter was then appointed as Smith's attorney and won him a reduced sentence of life imprisonment.

Whatever his past sins, there were some sitting on the kangaroo court who felt that the virulence being directed toward the defense attorney appeared to be in poor taste at best and, at worst, slanderous.

The prosecution went, literally, to every legal length to have Kanarek removed from the case. Beginning with Vincent Bugliosi's nearly one hour long denouncement and culminating in an unprecedented representation by District Attorney Younger to the California Supreme Court for a writ of mandate to order Judge Older to hold a hearing to determine Kanarek's competency, the persecution of Irving Kanarek appeared, to the impartial observer, to attain near paranoic proportions.

"We are prepared to present testimony from eight judges and numerous attorneys and court attaches," Younger said at a press conference prior to the California Supreme Court's refusal to issue the writ of mandate, "that Manson's counsel has a reputation for grossly obstructionist and dilatory tactics which have been prejudicial to the interests of his clients and to the people of this state.

"There is a suspicion," the District Attorney continued, "that some attorneys deliberately follow a course of conduct during a trial to increase the likelihood of reversal on appeal."

Although there was undoubtedly substance to the prosecution's contentions as to the defense attorney's past behavior, the plain fact was that up to the time of jury selection in Tate/La Bianca Kanarek, accused by Bugliosi before the press and jury of having "Diarrhea of the mouth," had not exhibited that condition.

True, on the few occasions when he questioned the prospective jurors he was less than brilliant. Sample exchange:

Q: Do you judge a man by the way you think or by the way he thinks?

A: By the way he thinks.

Q: Would you explain what you meant by the way he thinks . . . (Laughter in courtroom)

STOVITZ: Object. Improper *voir dire.*

OLDER: Sustained.

Q: Could you judge someone from Afghanistan if you didn't know their culture or background . . .

A: I don't know where Afghanistan is.

Q: Neither do I. I just picked the name. Now, you would have to evaluate what the people from Afghanistan think, what their own culture thought of what they might have done . . .

STOVITZ: Object. Improper *voir dire.*

OLDER: Sustained.

Q: Would it be difficult to judge a person from a different way of life?

A: Yes.

Q: How do you propose to judge someone from a different way of life?

OLDER: I'm going to sustain my own objection. Improper *voir dire.*

Q: Are there some things you would be incapable of judging?

STOVITZ: Object. Improper *voir dire.*

OLDER: Sustained.

And so it went. Kanarek seemed either to have no understanding of proper judicial procedure or to be playing games with the court. When later, at Manson's orders, he stopped questioning the jurors and began accepting some who were obviously inimical to his cause, the kangaroo court argued that he was not representing his client properly, that he was seeking instead to provide grounds for a successful appeal.

Physically, Kanarek is well cast for the role of the trial "heavy." Bearing a striking resemblance to Akim Tamiroff in both face and build he appears to function in a constant state of disarray. Loose papers flap from file folders tucked under both arms as, shirttail flying and trouser cuffs trailing the floor behind, he arrives in court late. His lack of punctuality was a

JUDGE CHARLES H. OLDER, " . . . A VERY HEAVY DUDE"

constant source of irritation to Judge Older; one morning, in a private session in chambers, his Honor lowered the boom.

OLDER: Mr. Kanarek you were late again this morning.

KANAREK: Your Honor, I believe I was three minutes late.

OLDER: You were not three minutes late; you were seven minutes late.

KANAREK: Well, I apologize to the court for being late, your Honor, I certainly am conscious of it. The parking situation is very difficult your Honor.

OLDER: You are not going to use that excuse that you cannot park, Mr. Kanarek. I really cannot accept the reason you have given me. I am going to fine you in contempt for being late. I am not going to take up the matter at this time. I am going to defer it.

(Later, in chambers, after the mid-morning fifteen minute recess)

OLDER: Before we resume with the trial matters I want to make an order with respect to Mr. Kanarek's failure to appear on time this morning.

KANAREK: Your Honor I wonder if I might have an attorney represent me in this matter?

OLDER: On your tardiness?

KANAREK: Your Honor enunciated it as contempt, your Honor, and I would like to have a hearing on it.

OLDER: Well, I had a hearing. You didn't mention anything about an attorney then. I simply wanted to enunciate a formal order on it now.

KANAREK: Your Honor, I would like to take evidence.

OLDER: Evidence on what?

KANAREK: As to actually the extent of my lateness. What I would like to have is counsel, your Honor, in this regard. I know that I am not in contempt if by contempt we mean willfulness.

OLDER: Are you now arguing the merits?

KANAREK: No, your Honor. I am just giving the court a reason. First of all, it is a criminal charge.

OLDER: No, it is not a criminal charge, it is a civil contempt.

KANAREK: Isn't it deemed in any situation wherein one can find themselves in custody in the county jail — it would seem that that has criminal overtones, your Honor.

OLDER: Do you have an attorney in mind, Mr. Kanarek?

KANAREK: Yes, your Honor.

OLDER: Who is that?

KANAREK: Mr. Fitzgerald.

OLDER: Does he agree to represent you?

FITZGERALD: I will represent him.

OLDER: All right. Let's proceed.

KANAREK: Very well. I would like to prepare him . . .

FITZGERALD: Could we put it over until maybe early this afternoon?

OLDER: All right, we will put it over until 1:45 this afternoon.

FITZGERALD: That is agreeable.

KANAREK: Thank you, your Honor.

(In chambers after lunch)

OLDER: Do you wish to proceed with the contempt matter?

FITZGERALD: Yes. (Asks for a delay because he has not had time to consult with his client.)

OLDER: Well, I have no objection to a continuance.

FITZGERALD: Well, would your Honor consider a week?

OLDER: I don't see any necessity for that. We are talking about a tardiness of seven minutes, disputed one way or the other for a minute or two. Let's not be absurd. We will put the matter over until Friday, two days from now at 8:15 A.M.

KANAREK: Thank you, your Honor.

STOVITZ: (Until now a silent witness to the proceedings) He can get a parking space at 8:15.

Later, at the trial within a trial, Paul Fitzgerald put on a spirited defense of his client, and Judge Older set aside his contempt motion.

Kanarek may present a bungling, at times even a clownish

image; it may be argued, however, as Polonius said of Hamlet, that his rantings and ravings have method in them. He drove the opposition to distraction, a condition notoriously ill-suited to reasoned argument, and managed on several occasions to break down the carefully cultivated Stovitz "cool." "A law-yer's duty is to defend his client," the Head of Trials observed after a shouting session with Kanarek, "not to turn the whole judicial procedure into a sideshow."

Most people would agree with Stovitz's observation, but, then, most people are not on trial for their lives. In Kanarek, Manson found what he may have been searching for all along, an educated man willing to play the game according to Charlie's rules, a man of the establishment willing to forsake it for . . . what? Apparently not money. Prestige? Well, the other attorneys were in it for prestige, why not Irving Kanarek?

Kanarek's background suggests more substance than that required of the court jester. The law is his second profession. As a chemical engineer he worked for North American Aviation on the Redstone project then decided on the study of law. He originally intended to become a patent attorney (rumors, which he refuses to confirm or deny, suggest that he holds engineering patents that enable him to try financially unrewarding cases) but, he maintains, it just happened that his first few clients were involved in felonies and he drifted into the practice of criminal law.

Kanarek, harassed legally and abused verbally, arouses somewhat the same emotions in at least one observer as does Leroux's *Phantom of the Opera;* he may seem a little cracked running around up there like that but one can't help but experience a sense of sympathy for his plight. Judge Older, despite some trying exchanges with the defense attorney both in chambers and in open court, appeared to be aware that the numerous public denunciations of Kanarek represented a potential source of bias that might reflect adversely on Charles Manson. Following public disclosure of the appeal to the California Supreme Court to test Kanarek's competency, Older addressed the prospective jurors:

"Mr. Kanarek," he said, "is to be considered like any other attorney. He is like any other attorney in this case. The act of the District Attorney in calling a press conference while this jury was being selected was an irresponsible act. But I admonish you that you are not to consider that act or any statement coming out of that conference as having any bearing whatever on any of the issues in this case."

Irving Kanarek's importance in Tate/La Bianca lies not in his person but in the fact that he is defending a client in a capital case whose significance goes far beyond the usual homicide. If his behavior obscures the issue without presenting an adequate defense, if he does, indeed, turn the trial procedure into a "sideshow," the cause of justice will hardly be served. A conviction will not act as a deterrent, should this be the "first of the acid murders," if, on appeal, the trial record is hopelessly beclouded with extraneous trivia.

However, up until Tuesday, July 14, 1970, the day the first jury of seven men and five women was sworn in four weeks and three days after the trial began, (as opposed to Kanarek-inspired estimates from the other attorneys of from three months to one year) no breakdown in the orderly trial process had occurred, due principally to the firm judicial hand of Judge Charles H. Older. How the jury was reacting to what it saw and heard and, equally importantly, to information that was expressly denied it but to which it may have had access, remained to be seen.

Chapter VII

DAY THIRTY-FIVE

If, in private, Deputy District Attorney Vincent T. Bugliosi displayed a sensitivity to his name that suggested the symptoms of an incipient neurosis, in the courtroom he projected a dedication to and impassioned belief in the righteousness of his cause that favorably impressed the jury.

Extroverted, the press called him "Vince," addicted to conservatively cut single breasted suits usually worn with a vest, the junior member of the prosecution team possessed a self-confidence that occasionally edged over into cockiness; he didn't suffer fools gladly but he never permitted his private opinions to interfere with his relationship to the jurors.

Vince Bugliosi just doesn't look like the kind of fellow who would want to harm anyone, let alone demand and, in an impressive number of cases win, the death penalty. If this nice clean-cut young man, the jury might well say to itself, thinks that these people are bad, then there must be something to it.

Straightaway the jurors began calling him "Sir," an honorific they generally denied defense counsel. There is nothing that a prosecutor trying an important case likes better than to have the jurors address him as "Sir." It indicates that they are properly respectful and of a frame of mind to give the required weight to their interrogator's veiled pronouncements.

From the beginning, Bugliosi hammered away at the concept of circumstantial evidence; a typical exchange with a juror:

Q: Now it is important that you understand the meaning of circumstantial evidence in this case.

A: Yes, sir.

Q: Let me give you an example of circumstantial evidence that is often used in our courts. Little Johnny Jones's mother tells him that he must not take any cookies from the cookie jar. (Bugliosi flashes a smile emphasizing the wholesomeness of his example. One would suspect that the inner Bugliosi is saying 'Any idiot should be able to get this,' but the public Bugliosi draws a reassuring return smile from the juror. The only thing that might have improved the example would have been the substitution of a slice of apple pie.) Now she goes into another room then returns to the livingroom to find little Johnny sitting on the floor eating a cookie. Now that is circumstantial evidence. Do you understand that?

A: Yes, sir.

Q: If Johnny had been actually seen by someone putting his hand in the jar taking the cookie that would be direct evidence. Right?

A: Yes, sir.

Q: But no one saw him. However, the fact that there was no one else around and that he was sitting there eating the cookie is circumstantial evidence that he took the cookie from the jar. Is that clear?

A: Yes, sir.

Q: So quite often (here Bugliosi slows his delivery and adopts a tone that indicates the seriousness of the point about to be made), circumstantial evidence is every bit as effective, if not more effective, than direct evidence. Is that clear?

A: Yes, *sir*.

Paul Fitzgerald in his *voir dire* wryly observed that little Johnny's brother could have come in, given him a cookie, and then left. This was taken, by some members of the panel at least, to be a facetious remark; when Bugliosi resumed his interrogation with the information that little Johnny, of course, didn't have a brother, the jurors got the message. Little Charlie didn't have a brother, either.

Jurors not excused for hardship were often excused for causes that varied from a newly joined member of Alcoholics Anonymous who told the judge that he was still in the shaking stage and would surely return to the bottle should he be sequestered in a hotel for six months, to a juror with an overly vengeful attitude. Judge Older addressed his standard "Do you entertain such conscientious opinions . . ." to this latter venireman and received this unusual reply:

A: Yes, I would (refuse to impose the death penalty), for the simple reason that I don't think it's harsh enough.
   There ought to be something worse than death, you know, for certain crimes.
   If it is punishable by death or life imprisonment, it is not bad enough, you know. They ought to be given a worse punishment than that.

At the invitation of the court, Paul Fitzgerald inquired:

Q: You indicated to the court that your feelings in connection with the death penalty were that in some respects the death penalty was not harsh enough. Is that correct?

A: That's right.

Q: What did you have in mind, the rack and screw?

A: Well, I am not a sadist, but something like that. I mean, you know, well, let's say for example, you know, in a case where someone was brutally, you know — let's say they were kidnapped and then tortured, or something like that, where they take the guy in and he goes through his trial, they might give him life imprisonment and he gets out at the end of seven years, and that is nothing.

Whereupon counsel approached the bench and out of the hearing of the prospective jurors and the press Irving Kanarek moved for a mistrial on the grounds that the venireman's statements prejudiced the whole jury panel against life imprisonment. The motion was denied, everyone returned to their places and Aaron Stovitz decided to milk the situation for what it was worth. Stovitz addressed the prospective juror:

Q: You are faced with these two decisions, life imprisonment, whatever that may be, or the death penalty.
   Do you think that your frame of mind is such that you are unalterably opposed to imposing the death penalty because you feel that is not sufficient punishment under the facts of the case?

FITZGERALD: (Jumping to his feet) Object, your Honor. That is misconduct and I will cite Mr. Stovitz for misconduct.

Everyone then approached the bench where the defense asked for an assignment of misconduct because Stovitz's "whatever that may be" implies that a life sentence doesn't mean life imprisonment, as well as an admonishment to the jury. Irving Kanarek asked for a mistrial. The following privileged exchange, like most of the other bench and in chamber conferences, revealed here for the first time, took place:

OLDER: The motion for a mistrial will be denied.

REINER: Excuse me. The court has not ruled on our request for an assignment of misconduct and admonition to the jury. I think the court has indicated its feelings but there has been no ruling on those requests.

OLDER: I find no misconduct. Anything further?

REINER: Thank you. I assume, then, the court will not admonish the jury?

OLDER: Where do you get that assumption? I have already told you that they have been admonished in the first place on precisely that subject, and I have not said I would not admonish them.

REINER: I meant with respect to Mr. Stovitz.

OLDER: Don't assume. If you want to ask me, ask me, but don't make assumptions for the record.

REINER: I did ask it directly.

OLDER: The answer is, I will.

REINER: Advise the jury with respect to Mr. Stovitz?

OLDER: No. No.

Judge Older then admonished the prospective jury to disregard the inference that the verdict of life imprisonment may or may not constitute a life sentence.

Most of the jurors who were excused had pleaded hardships or expressed opinions that made their departure almost a foregone conclusion. Some, however, who were finally sworn on the original panel of twelve, responded in *voir dire* in a manner that seemed, to some observers, to be highly prejudicial. Here, for example, Ira Reiner questions Anlee L. Sisto, an electrician in the suburban Downey school district.

Q.   With respect to the information, such as it was, that came to you from the media, Mr. Sisto, would it be a fair statement to say that the sum and substance of such media information was to the effect that the defendants or some of them may have been guilty of the crimes for which they have been charged?

A: Yes, I would have to say yes.

Q: And would it also be a fair statement to say that you did not receive any information or any suggestions from the media to the effect that the defendants may not be guilty; is that true?

A: I recall of none.

Q: So, it would be a fair statement to say that the totality of all information that you received prior to the time that you were called as a prospective jury member was to the effect that the defendants were guilty?

A: Yes.

Q: Would it be a fair statement to say that prior to the time that you were called as a prospective juror in the case, it was your tentative, if not firm, judgment that the defendants probably were guilty of these crimes?

A: Yes.

Q: And nothing has occurred since that time upon which you could base a change of opinion?

A: No, I don't believe so.

Q: So your opinion today is the same as it has been during the last few months?

A: Yes, I would say so.

Q: Thank you very much.

Why was Mr. Sisto not challenged? The fact that he was not lends credence to District Attorney Evelle Younger's implication that the trial might be conducted with an eye to an appellate court, that the attorneys were actually jeopardizing the rights of their clients in this trial—in effect, conceding it —in the hope that their omissions, errors and general sloppy handling of the case would result in the verdicts being reversed.

Why, to pursue the thinking a step further, would any attorney want his client to be found guilty and then have his own work cited as a reason for a new trial? Because in Tate/La Bianca the defense, for a variety of reasons ranging from pretrial publicity to private conviction, felt that theirs was a lost cause and that most of their colleagues felt the same. There would be no stigma attached to losing, each man would have gotten his share of notoriety and the clients would be afforded a second opportunity—with a new batch of eager attorneys— to establish their innocence.

Does that sound cold-blooded? Let's take another look at Mr. Sisto's commendably frank testimony and what might have happened as a result of it. Each defense attorney has five peremptory challenges with which he can excuse a prospective juror without cause. (If he excuses for cause, such as hardship or bias, he must prove his contention to the satisfaction of the judge, not an easy task when jurors are walking in and out of the court in a seemingly endless stream.) In addition, the four defense attorneys have twenty additional peremptory challenges which they can only exercise collectively; if one refuses to exercise a collective challenge, none may do so. The prosecution also has a total of forty peremptory challenges.

Ira Reiner exercised his five personal peremptory challenges but his colleagues refused to exercise any of the twenty joint challenges. Paul Fitzgerald exercised one of his personal challenges, Irving Kanarek and Daye Shinn none. This does not necessarily make Ira Reiner a shining example of legal virtue, battling for his client's life despite the dastardly motives of his co-counsel; he may simply have been less realistic than they. But he did challenge Mr. Sisto for cause and, when in later questioning the juror assured the court that he would take its instructions and view the evidence with an open mind, had that challenge denied.

The prosecution, leery of being accused of delaying tactics and increasingly pleased with the make-up of the panel, exercised its peremptory challenges sparingly, ending up with twenty-nine not used.

In fairness, Ira Reiner did try harder. He asked for, and was granted, a secret session in chambers from which even the defendants were excluded. This is what transpired:

REINER: It is a matter of common knowledge among those of us who practice in the criminal courts that the District Attorney's office has access to information not available to defense counsel in selecting peremptory challenges.

I am referring specifically to two things.

They have what is called a "bounce sheet" in the

FOR THE DEFENSE: REINER, FITZGERALD, KANAREK AND SHINN

District Attorney's office, indicating the entire voting record of all prospective jurors in all prior cases on which they have sat.

This information is available to counsel in civil cases generally but is not available to defense counsel in criminal cases. I would ask the court to order the District Attorney's office to run a make on each prospective juror to determine whether they have a criminal record, and they exercise this and use this in determining whether they shall or shall not exercise a peremptory challenge. I think, checking the criminal records, not from the District Attorney's office, but employing the services of the Los Angeles Police Department to make such checks, is improper.

STOVITZ: In answer to counsel's first inquiry, we do not keep a list of all the jurors and how they voted on previous cases. We do have a list of oddball jurors who have hung up juries 11 to 1 or 10 to 2. These come out, oh, whenever a deputy has such a case. If counsel wants to see our list, going back for six months, I will be glad to show counsel that list of oddball jurors.

REINER: I am referring to jurors, of course, who have not previously served, but those on the present jury panel of which the District Attorney has information. Does your office include all prospective jurors?

STOVITZ: The offer is that if we become aware of any criminal record of any of the jurors and if your Honor feels this is information that should be turned over to the defense, we have no objection to turning that information over to the defense.

Reiner repeatedly attempted to separate his client, Leslie Van Houten, from the other defendants, in the minds of the prospective jurors. Admonitions such as: "Do you fully understand that I am representing Miss Van Houten and only Miss

Van Houten?", "When I speak in this courtroom I am speaking only for Leslie Van Houten," and "Whatever evidence is presented against the other defendants applies only to them and does not necessarily involve Leslie Van Houten," became commonplace.

One question that the defense attorney repeatedly asked revealed the difficulties under which he was operating and foretold his ultimate dismissal from the case. "Would you," Reiner asked each juror, "find Leslie Van Houten 'Not guilty' if the evidence so indicated *even though she herself expressed a desire to be found guilty?*" Patently, one of the most unusual *voir dire* questions in the practice of criminal law.

The question, in effect, told the jury that the defense counsel did not have the confidence of the defendant and even carried a strong implication of possible guilt. Miss Van Houten, at nineteen the youngest of the defendants and charged with only two counts of murder (the La Bianca slayings) as opposed to seven counts for each of the other three, appeared determined to sabotage her attorney's efforts. She began standing up in court and asking to be heard. Judge Older, after pointing out on several occasions that she must speak through her counsel, finally gave her permission to address the court.

"Mr. Reiner is not speaking for me, he is speaking for himself," the defendant said on one occasion. "His voice is not my voice. He can't speak for me."

Judge Older asked her what she had in mind.

"I want Mr. Reiner removed as my attorney," she replied. "I don't want him to represent me."

The court denied her request then and on one subsequent occasion. Finally, she submitted a written petition asking that Reiner be relieved and that Ronald Hughes, for a brief time Manson's attorney, replace him.

Judge Older took the matter into chambers and asked if either the defendants or their attorneys wished to be heard.

STOVITZ: Just speaking as *amicus curiae,* your Honor, I know that Miss Van Houten has graduated from high school. At least I think she has.

I know she should be made aware of Mr. Hughes's background with respect to what murder cases Mr. Hughes has been involved in, and his background as to what criminal cases he has defended.

HUGHES: I will volunteer . . .

MANSON: We know all these things, he (Stovitz) just wants to bring this out.

STOVITZ: He has just, within the last year and a half . . .

HUGHES: Within the last year past . . .

STOVITZ: Within the year been admitted to the practice of law in the State of California. Prior to that I don't believe he was admitted to practice in any other state. He did work for a short time in the Public Defender's office. Is that right?

HUGHES: That is correct.

STOVITZ: As a clerk?

HUGHES: Law clerk.

STOVITZ: To my knowledge, being Head of Trials in the District Attorney's office, I have not heard of Mr. Hughes defending any felony cases in the past year and a half.

OLDER: Are you acquainted, Miss Van Houten, with these facts?

VAN HOUTEN: Yes, I am very familiar with them.

OLDER: You understand that, relatively speaking, Mr.

LESLIE VAN HOUTEN CHANGED ATTORNEYS IN MID-TRIAL

Hughes has not had a great deal of experience in the criminal field?

VAN HOUTEN: Yes.

OLDER: That does not disqualify him because everyone has to start sometime.

VAN HOUTEN: Right.

OLDER: On the other hand, you should bear this in mind, that this is a case which has complications of many different kinds. You need an attorney who has the intelligence, the ability and capacity and desire to represent you to the fullest.

VAN HOUTEN: (Nods in affirmative)

OLDER: There are many attorneys in the criminal field who have far more experience than Mr. Hughes in murder cases and all types of cases. Notwithstanding all of this you still wish to have Mr. Hughes as your attorney?

VAN HOUTEN: Yes, I do.

Judge Older then granted the request. On July 17, 1970, three days after the jury panel of twelve had been sworn but before the six alternates had been selected, Ronald Hughes, who had yet to try his first criminal case, became Leslie Van Houten's attorney of record. It was an odd substitution by any standards; a man with no experience for one who vigorously, in the context of the general defense, pleaded her cause. And a prosecution attorney who attempts to protect a defendant's interests.

I asked Ira Reiner how he felt about the whole thing.

"I wanted 'out' a long time ago," he told me. "This thing is killing me financially. I'm in practice by myself and there is simply no money coming in."

Why did he get into it in the first place?

"For the publicity," he admitted. "But I never thought it would go this long. I figured I'd be in this for two or three months, enhance my reputation, get out and possibly get some big referrals."

There had been speculation that Reiner, a handsome man with a deep, very masculine voice and salt and pepper speckled dark hair, had originally been appointed by Miss Van Houten because of a physical attraction. I asked him about it.

"Bullshit," he replied amiably. "Oh, there may have been something like that vaguely in the back of her mind but I was hired because they thought I would go along with the general defense." He shrugged. "I found that I couldn't do it. I had to put on the best defense I knew how."

Why hadn't he pulled out before this?

"Two reasons. First, the court wouldn't let me, and second," the attorney made a visible effort to compose himself, "I just might have gotten her off. The key to her case is separating her from the others," he continued earnestly. "They don't really have anything on her except possibly Linda Kasabian's uncorroborated testimony. But she wouldn't do it; she wouldn't give herself that chance."

I asked why.

Reiner shook his head slowly. "I don't know. I really don't know. Charlie tells her to do it, and she does it."

Could it be, I suggested, that Manson knows that he would gain strength by having that kind of loyalty displayed? That Hughes will take his orders and not give Leslie Van Houten a proper defense and that the jury, possibly reluctant to convict three young girls, might permit some of that charity to rub off on the Family leader?

"Although I'm no longer attorney of record," Reiner said, "I'm still bound by the court's gag order. I can't answer that."

Later, in his sixth-floor office puffing a reflective cigar after the Hughes substitution, Aaron Stovitz spoke about women being tried for capital offenses.

"It is virtually impossible," he admitted, "to get a jury to convict a woman in certain types of crimes, quite aside from the death penalty. I prosecuted a case where a woman shot her husband. Sure, he was a mean guy and physically abused her. He ran a service station and at night he'd bring home all the mechanics' overalls—you know, full of grease and oil—for her to wash." Stovitz's brow furrowed. "Every night," he repeated.

"She had six children to look after," he continued, "and he'd bring home some of his employees to dinner without telling her. If she complained he'd tell her that he worked hard, was tired and to shut her mouth. Sometimes he shoved her around, maybe even slapped her a couple of times. The woman never went out, except to shop for groceries, had no time to herself. She couldn't even watch T.V. at night because she had the overalls to do.

"Naturally," the D.A. said, "she let her appearance go a little. Then her sister came to stay with them for her vacation. Her sister was younger, worked in an office, took care of herself. The sister sat around all day filing her nails. One night the husband came home, changed his clothes, and asked the sister to go down to the corner with him for a beer. After that the husband began coming home earlier, ridiculing his wife in front of the sister, and taking the sister out . . . you know," Stovitz shrugged, ". . . because she was on vacation.

"Well," he took a long puff on his cigar, "one morning while the sister was still asleep the husband got up to go to work and his wife was getting his breakfast. They had words about the sister. The husband said some nasty things, slammed the front door and started down the walk. The wife goes to his drawer where he kept his socks, takes out this pistol he owns—a long barreled twenty-two caliber—and goes to the front door. The guy turns at the end of the walk," Stovitz arches his eyebrows in amazement, "a good thirty feet away, and starts to say something. She raises the gun, pulls the trigger once and down he goes, dead, right through the forehead.

"One shot," the D.A. said reflectively. "As I pointed out in my summation, there was no immediate or even implied threat to her; the guy was thirty feet away and didn't even have a chance to open his mouth. She lets him have it." He heaved a deep sigh and flicked some ash into a tray on his desk. "Acquittal," he announced resignedly.

The situation in Tate/La Bianca had altered appreciably. Judge Older, having agreed to the attorney substitution on condition that there be no delays, conducted business as usual in chambers with the selection of six alternate jurors.

That made the current line-up: Fitzgerald, Shinn, Kanarek and Hughes opposing Stovitz and Bugliosi with Fitzgerald, generally considered to be the most competent of the defense attorneys, apparently not putting out anything like a maximum effort.

"The lackadaisical attitude of defense counsel is, to my mind, unprecedented," J. Miller Leavy, famed prosecutor of Barbara Graham, L. Ewing Scott and Caryl Chessman and now the Trials Division elder statesman, told me. "I've tried some bizarre cases but I've never seen the defense behave like this."

The outlook for the defense appeared to be gloomy indeed. Four able attorneys, united in their efforts and certain of their direction, would have found the prosecution team a formidable adversary; under the present circumstances the scales of justice seemed heavily tipped in favor of the people.

On July 21, 1970, the six alternate jurors were sworn and Judge Older set July 24, at 9:45 A.M., thirty-eight days after the trial began, to hear the first of the opening statements.

Chapter VIII

DAY THIRTY-EIGHT

The predictably sunny and warm July day dawned unpredictably overcast and cool on July 24, 1970, the day the Deputy District Attorney Vincent Bugliosi delivered his opening statement in Tate/La Bianca. This was viewed, typically, by the press as either a portent of doom for the defense's cause or as a suggestion that surprise twists inimical to the prosecution's case were to be expected.

All the anticipation, the painful eking out of inches of copy or seconds of airtime, the grasping at rumors *of* rumors, made for a state of sustained expectancy in crowded Department 104 that day as Bugliosi, wearing a businesslike gray single-breasted suit and vest accepted Judge Older's offer and rose to make his opening statement.

He had already been upstaged. Charles Manson, dressed in prison denims, white patches showing where the back pockets should be, appeared in court minutes before with an "X" scratched on his forehead. A written statement that the defendant issued during the noon recess to clarify the "X" gives, as we shall see, a fascinating insight into his mental processes.

For the moment, however, the floor is Bugliosi's. The prosecutor began by explaining that he was about to show what the people meant to prove and, in part, how they meant to prove it. Immediately Irving Kanarek began harassing him with a form of verbal sniping that was at least partially effective.

BUGLIOSI: Your Honor, defense counsel, ladies and gentlemen of the jury. (To the jurors) I know that you have sat through an almost interminable *voir dire* and I apologize for all the repetition. By now, I'm sure, you probably have some idea of what this is all about.

KANAREK: Object. That is not a proper opening statement.

OLDER: Overruled.
    (A few minutes later.)

BUGLIOSI: I believe in making a short opening statement. However, I must warn you that the prosecution's summation at the end of the trial will last much longer.

KANAREK: Object. Your Honor, he cannot say that at this time.

OLDER: Overruled.

BUGLIOSI: (Turns with great deliberation to look at Kanarek, then turns back and resumes.) As you know, there are eight counts to the Grand Jury indictment in this case. The first seven are murder counts, the eighth count charges the crime of conspiracy to commit murder.
    Defendants Charles Manson, Susan Atkins and Patricia Krenwinkel are charged in the indictment with all seven murders, that is, the five Tate murders on August 9, 1969 and the murders of Mr. and Mrs. La Bianca on August 10, 1969. Each of these three defendants are also charged with the eighth count of conspiracy to commit murder.
    Defendant Leslie Van Houten is not charged with the

first five murder counts of the indictment, the five Tate murders. She is only charged with the murders of Mr. and Mrs. Leno La Bianca in counts six and seven of the indictment.

So I would remind you that any evidence at this trial which pertains solely to the five Tate murders, should not be considered by you against Miss Van Houten for the simple reason that she is not charged with these murders.

KANAREK: Objection. Mr. BUGliosi is being argumentative.

OLDER: Overruled.

BUGLIOSI: (The hard "G" name pronunciation did it; he takes a long, slow drink from a water glass, composes himself with some effort, and resumes) I will get through these opening statements despite the discourtesy of defense counsel.

In the early morning hours of August 9, 1969, Susan Atkins, Patricia Krenwinkel and Charles Watson murdered five human beings at the Roman Polanski residence, a secluded home at the top of a long, winding driveway, located at one-zero-zero-five-zero Cielo Drive, Los Angeles.

Those five victims were: Sharon Marie Polanski, whose stage name was Sharon Tate, Abigail Folger, Voityk Frykowski, Jay Sebring and Steven Parent.

As I've indicated, the Tate murders took place in the early morning hours of August 9, 1969. Later that same day, in the late evening of August 9, 1969, another defendant, defendant Leslie Van Houten, joined in the continuing conspiracy to commit murder. Pursuant to that conspiracy, in the early morning hours of August 10, 1969, these defendants murdered Rosemary and Leno La Bianca at their residence located at three-three-zero-one Waverly Drive, in the Los Feliz District area of Los Angeles.

Then the thirty-five year old prosecutor began showing the

VICTIM SHARON TATE PLEADED FOR HER BABY'S LIFE

form that had earned him the assignment to this important case.

BUGLIOSI: What kind of diabolical, satanic mind would con-
template or conceive of these mass murders? What kind
of mind would want to have seven human beings brutally
murdered?

We expect the evidence at this trial to show that defendant Charles Manson owned that diabolical mind.
Charles Manson, who, the evidence will show, at times
has had the infinite humility, if you will, to call himself
Jesus Christ.

The speaker paused here, obviously overcome by the enormity of that suggestion. He drained the water glass and handed
it to his superior Aaron Stovitz who imperturbably walked
around the defendants to the water cooler and filled the glass
while his colleague resumed. They didn't always see eye-to-
eye in private, these two, but in court they made a great team.

BUGLIOSI: Evidence at this trial will show defendant Manson
to be a vagrant wanderer, a frustrated singer and guitar-
ist, a pseudo philosopher, but most of all, the evidence
will show him to be a killer who cleverly masqueraded
behind the common image of a hippie, that of being peace
loving.

As the deputy district attorney went on to outline testimony
that Linda Kasabian, also indicted for the murders but expected to be granted immunity, would keep the listener's mind
locked on the phrase "peace loving," and memory drifted back
to another trial just recently completed, the conviction of
Family member Robert Beausoleil for the murder of Gary
Hinman, a musician. Beausoleil, testifying in his own defense
during that trial, remembered displeasing Charles Manson and
recalled, on the witness stand, the consequences.

Beausoleil, questioned by his attorney, Leon Salter, told of nearly being taken for a ride by Manson.

Q: Did he say anything to you at that time?

A: Yes. He asked me if anything was bothering me.

Q: What did you say?

A: I told him there wasn't anything bothering me but that I had been thinking of leaving.

Q: And what did he say?

A: Well, he got mad . . .

Q: What did he say then?

A: He said that I knew too much about several underaged girls that were there and where the camp was and about him killing a Black Panther. And he said I knew too much generally.

Q: Did he then say something to you?

A: Well, we had started—he started driving again. He was still talking and telling me that I knew too much about stolen dune buggy parts and different things like that. And that when he said that he didn't—he shouldn't let me leave.

Q: Will you tell the jury what he said, or threats he made?

A: He told me that he shouldn't let me leave—or should I say what he said?

Q: Say the words he used.

A: He said: "What I ought to do is just cut your mother-fucking throat."

Q: Did he have any weapons on him?

A: Yes, he did.

Q: What weapons did he have?

A: Well, there was a bayonet, a military bayonet, stuck in the steering column of the dune buggy he was driving. He had a—this was supposed to be the gun that he had killed the Black Panther with, it was a .22 pistol. I think that's what it was. And he had that between his legs on the seat.

And he had a little knife that he always had, had it in a sheath at his ankle. He had on those buckskin pants, those frilled buckskin pants, and there is a sheath built into it. He had one of the girls sew a sheath into the ankle.

But back to the present, as the peace loving Charles Manson stares vacantly at his accuser, Vincent Bugliosi.

BUGLIOSI: The evidence will show Manson to be a megalomaniac who coupled his insatiable thirst for power with an intense obsession for violent death.

Then the deputy district attorney launched into his controversial Helter Skelter motive theory. After first explaining that the prosecution did not have to establish any motive in the case, Bugliosi postulated not one, but several.

BUGLIOSI: In this trial, we will offer evidence of Manson's motive for ordering these seven murders. There was more than one motive.

Besides the motives of Manson's passion for violent death and his extreme antiestablishment state of mind, the evidence at this trial will show that there was further motive which was almost as bizarre as the murders themselves.

Very briefly, the evidence will show Manson's fanatical obsession with Helter Skelter, a term he got from the

English musical recording group, the Beatles. Manson was an avid follower of the Beatles and believed that they were speaking to him through the lyrics of their songs. In fact, Manson told his followers that he found complete support for his philosophies in the words sung by the Beatles in their songs.

KANAREK: Objection, your Honor. Now he's making *our* opening statements for us.

OLDER: Overruled.

BUGLIOSI: To Manson, Helter Skelter, the title of one of the Beatles's songs, meant the black man rising up against the white establishment and murdering the entire white race, that is, with the exception of Manson and his chosen followers, who intended to "escape" from Helter Skelter by going to the desert and living in the Bottomless Pit place Manson derived from Revelation 9, the last book of the New Testament from which Manson told others he found further support for his philosophies.

The evidence will show that although Manson hated black people, he also hated the white establishment, whom he called "Pigs."

The evidence will show that one of Manson's principal motives for the Tate/La Bianca murders was to ignite Helter Skelter, in other words, start the black-white revolution by making it look like the black people had murdered the five Tate victims and Mr. and Mrs. La Bianca, thereby causing the white community to turn against the black man and ultimately lead to a civil war between blacks and whites, a war Manson foresaw the black man winning.

Manson envisioned that black people, once they destroyed the white race and assumed the reins of power, would be unable to handle the reins because of inexperience and would have to turn over the reins to those white people who had escaped from Helter Skelter, that is, turn over the reins to Manson and his followers.

Bugliosi then summarized other evidence that would be presented, covered in detail in the succeeding pages, and concluded:

BUGLIOSI: Mr. Stovitz (Aaron Stovitz nodded his appreciation of this, his first credit) and I intend to prove, not just beyond a reasonable doubt, which is our only burden, but beyond all doubt, that these defendants are guilty of these murders. In our final arguments to you at the termination of the evidence, we intend to ask you to return verdicts of first degree murder against each of these defendants.

Mr. Stovitz and I feel confident you will give your full, undivided attention to all of the evidence during the trial so that you can give both the people and the defendants the fair and impartial verdict to which they are both entitled.

Thank you very much.

Defense reaction to the opening statement ranged from the frankly irreverent, "He's going to have to prove that Manson really is Jesus Christ and then that Jesus Christ committed all those terrible crimes," of Ronald Hughes to the calculated riposte of Paul Fitzgerald. "I think his opening statement went well beyond the bounds of propriety," Patricia Krenwinkel's attorney told me. "It was a slanderous, inflammatory megalomaniacal performance. This trial has degenerated into some form of name-calling."

A great many members of the press were skeptical; they felt that the prosecutor should have left well enough alone, proven his case, and let it go at that. "You start crapping up the jurors's minds with all that junk," a correspondent for a large western daily confided, "and they're liable to begin confusing proof of crime with proof of motive." His published story the next day solemnly proclaimed the staggering implications of the prosecution theory.

It had been the policy of the Los Angeles County Sheriff's office charged with trial security to search the person of anyone who appeared to them to be potentially dangerous to the defendants or the court. This was widely interpreted as being a shake-down rule directed principally against people with long hair and wearing hippie-style clothing. Personal observation over an extended period of time convinced this writer that, although it was true that no suspected hippie got, unsearched, into the few public seats available, a great many citizens of the more solid persuasion were subjected to the same kind of "pat down," a superficial check for obvious weapons, or, in some cases, were submitted to a much more personal check. The bailiffs did not want to lose either judge or prisoners and, although the security was not as intense as during the Sirhan trial where the press was subjected to daily searches, a sense of alertness to possible danger prevailed.

When, following Vincent Bugliosi's opening statement, the prosecution called as its first witness Paul J. Tate, the late Sharon Tate's father, a new dimension was added to the security problem. Tate, in his middle forties and a recently retired lieutenant-colonel in U.S. Army Intelligence, looked and acted like a tough customer. A trim, bronzed man of medium build, the victim's father sported mod clothes and a stylish Jay Sebring haircut, smoked good cigars and appeared to view the corridors and courtrooms of the Hall of Justice the way a Green Beret might size up the enemy headquarters into which he had infiltrated and against which he was prepared to move at any time.

The sheriff's detail guarding Judge Older's court, most of them ex-military men, paid Tate the supreme compliment of

PAUL TATE, WAS HE PLANNING A FATHER'S REVENGE?

one of the most thorough shake-downs many observers had been privileged to witness. Well aware that following his daughter's death Tate had "gone hippie" and roamed through Southern California on a personal search for her killers, the guardians of the incarcerated Family treated him most gingerly. And not without reason. Tate himself had been trained to kill.

As one deputy told me just after the ex-colonel's first courtroom appearance (he attended occasionally after that as a spectator), "He (Tate) could take out all four of 'em (the Family) before we could start to move." There was some concern that the late actress's father, running into members of the Family still at liberty, might have "dropped one or two," in the words of the deputy but, the lawman added with a fatalistic shrug, there was not much anyone could do about that eventuality.

Tate's actual testimony was limited to identifying pictures of his daughter, Thomas Jay Sebring, Voityk Frykowski and Abigail Folger, and to recalling that the last time he saw his daughter alive was on July 20 and 21, 1969 when they watched the moon landing together. He was excused with the stipulation that he be recalled and promptly indicated to the prosecution that, testify or not, he would be in the courtroom for the duration of the trial. During his brief period on the stand he glanced at the defendants only once or twice, appearing hardly to notice them; Manson did not attempt to put the whammy on him and appeared unnaturally subdued. Here was a man, the father of a girl Manson had allegedly ordered to be brutally murdered, who talked his language: violence; the bearded leader could well have been uneasy in the presence of an establishment figure who could conceivably set aside man-promulgated laws to meet the Family on its own terms.

The second witness, Wilfred E. Parent, father of the young boy who was shot in his car while leaving the Tate grounds after visiting William Garretson in the guest cottage, restored the courtroom to a sense of normalcy by behaving the way a bereaved father might be expected to; Aaron Stovitz on direct examination:

Q: Mr. Parent, what is your business or occupation, sir?

A: I'm a construction superintendent.

Q: Your Honor, I have a photograph of a young man and a young girl, may this photograph be marked as Exhibit 5 for identification?

OLDER: It will be so marked.

Q: I show you Exhibit 5 for identification, do you recognize the young man depicted in that photograph?

A: Yes I do, that is my son . . .

Mr. Parent never got beyond those words; he broke down on the stand, brought his hand to his face and chokingly apologized for his behavior. Stovitz got him a glass of water and Parent composed himself and identified his son and his girl friend, Tina. He then identified a picture of his son's car, told of his employment as a salesman of high fidelity and stereo sound equipment, and was excused.

Counsel were then called to the bench in connection with the following statement supposedly written by Charles Manson and released to the press.

> *I am not allowed to be a man in your society.*
> *I am considered inadequate and incompetant (sic)*
> *to speak or defend myself in your court. You have*
> *created the monster. I am not of you, from you, nor*
> *do I condone your wars or your unjust attitudes*
> *towards things, animals and people that you won't*
> *try to understand. I haved (sic) Xed myself from*
> *your world. I stand in the opposite to what you do*
> *and what you have done in the past. You have*
> *never given me the constitution you speak of. The*
> *words you have used to trick the people are not*
> *mine. I do not accept what you call justice. The lie*
> *you live in is falling and I am not a part of it. You*
> *use the word God to make money.*

MANSON TRIES TO EXPLAIN

You! Look at what you have done and what you are doing. You make fun of God and have murdered the world in the name of Jesus Christ. I stand with my X with my love, with my god and by myself. My faith in me is stronger than all your armies, governments, gas chambers or anything you may want to do to me. I know what I have done and your courtroom is mans (sic) game. Love is my judge. I have my own constitution; its (sic) inside me.

No man or lawyer is speaking for me. I speak for myself. I am not allowed to speak with words so I have spoken with the mark I will be wearing on my forehead. Many U.S. citizens are marked and don't know it. You won't let them come from under your foot. But God is moving. Moving, and I am a witness.

I have tried to stand on the constitution but I am not afforded the rights another citizen may enjoy. I am forced to contend with communicating to the mass without words. I feel no man can represent another man because each man is different and has his own world, his own kingdom, his own reality. It is impossible to communicate one reality through another into another reality.

(signed) Charles Manson

Nathaniel Branden, one of the nation's foremost psychologists and author of the bestselling *The Psychology of Self-Esteem* was asked his opinion of Manson's statement.

"In appraising the psychological significance of this statement," the psychologist said, "there are two facts that one must keep in mind. The first is that its author is an avowed irrationalist — he has expressed his contempt for reason, logic and conceptual thought on many occasions and in many ways. The second is that he is on trial for first degree murder — a wanton, senselessly brutal murder of a group of innocent human beings of whom he had no knowledge and with whom he had no connection.

"The staggering irrelevance of his statement in the context of the legal charges confronting him, and its projection of vacant grandiosity, immediately suggests a diagnosis of paranoid psychosis or pre-psychosis. This is the obvious diagnosis and it may be the correct one. Having never examined its author," Branden pointed out, "I am not in a position to say.

"However," he assured the questioner, "an alternative interpretation can be given. And that is, that the statement represents a calculated attempt to create the illusion of psychosis in order to diminish or remove the author's moral and legal responsibility for the murders with which he is charged, and thus to diminish the severity of the sentence accordingly.

"It scarcely needs to be argued that a man capable of inspiring or precipitating the murders for which he is on trial, is mentally unbalanced to some extent. His action is clearly not that of one who is in rational contact with reality. This does not mean — and," Branden emphasized, "I wish to stress this — that he is therefore innocent of moral responsibility. There are people who wilfully choose to sever contact with reality. Among other things, this can permit them to act out their malice and hatred — while allowing them to be blinded to the full meaning of what they are doing. This does not make their action any less criminal or any less deserving of severe legal punishment."

Judge Older's courtroom demeanor, which suggested a Job-like temperament, obviously was taking a toll on his private emotions. His Honor's temper was wearing thin, as this private exchange suggests:

OLDER: The bailiff informs me that Mr. Shinn just gave a copy of this document, a typed one-page document, it has the name Charles Manson at the bottom, to the press, is that right, Mr. Shinn?

SHINN: Most of them had it already, your Honor.

OLDER: How did you know that?

SHINN: I was informed this morning.

OLDER: Why did you have to give it to them?

SHINN: I did not hand it out this morning.

OLDER: You just now handed it to someone.

SHINN: Yes.

OLDER: Apparently you thought he did not have a copy.

SHINN: Yes.

OLDER: What is the purpose of it?

SHINN: I don't know.

OLDER: Then why did you hand it to him?

SHINN: He asked me for it. They were handed out this morning and he asked me for this one.

OLDER: I am going to have this marked as an exhibit; we will mark it as a special exhibit, the court's special exhibit I. It will become part of the record but it will not be shown to the jury.

    I am interested in knowing what your motive is in handing out a copy of this to the press, Mr. Shinn.

SHINN: They asked me for it and I gave them a copy.

OLDER: Did Mr. Manson write this?

SHINN: That I don't know, your Honor.

OLDER: Are you intending to prejudice your own case, Mr. Shinn?

SHINN: No, your Honor.

OLDER: I am at a complete loss to understand why you would give something like this to the press. It appears to me that you are not much concerned about the type of publicity that is given to the press, or whether it affects your client or not.

SHINN: Your Honor, if I initiated it, that would be a different story.

OLDER: Apparently it was initiated by you just now because someone saw you hand it to a member of the media.

All right, let's proceed.

The next witness, Winnifred Chapman, identified herself as a cook and a cateress who worked as a cook and a

MAID WINNIFRED CHAPMAN DISCOVERED THE BODIES

housekeeper for the Polanskis. A small, high-strung woman given to curt answers from the witness stand, Mrs. Chapman appeared to fully appreciate the importance of her role as the discoverer of the dead bodies at the Tate residence on the morning of August 9, 1969. Her left arm and wrist partially bandaged as the result of an auto accident, she indicated that she was in pain and could not answer questions for too long. At one point, at the request of Vincent Bugliosi the court granted a five minute recess so that she could pull herself together.

The most significant part of her early testimony centered around the front and back doors of the main house on which fingerprints of Charles "Tex" Watson and Patricia Krenwinkel supposedly were found by the police. Bugliosi is inquiring:

Q: On the date August 8, 1969, a Friday (the day before the murders) did you have occasion to wash the front door?

A: I did wash it.

Q: About what time of day did you wash the front door?

A: Before lunch.

Q: Why did you wash the front door?

A: Well, it was splattered. The dog had marked it up. So I just cleaned the whole door.

Q: Did you frequently wash the outside of the front door?

A: Yes.

Q: A couple of times a week?

A: Your Honor, this is too much. Too much.

OLDER: Do you feel all right?

BUGLIOSI: Do you feel all right?

A: Well, I will try to go on a little further, but not much longer.

BUGLIOSI: Calm down.

The prosecutor then showed Mrs. Chapman a picture of the doors leading from the back master bedroom onto the pool area.

Q: Do you recall ever washing the inside of this back door to the master bedroom?

A: Yes.

Q: How often did you normally wash the inside of the back door?

A: A couple of times a week. I got all the prints off of it.

This answer drew loud laughter, especially from the attorneys at the defense table who had been making the point as often as possible that the witnesses had been interrogated to the point of being coached by various members of the police and district attorney's office. After a cross-examination by defense attorneys Fitzgerald, Shinn and Hughes during which it was ascertained that, a: Mrs. Chapman had washed prints off other articles of furniture; b: she knew what a marijuana cigarette looked like; and c: she had never seen any video tape equipment in the Polanski residence, she was excused subject to being recalled.

The next witness, twenty-year-old William Garretson, who lived in the so-called guest cottage behind the main house (it was actually owned by Garretson's employer, Rudy Altobelli) and the only living person found on the grounds the morning of the murder, was questioned closely about his

actions on the night prior to, and morning of, the murders
by Vincent Bugliosi. After establishing that Garretson's sole
duties were looking after the absent Altobelli's three dogs,
the deputy district attorney inquired:

Q: Do you recall what you did that evening, August 8,
1969, a Friday?

A: Yes.

Q: What did you do that evening?

A: I went down to Sunset Boulevard.

Q: How did you get there?

A: Hitchhiked.

Q: All right, what happened when you got down to Sunset
Boulevard?

A: I purchased a T.V. dinner and some cigarettes and
some Pepsi-Cola.

Q: And what time did you return?

A: Around 10:00 o'clock.

Q: When you returned at approximately 10:00 P.M. did
you see anyone else on the premises?

A: No, sir. I did not.

Q: How did you enter the premises, through the gate here
as depicted on the diagram? (Referring to a large drawing
of the main house, grounds and guest cottage erected in
court)

A: Yes.

Q: How did you open the gate?

A: You had to push a button right before you get to the gate, it would be on the left side.

Q: Is the button near the telephone where I am pointing now?

A: Yes.

Q: And this would activate the gate and open it, is that correct?

A: Yes.

Q: How long would the gate stay open? Would you have to close it or would it automatically close?

A: No. I would say about fifteen to twenty seconds, something like that.

Q: When you arrived back at the premises did you notice any telephone wires on top of the gate or on the ground or anything like that?

A: No.

Q: Did everything seem to be in order?

A: Yes.

Garretson then explained that he walked up a path to the guest house that did not take him across the front of the main house and that he was unaware of any noise or lights in the vicinity of the main house. The prosecutor then turned his attention to Garretson's late night visitor.

Q: Did you have any visitors that night in your guest house?

A: Yes, I did.

Q: Who was that?

A: Steven Parent.

Q: At about what time did Mr. Parent arrive?

A: Around 11:45 P.M.

Q: Just before midnight?

A: Yes.

Q: Did he arrive by himself?

A: Yes, he did.

Q: What was the nature of Mr. Parent's visit to you?

A: He brought a radio with him, a clock radio, and he wanted to know if I would like to buy the one that he had, buy it or one that he could get, you know. He worked in an appliance place or something that dealt with radios and stereos.

Q: Did you buy the radio from him?

A: No.

Q: I take it that he eventually left your guest house?

A: Yes. He made a phone call though, before he left.

Q: About what time did he make a phone call?

A: About 12:00 o'clock.

Q: What did you do after Mr. Parent left?

A: I wrote a few letters and listened to the stereo.

Q: Okay. Did you eventually fall asleep that night?

A: No.

Q: Did you fall asleep at all?

A: No. I was going to make a phone call before dawn.

Q: Did you make the phone call?

A: No.

Q: Why not?

A: The line was dead. I mean, not the line, the phone was dead.

Q: Did this frighten you at all?

A: Yes.

Q: Did you do anything about it?

A: No.

Q: Did you fall asleep around dawn at all?

A: Yes.

Q: But throughout the night you were awake?

A: Yes.

Q: Listening to your stereo?

A: Yes. And writing letters.

Q: Did you hear any gunshots during the night?

A: No.

Q: Did you hear any loud screams during the night?

A: No.

Bugliosi then elicited the information that the three dogs in Garretson's charge usually barked when someone approached the guest house but not, to his knowledge, when someone approached the main house. On cross-examination Paul Fitzgerald pursued the young man's nocturnal habits.

Q: What time was it that you actually went to bed, went to sleep that is?

A: I couldn't really say but it was just before daybreak. I mean, daybreak.

Q: And did Christopher (one of the dogs) wake you up?

A: Yes.

Q: All three dogs were inside the guest cottage that night; is that right?

A: Yes.

Q: Did you say anything to Christopher when he started to bark and woke you up?

A: I told him to be quiet.

Well, he started barking, you know, I told him to shut up, and then I looked up and there was a policeman outside in the patio pointing a rifle at me by the picnic table.

Q: What did you do then?

A: I didn't know what to do.

Q: What happened next?

A: Another one came and pointed another rifle, and then another one, and he was pointing a pistol, and he kicked in the door, and Christopher bit him on the leg.

The courtroom erupted into laughter with Judge Older uncharacteristically joining in.

Q: What happened to Christopher?

A: I told him to stop it.

More laughter; the kind of laughter that is as much a release from tension as it is a manifestation of enjoyed experience.

Q: What happened next?

A: Well, then they drug me onto the patio and threw me down on my stomach. And I asked them what was wrong. And they told me to shut up, they would show me.

Q: Were you shown?

A: Yes.

Q: What were you shown?

A: Two bodies on the front lawn and one in the car.

Garretson, closely squired by attorney Robert Cohen who is handling his lawsuits against the police and numerous John Does for false arrest, was then excused and ordered to return for questioning the following Monday. He, and the other prosecution witnesses subsequently called were to be completely overshadowed by the appearance of the people's principal, some said their only, witness. All that was past was truly prelude when, on Monday, July 27, at 2:00 P.M., Linda Kasabian, herself accused of seven counts of murder and one count of conspiracy to commit murder, took the stand under a promise of immunity, against her former Family.

Chapter IX

DAY FORTY-ONE

The sight of Linda Kasabian, ex-Family member and now, in Vincent Bugliosi's words, the people's "star witness," stepping through the holding-room doors into the courtroom at 2:00 P.M. on Monday, July 27, 1970 unleashed the agonizingly suppressed vigilantism of Irving Kanarek. Protestations on grounds of irrelevancy, immateriality and impropriety streamed from the stocky defense attorney's mouth in an unprecedented flow of legal flatulence.

He began in spectacular fashion, without waiting for the court clerk to finish his standard request of a witness: "Would you raise your right hand, please."

KANAREK: (On his feet and shouting) Object, your Honor, on the grounds this witness is not competent and she is insane!

Judge Older swivelled his chair around, frowning in astonishment.

BUGLIOSI: (On *his* feet and shouting) Wait a while, your Honor, move to strike that and I ask the court to find

117

him in contempt of court for gross misconduct. This is unbelievable on his part.

OLDER: If you have anything to say, Mr. Kanarek, come to the bench.

KANAREK: Very well, your Honor.

OLDER: The jury is admonished to disregard Mr. Kanarek's comments.

Older, obviously restraining himself, faced the attorneys out of hearing of the jury and press.

FITZGERALD: I think I can more succinctly state the objection, if I might, with leave of the court.

It is our contention that this witness is incompetent to testify as the result of unsoundness, and we are willing to make an offer of proof in that respect.

OLDER: Make your offer.

FITZGERALD: Basically, our position is as follows: That Linda Kasabian — and we will offer to prove this by various witnesses, and I will state them separately at the conclusion — that Linda Kasabian, due to prolonged extensive illegal use of LSD is a person of unsound mind, is mentally ill, is insane, is unable to differentiate between truth and falsity, right or wrong, good or bad, fantasy and reality, and is incapable of expressing herself concerning the matter so as to be understood.

In connection with our offer of proof, we would like to incorporate by reference and resubmit to the court a motion, declaration and points and authorities filed on behalf of the defendants on June 12, 1970.

We would make a further offer of proof that Dr. A. R. Tweed, whose declaration is attached to that motion, is an expert in the diagnosis and treatment of mental, emotional and psychiatric disorders, and he will testify as to the matter contained in his declaration.

LINDA KASABIAN, THE PEOPLE'S STAR WITNESS

Dr. A. R. Tweed, a psychiatrist who identified himself as a medical examiner for the Superior Court, County of Los Angeles, declared:

"The statements ascribed to Mrs. Kasabian of having supernatural powers while under the influence of LSD as well as her feelings of deep depersonalization when not directly under its influence is not only medically possible but highly probable with doses much smaller and with fewer times used than described.

"That further it is a confirmed fact that even one ingestion of LSD could cause an immediate bad reaction or return of what is called a flashback many times even several months later without further use.

"That the habitual long-term use of LSD for pleasure or escape produces the possibility for the impairment of good sense and maturation.

"That individuals so affected may become confused and disorganized and are usually markedly suggestible."

At the time of Dr. Tweed's original statement Fitzgerald also delivered an indictment of what, in his opinion, LSD could do to people who ingested it: "Lysergic acid is defined and classified as a hallucinogenic drug; a hallucinogenic drug itself, it is my understanding, artificially or chemically induces fantasy, and that is the crucial area of this motion, I think, that the chemical fact of lysergic acid is to distort reality and to blur distinctions between reality and fantasy.

"The drug itself induces mental states that are quite similar to psychoses, and some authorities feel the prolonged use of lysergic acid actually induces insanity, and results in organic brain disorder and disturbance.

"Certainly lysergic acid disturbs and distorts emotions. It disturbs and distorts organized thought processes. It disturbs and distorts memory, and disturbs and distorts recollections.

"It also disturbs and distorts the ability of a person to recollect and communicate about things they have perceived, and it is a drug that distorts perception itself.

"I think that when one is under the influence of lysergic acid diethylamide or the prolonged residual effect of LSD, that is in essence uncontrollable; that the person who has ingested the lysergic acid diethylamide presently is unable to control his mental or thought processes.

"There is substantial medical and scientific evidence to the effect that actual drug states are subject to recurrence without notice or warning. This is the so-called flashback effect of lysergic acid.

"It has been documented in several places that lysergic acid has residual effects to the organic brain processes. There has been a great deal of concern that at least in one mental area, at least in one physical-mental area it destroys the normal function of the chromosomes.

"It has led to permanent brain damage in large doses.

"It has led to permanent disturbances of motor functions, to permanent disturbances in intellectual functions. It also led to the disturbance of the so-called super-ego functions, which is the conscience or moral functioning area of the brain."

These statements are of considerable importance because at this time of the trial, with prosecution witness Linda Kasabian yet to take the stand, the defense is attempting to lay a foundation for its own case. This writer, anticipating the defense position, had done considerable research into the nature of the drug d-lysergic acid diethylamide tartrate and, as the trial progresses and the testimony warrants it, will intersperse facts impartially presented so that the reader may better understand the conflicting testimony.

Remember, Paul Fitzgerald referred to this in the beginning as, "The first of the acid murders." It is vital for our understanding of this case, and perhaps for our ultimate survival, to know all there is to know at present about LSD. As we shall see, defense or prosecution claims to the contrary, there is not all that much to know; what is very important is the unusual opportunity that Tate/La Bianca has presented: a chance to measure the observable effects of the drug in relation to a criminal act being debated in a public forum. A time for speculative projection will come later in this volume; now we must follow closely what is said and attempt to give it the proper interpretation. If we don't want carloads of people riding around in every city and town (as the prosecution will contend happened in Los Angeles), selecting you or me as random murder victims, we will do well to find out what role acid played in this landmark case.

Now we are back in Judge Older's court, at the bench, listening to Paul Fitzgerald continue to plead the defense case against the testimony of Linda Kasabian.

FITZGERALD: Two additional witnesses will testify as to their opinions concerning her sanity and/or mental illness.

OLDER: Who are these witnesses by whom you expect to prove matters stated in your offer?

STOVITZ: I'd like, at this time, to ask your Honor to remind counsel that it is quite unethical to take up a matter like this in the presence of the jury.

OLDER: There is no question about it, and your conduct is outrageous, Mr. Kanarek.

KANAREK: If I may respond. Your Honor, it is a legal ground.

OLDER: That is not the point. You understand what the point is. It should have been done outside the presence of the jury.

FITZGERALD: I would offer for the court's consideration an additional declaration by June Emmer. This witness purports to be a close friend and personal acquaintance of Linda Kasabian, and spent the month of October, 1969, in her presence.

That Linda Kasabian made certain admissions and statements concerning her activities in California, and certain admissions and statements regarding the use of lysergic acid.

Also, in support of the motion I have a declaration under Florida law, an affidavit of Rosaire Drouin who purports to be the father of Linda Kasabian who in this affidavit sets out material indicating that his daughter the witness, Linda Kasabian, has extensively used the drug LSD.

OLDER: Do you expect to prove all of the facts of your offer of proof by these two witnesses?

FITZGERALD: We make an offer of proof as to a witness, Charles Melton, who is present in court and will testify as to personally taking LSD with Linda Kasabian on at least six occasions and will testify to her bizarre conduct under the influence of LSD.

We don't claim she is under the influence of LSD at this time, but if we could call Dr. Tweed as a witness we would be able to demonstrate to the court the residual effects of LSD are such as to render someone incompetent as a witness, and Dr. Tweed has so stated in his affidavit to the court.

OLDER: I have heard nothing so far that leads me to
    believe that there is anything in your offer of proof
    which has any connection with the competency of this
    witness to testify.
        Mr. Kanarek, if you do that once more in open
    court in front of this jury I am going to take action
    against you.
        Is there any objection to the offer of proof?

BUGLIOSI: Yes, your Honor.

OLDER: The objection is sustained. You may proceed.

This private exchange at the bench is reported here to
indicate how an attorney, without the public's knowledge,
can delay the orderly procedure of a trial. As far as the jury
and press knew, Mr. Kanarek's objection was being given
weighty consideration by the court when, in fact, it was Paul
Fitzgerald's presentation that was being heard. Whether or
not this constituted a deliberate defense strategy to make
Kanarek the villain in open court and Fitzgerald the rational
pleader at the bench or in chambers was not clear; what was
clear was the emergence of Kanarek the obstructionist, the
ogre paraded before us so unsuccessfully by the district attorney's office.

Linda Kasabian, her light brown hair trailing in two braids
over her shoulders and wearing a blue and red peasant dress,
was duly sworn. From the very first her eagerly awaited
testimony was challenged by Manson's attorney. Vincent
Bugliosi inquired:

Q: Linda, you realize that you are presently charged with
seven counts of murder and one count of conspiracy to
commit murder?

A: Yes.

Q: KANAREK: Immaterial, your Honor, I object on the grounds I would like to approach the bench.

OLDER: Overruled, let's proceed.

KANAREK: I have a motion to make, if your Honor does not wish me to do it in the presence of the jury I will do it whichever way your Honor wishes.

OLDER: State your motion.

KANAREK: My motion is . . . your Honor wishes me to do it in the presence of the jury?

OLDER: State your motion.

KANAREK: The motion is for a mistrial.

OLDER: I did not want to hear your grounds, just the motion.
The motion will be denied.
Let's proceed.

KANAREK: May I state the grounds at the bench?

OLDER: Is this something in addition to what you have already stated, Mr. Kanarek?

KANAREK: Yes.

OLDER: All right, you may.

The following took place at the bench, outside of the hearing of the jury and press.

OLDER: Make your motion.

KANAREK: The motion, your Honor, is for a mistrial. I ask your Honor to consider the fact that she is named a defendant. It is reversible error for the district attorney to call a defendant to the witness stand.

OLDER: That is the ground? That is all?

KANAREK: This witness has not been granted immunity and I am sure the court agrees with me.

OLDER: Anything further?

KANAREK: No.

OLDER: All right. The motion is denied. Let's proceed.

Everyone back to open court. Bear in mind that Bugliosi had asked *only one question* on direct examination. Kanarek's purpose, it would seem, was twofold. First he was objecting for the record, for the appeal; second he was objecting to rattle the witness, Linda Kasabian; although she appeared to be calm there was no question but that the combination of being under the eyes of the international community and, more immediately, of the Family, would take a toll. Almost from the beginning the Family tried to catch her eye, to communicate with her. Certain signs had meaning to the observer. The girls would run their fingers rapidly over their lips in a blabbering motion that, to Linda — in the words of her attorneys Gary Fleischman and Robert Goldman — signified that she was a blabbermouth. They would run their fingers straight up and down their noses in a motion that meant lies were being told. On the second day of her testimony Manson, during one session at the bench when the attorneys were preoccupied, was heard to say "You're lying, Linda. You lied three times." (About the Tate murders.)

She was heard to answer clearly and with sincerity. "No, I'm not, Charlie. And you know that."

On another occasion Susan Atkins mouthed the words, "You're killing us."

To which Linda replied in a whisper quite audible to the jury: "I'm not killing you. You've killed yourselves."

The problem at the beginning was to get any testimony at all; Bugliosi, after establishing that Linda Kasabian would be granted immunity for testifying, asked her if she had any other reason for being on the stand.

KANAREK: I object on the grounds, your Honor, that it is immaterial, conclusionary, calls for hearsay, assumes facts not in evidence. Clearly your Honor, her reasons are immaterial. She is called as a witness.

OLDER: I don't want to hear any arguments.

KANAREK: Those are the objections. May I approach the bench to make an argument?

OLDER: No.

KASABIAN: I strongly believe in truth, and I feel the truth should be spoken.

KANAREK: May I have that read back, your Honor?

OLDER: Read the answer.

KANAREK: Well, then, I ask that that be stricken. It is a self-serving declaration.

OLDER: Overruled.

After tortuously taking her through her background from the time she was born on June 21, 1949 in Biddeford, Maine through her on-again, off-again marriage to Robert Kasabian, Bugliosi got down to the business at hand. Here, with many of the repetitive objections and other matter extraneous to this narrative omitted, is how the testimony evolved:

Q: Did you ever go to live at the Spahn Movie Ranch in Chatsworth, California?

A: Yes, I did.

Q: I show you people's 28 for identification. Linda do you know whose photograph that is?

A: Yes, I do.

Q: Who is shown in that photograph?

A: Gypsy.

Q: Do you know her by her real name?

A: Kathy.

Q: Does the name Katherine Share ring a bell?

A: Yes.

Q: You know her as Gypsy and Kathy?

A: Also she told me Minine or Minone.

Q: Did Gypsy have anything to do with your going to the Spahn Ranch?

A: Yes, she did.

Q: How was that?

A: She told me about a beautiful man that we had all been waiting for.

Q: Did you start to live at the Spahn ranch?

A: Yes, I did.

Q: When did you meet Charles Manson for the first time?

A: The next night.

Q: That would be July 5, then?

A: Right, and he was up and back at the ranch, in a cluster of trees, and he was working on a dune buggy.

Q: Did you have a conversation with Mr. Manson on this first occasion?

A: Yes.

Q: What did he say to you?

A: He asked me why I had come. I had told him that my husband had rejected me and that Gypsy told me I was welcome here as part of the Family.

Q: After you told Mr. Manson why you had come to the Spahn Ranch, did he do anything . . .

A: Yes, he felt my legs and seemed to think they were okay or whatever.

Q: Where did you stay that night?

A: In a cave up in back of the ranch.

Q: When was the next time you saw Mr. Manson?

A: The next night or maybe the night after, I am not sure.

Q: Where did you meet Mr. Manson on this following occasion?

A: Inside the cave.

Q: What took place at that time?

It must be remembered that all through this testimony Irving Kanarek is registering an objection after almost every question. He did so following the last question and it was sustained. But Kanarek was plainly getting on Judge Older's nerves, as this next exchange indicates. Again Bugliosi inquires:

Q: You mentioned earlier, Linda, about a Family. Is that what the people were called out at the Spahn Ranch?

A: Yes.

KANAREK: Objection on the grounds it is assuming facts

not in evidence. There is no evidence of any Family. What they are called is hearsay, your Honor.

OLDER: Mr. Kanarek, I told you before I just want the motion or the objection and grounds without the argument.

KANAREK: And I respectfully ask the court to ask the witness . . .

OLDER: Sit down, sir.

KANAREK: . . . not to respond . . .

OLDER: Sit down, sir.

All was not smooth sailing for the prosecution, either. After several questions by Bugliosi using the term "Family," trying to establish Manson's dominance over it, had been objected to and the objections sustained, the junior deputy district attorney asked to approach the bench.

The following discussion was held out of the hearing of the jury and press.

BUGLIOSI: Your Honor, with all . . .

HUGHES: I find it highly prejudicial, that we go to the bench whenever Mr. Bugliosi wishes and not when Mr. Kanarek asks.

OLDER: Don't interrupt. Mr. Bugliosi was talking.

BUGLIOSI: With all deference to the court I don't understand why I cannot put in Manson directing . . .

HUGHES: I cannot hear this.

BUGLIOSI: I cannot understand, with all deference to the court how the court is not permitting me to put on evidence that Manson was in charge of the Family.

I have the highest regard for the court. I want the court to know that.

At this particular point, your Honor, I am shocked at the court's position. This is our case against Manson.

OLDER: That is not a legal argument, Mr. Bugliosi, as you well know.

BUGLIOSI: I agree with the court on that.

OLDER: The questions called for hearsay. I find no exception under which it might come in. That is the reason I sustained the objection.

BUGLIOSI: The only way I can prove Manson was the head of the Family is that he directed everyone to do things. I am just at a loss for words.

OLDER: I think perhaps a good deal of it can be solved by phrasing your questions in some other manner.

As the court adjourned for the day some small in-fighting was taking place between defense and prosecution that escaped general notice. For several days members of the Family, long-haired, bearded and dressed in extremely casual fashion had been attempting to gain access to the courtroom. By order, the defense is allotted four precious permanent seats, as is the prosecution. The prosecution, it can be assumed, did not want four bedraggled specimens giving Linda Kasabian a collective whammy while she was testifying. Accordingly, as each member applied for admission, he or she (or, as one bailiff suggested facetiously, it) was served with a subpoena as a witness for the prosecution. Since witnesses were automatically excluded from the courtroom if they were going to testify on evidence being heard, the ploy worked.

Ronald Hughes, as we shall see in the next day's testimony, struck back with what courtroom observers dubbed a feeble, if not downright juvenile, response.

Chapter X

DAY FORTY-TWO

The next day, Tuesday, July 28, Vincent Bugliosi, despite the incessant objections by Irving Kanarek, led Linda Kasabian through a description of her first encounter with Charles Manson. Bugliosi inquires:

Q: Did you indicate yesterday that after the first time you met Mr. Manson you saw him the following night; is that correct?

A: Yes.

Q: Where were you this night when Manson saw you?

A: In a cave in back of the ranch.

Q: Did anything take place between you and Mr. Manson in the cave?

A: He made love to me and we had a slight conversation.

Throughout this testimony Linda Kasabian sat with her hands folded in her lap, answering the last question as she had done all the others, in a quiet, unemotional voice. The

KRENWINKEL, VAN HOUTEN, ATKINS AND MANSON

three girl defendants, now each with "X" scratched on her forehead, stared at her but she appeared not to notice. Whenever the attorneys were called to the bench, which was frequently, her two lawyers, Fleischman and Goldman, immediately escorted her off the stand and led her to a seat where she was partially shielded from the defendants' view.

Q: What conversation did you have with Mr. Manson while you were making love, or about that time?

A: I don't recall the complete conversation, but he told me that I had a father hang-up, and I said . . .

Q: This is after you had sexual intercourse with him?

A: No. I think it was before.

Q: Did this impress you when he said you had a father hang-up?

A: Very much so.

Q: Why?

A: Because nobody ever said that to me, and I did have a father hang-up. I hated my stepfather.

After establishing that Manson had set up a camouflaged campsite containing dune buggy parts some two miles from a waterfall behind the Spahn Ranch, the prosecutor asked:

Q: Was a walkie-talkie system set up at this campsite?

A: Yes, it was.

Q: Do you know who ordered that the walkie-talkie system be set up?

A: Charlie did.

Q: Did he indicate why he wanted a walkie-talkie system?

A: Yes. We had been spotted. Maybe it was the fire department, or some trucks were going back and forth, and we had been spotted. So, we had a walkie-talkie system set up a little ways from the camp that we would make phone calls if they would come by, you know, to let people at the camp know.

Q: What was the setup of the walkie-talkie system?

A: Well, there was a road leading up to the campsite, and right at the beginning of this road a part of the walkie-talkie system was set up, and then there was a wire going all the way down to the road, camouflaged, leading to another part of the walkie-talkie system at the camp.

Q: Were there any guard shifts at the second camping site?

A: Yes.

Q: Who acted as guards?

A: All us girls in different shifts.

Q: What were you guarding?

A: Actually just like a watch-out tower, we would sit there with the walkie-talkie system, watching out if a truck went by or if, you know, somebody came walking through that would spot us.

Q: Did Charlie ask you girls to do anything while you were at the second camping site?

A: First he instructed us to make little witchy things to hang in the trees to show our way from the campsite to our road in the dark.

Q: What witchy things?

A: Things made from weeds, rocks, stones, branches, some kinds of wires, I don't know, all different little things.

Q: Why do you use the word "witchy?"

A: All the guys, Charlie called us witches.

Q: Okay, were there any male visitors who came to the ranch and visited the Family?

A: Yes.

Q: Did Charlie ever tell you girls to do anything with these male visitors?

A: Yes, he told us to make love to them, and try to get them to join the Family, and if they would not join the Family, not to give them our attention, not to make love to them.

Here Kanarek made a motion for a mistrial on the grounds that the testimony impugned Mr. Manson's moral character and integrity. The motion was denied and Bugliosi resumed.

Q: Where did you get your food from?

A: We used to go on garbage runs.

Q: What do you mean by garbage runs, Linda?

A: We used to go in the back of supermarkets and restaurants, into the garbage cans and take the throw-away food, take them home, clean them up and eat them.

Q: Did Charlie ever say anything about what type of food you should eat?

A: Not really. He used to really dig zusus.

Q: What are zusus?

A: Candy and ice cream.

Q: Linda, do you know what a sexual orgy is?

A: Yes, I do.

Kanarek objected and asked to approach the bench. It became abundantly clear that Judge Older, a model of restraint in open court, was doing a slow burn in private. Kanarek, who had been matching question and objection with increasing frequency, was the principal target of the jurist's wrath. Out of the hearing of the press and jury, Older spoke his mind:

OLDER: Let me tell you something, Mr. Kanarek, and I want you to get it straight right now. I do not want you to interrupt. I don't want you to interrupt me; I don't want you to interrupt another attorney and I don't want you to interrupt the witness. Do you understand, sir?

KANAREK: Yes, your Honor.

OLDER: You will be given every opportunity to state whatever you want to discuss, but you are not going to continually interrupt.

KANAREK: I understand.

OLDER: Now just a minute, that means right now also.

KANAREK: Yes.

OLDER: If you continue to interrupt I'm going to find you in contempt. I want you to clearly understand that. When I am speaking, don't interrupt.

KANAREK: Well, your Honor, it's certainly not intentional.

OLDER: I believe it is.

KANAREK: Not to interrupt the court. The point is, your Honor, if Mr. Bugliosi solicits a question . . .

OLDER: You heard what I said. Now, I mean it.

KANAREK: Then Mr. Manson is being denied due process.

OLDER: Do you have anything else to say?

KANAREK: May I make the record, your Honor is interrupting me.

OLDER: There is no record to make.

KANAREK: The point is . . .

OLDER: Now, Mr. Kanarek, I order you to stop talking this moment, do you understand, sir?

KANAREK: Very well.

Whereupon, after argument over the propriety of the use of the term "sexual orgy," Judge Older denied its use and the trial resumed in open court and Vincent Bugliosi inquired:

Q: There was a back house at the Spahn Ranch?

A: Yes.

Q: A little past mid-July, 1969, did a large group of members of the Family and guests gather at the back house?

A: Yes, they did.

Q: About how many people?

A: As many people as there were in the Family — maybe twenty — and I believe there were three or four guests.

Q: About what time of day was it?

A: It was nighttime.

Q: What took place at the back house?

A: There was one particular girl — I don't remember her name — she was fairly young, I'd say maybe sixteen, and she was very shy and very withdrawn, and I remember she was lying in the middle of the room, and Charlie took her clothes off and started making love to her and kissing her and, you know, she was trying to push him off, and he just sort of pushed her back down and kissed her. And at one point she bit him on the shoulder, and he hit her in the face, and then she just sort of let go and got behind it, or whatever.
        Then he told Bobby Beausoleil — no, excuse me — yes, he told Bobby Beausoleil to make love to her, and he told everybody to touch her and to kiss her and to make love to her. And everybody did.

During this recital Linda Kasabian's tone reflected mild interest in what had transpired. She appeared to be merely reciting a commonplace event, the way another girl of her

LINDA TELLS OF A FAMILY SEX ORGY

age might talk about going to a beach party. The courtroom stirred restlessly after she was through but Linda seemed quite at ease. Mr. Kanarek made three motions in rapid succession, ending with a motion for mistrial. All were denied and Bugliosi continued.

Q: You say everyone made love to her. Are you referring to the male members of the Family?

A: Everybody that was in the room. Yes.

KANAREK: Well, your Honor, may I have a continuing objection and a continuing request to admonish, because this is most prejudicial what Mr. BUGliosi is eliciting.

BUGLIOSI: The "G" is silent, sir. It is Bugliosi. (Titters from the press.)

KANAREK: I am sorry.

OLDER: Let's proceed.

Q: (By Bugliosi): After everyone touched the girl, then what happened?

A: Then he told everybody to make love to everybody else.

Q: When you say "he" are you referring to Charles Manson?

A: Yes.

Q: Could you define in more detail what you mean by making love?

A: Well, we all shed our clothes, and we were laying on the floor, and it was just like — it didn't matter who was beside you, if it was a man or woman, you just touched each other and made love with each other, and the whole room was like this. It was sort of just like one.

Q: Was everyone nude?

A: Yes.

Q: Was there sexual intercourse?

A: Yes. That is what I just said.

Q: In your stay at the ranch did you ever have discussions with Charles Manson?

A: Yes.

Q: Did he ever say anything about how not to get caught?

A: Yes. He used to say "If you don't get caught, you won't get it caught thought in your head."

Q: Did he ever say anything to you about willing to kill or be killed?

A: Yes. He used to say "If you are willing to be killed, then you should be willing to kill."

Q: One day in the woods at the Spahn Ranch did Mr. Manson indicate to you that he was someone other than Charles Manson?

A: Yes. I remember he took me in his arms and said, "Don't you know who I am?"

Q: Did Charles Manson ever talk to you about the Beatles?

KANAREK: Object on the grounds of hearsay, conclusion, foundation — improper foundation as to who was present, the time when it occurred.

OLDER: Place?

KANAREK: Place, right. Thank you, your Honor.

OLDER: Overruled. (Laughter in the courtroom)

KASABIAN: Yes. There was a certain passage in one song where he said that he thought he heard — or did hear, I am not sure if it was thought or whatever — that the Beatles were calling to him, saying, "Charlie, Charlie, send us a telegram," or "Put out a song," or something. Yes, he felt that the Beatles were calling him.

Kanarek kept up his interminable objections until, at one point, Manson addressed Judge Older:

MANSON: May I object to my lawyer's objections?

OLDER: No, you may not, sir.

After describing how Manson ordered the children at the Spahn Ranch hidden because the Black Panthers were going to come and do them harm and how armed guards were posted nightly, Miss Kasabian told of Manson's reaction to black people coming to the ranch to rent riding horses.

KASABIAN: Well, they knew that we were super-aware, much more than other white people, and they knew we knew about them and that they were eventually going to take over, his whole philosophy on the black people, that they wanted to do away with us because apparently they knew that we were going to save the white race or go out to the hole in the desert.

Q: (By Bugliosi): Did Mr. Manson mention the term Helter Skelter to you?

A: (By Miss Kasabian after five separate objections by Kanarek): Yes. It is a revolution where blacks and whites will get together and kill each other and all non-blacks and brown people and even black people who do not go on black people's terms . . .

Q: Did he say who was going to start Helter Skelter?

A: Blackie. He used to say that Blackie was much more aware than whitey and super together, and whitey was just totally untogether, just would not get together; they were off on these side trips, and blackie was really together.

KANAREK: I ask that the answer be stricken on the basis that it is gibberish, your Honor, you cannot understand it.

BUGLIOSI (to Kanarek):   Why don't you talk to your client about it?

OLDER: I admonish counsel to not engage in colloquy.

Bugliosi then got down to the events leading up to the fatal night and morning of August 8 and 9, 1969.

Q: During the day of August 8, do you recall Mr. Manson saying anything about Helter Skelter?

A: Yes, I believe that was the day he got back from Big Sur. He was telling us about his trip and that people were really not together, they were just off on their little trips, and they just were not getting together. So he came out and said, "Now is the time for Helter Skelter."

Mrs. Kasabian then described how, after dinner, Manson told her to get a change of clothing, a knife and her driver's license, and to go with Susan Atkins, Patricia Krenwinkel and "Tex" Watson (also equipped with changes of clothing as well as three knives and a revolver) and "to do what he told me to do." As they were driving away from the Spahn Ranch Manson stopped the car, stuck his head in the window and told them to leave a sign. Then he said: "You girls know what I mean, something witchy."

Court recessed for lunch. At 2:00 P.M. counsel approached the bench and in a private conference Ronald Hughes expressed his displeasure at the press seating arrangements.

HUGHES: I make a motion now that the press, that this whole preconceived notion of, you know, the numbered seats, that this all be changed, that people, if they want to come into this courtroom, that they queue up like any other courtroom and first come first served, getting there, that there be no priorities given to any person.

OLDER: I prefer that the matter be placed on an organized, orderly procedure, and that is the reason it was done that way.

HUGHES: Your Honor, Auschwitz was a very orderly procedure and we cannot say that is a fair procedure.

OLDER: (Obviously annoyed) If that is an argument, sir, it goes over my head.

But Hughes showed, soon after, that his capacity for the inept remark was exceeded only by his flair for the inelegant gesture. As soon as Judge Older had called the court to order in open session Hughes stood up:

HUGHES: Your Honor, I caused to be served on Mr. Stovitz a subpoena, a copy of which — the original has been filed with the clerk, and we would call him later as an impeachment witness.

OLDER: Just a moment, sir. If you want to make a statement like that, approach the bench. I want to hear it up here.

STOVITZ: I have no objection, your Honor. I have been served with a subpoena to appear as a witness in this trial and if the defendants want to call me as part of their case, I will be available.

HUGHES: Then we would wish to exclude Mr. Stovitz.

STOVITZ: Exclude me from the trial?

HUGHES: Yes. Until Mrs. Kasabian's testimony is over.

OLDER: The motion is denied. Let's proceed.

Hughes also indirectly provided a reassuring domestic touch to a trial packed with somber testimony dealing with orgiastic sex and murder. He employed an investigator, long-haired William Swinney (as in Piggy), whose wife took to breast-feeding their infant baby while sitting on the floor of the corridor outside the courtroom, right beside the men's lavatories. If nothing else, Ronald Hughes was throwing himself wholeheartedly into the life-style of the Family member he was defending.

The defense attorney's concern with the public's lack of access to seats in the courtroom brings up a disturbing point: with few exceptions the behavior of those members of the citizenry who managed to be seated during the trial was, in this writer's opinion, atrocious. Henry L. Mencken's favorite description of his fellow citizens as the "booboisie," comes to mind.

The public's right to know became, once seated in Department 104, the right to gawk, poke, titter, whisper and, if there was a break in the "action," to express their annoyance at the cost of the trial. Minds dulled to a state of collective numbness by a decade of "Perry Mason," they gazed uncomprehendingly at the drama unfolding before their eyes. They sought, usually from some unfortunate reporter in an adjacent seat, the cast of characters.

"That's Krenwinkel," a perspiring juggins would poke his corseted mate excitedly. "And the one to her right is Van Houten."

There were always a few seats at the rear of the courtroom set aside for the casual passer-by. In addition to these a rule was promulgated that, should a regularly assigned press seat not be occupied by mid-afternoon it would be allotted on a first-come, first-served basis. This placed many an excited old lady from Pasadena next to a hard-working journalist intent on practicing his craft.

One favorite method of retaliation for the unwelcome barrage of questions consisted of giving the wrong names to the various defendants.

"Which one is Atkins?" might be answered by indicating Leslie Van Houten. "I just *knew* it," the visitor would cackle contentedly. "I read that confession and she just *looks* like she could do all those things."

The supreme thrill, especially for ladies in their forties from out-of-town, was to be frisked.

"Did they search you?" was a frequent question, usually stage-whispered over three rows of seats to a companion from Dubuque.

"They looked in my purse," the friend would hiss back.

"They took me into a *room*," number one would reply. "And searched me all over!"

Excited suggestive giggles; the orgasm according to Charles Manson who, through the unwitting agency of the female members of the Los Angeles County Sheriff's department, provided members of another kind of family with their thrill to remember.

"My wife," one T.V. viewing statistic confided to me: "it's her time of the month, you know, and they searched her. They feel all the way up. She was really embarrassed." The stranger sighed resignedly and craned to see the show.

The four Family emissaries, Mrs. Kasabian revealed, all dressed in dark clothing, drove directly to a "house on a hill" of whose location she was unaware, for a purpose that she was not privy to. Vincent Bugliosi asked her what she thought they were going to do.

A: I thought we were going on a creepy-crawl mission.

Q: A creepy-crawling mission?

A: Yes.

Q: What is a creepy-crawling mission?

A: A creepy-crawling mission is where you creepy-crawl into people's houses and you take things which actually belong to you in the beginning, because it actually belongs to everybody. I remember one specific instance where the girls

made Charlie a long, black cape, and one of the girls was
fitting it to him, and he sort of said, "Now when I go creepy-
crawling, people won't see me because they will think I am
a bush or a tree."

The press laughed at this but Manson didn't think it was
at all amusing. He sat staring straight ahead, tugging at his
hair. The girls, taking their cue, looked properly sober.

Linda Kasabian was not long in doubt as to the purpose of
the car ride up the hill. The courtroom tensed as her voice,
calm and almost expressionless during her recounting of her
own sex experiences, began to change pitch. Bugliosi inquired:

Q: What was the first thing that happened after you arrived
on top of the hill?

A: Tex turned the car around and parked the car beside a
telephone pole.

Q: What is the next thing that happened?

A: He got out of the car; he walked around the back of
the car. I don't know if he had wire cutters or what, I don't
know, but I remember he climbed the pole, and I saw the
wires fall. Then he came back and got back in the car.

Mrs. Kasabian then testified that Tex turned the car around,
drove down the hill a short ways, parked it where the driveway met the street, and all four walked back up the hill.
Here her voice broke perceptibly and the press and jury
strained forward in anticipation. The prosecutor continued:

Q: What happened after you, Katie, Sadie and Tex walked
up the hill?

A: We climbed over (a sob escaped from her throat) — we
climbed over a fence and then a light started coming towards
us and Tex told us to get back and sit down.

OLDER: Are you able to go on, Mrs. Kasabian?

A: Yes, I am. (But the words came out in a rush, now, no longer serenely measured but punctuated with anguished cries and tears.) And a car pulled up in front of us and Tex leaped forward with a gun in his hand and stuck his hand with the gun at the man's head. And the man said. "Please don't hurt me, I won't do anything."

And Tex shot him four times.

Q: After Tex shot the driver four times what was the next thing that happened?

A: The man just slumped over. I saw that, and then Tex put his hand in the car and turned the ignition off. He pushed the car back a few feet then we all proceeded towards the house and Tex told me to go in back of the house and see if there were open windows or doors, which I did.

Q: Did you find any open doors or windows in the back of the house?

A: No. I came around from the back and Tex was standing at a window, cutting the screen, and he told me to go back and wait at the car, and he may have told me to listen for sounds, but I don't remember him saying it.

And I waited for a few minutes (at the car), and then all of a sudden I heard people screaming, saying "No, please, no." (The witness broke down completely; sobbing openly while trying to speak.) It was just horrible. Even my emotions cannot tell you how terrible it was.

I heard a man scream out "No, no." Then I just heard screams, just — I don't have any words to describe how a scream is. I never heard it before. It was just unbelievably horribly terrible.

Q: Were these the screams of men or women or both?

A: It sounded like both.

Q: Were the screams loud screams or soft screams, or what?

A: (Loudly) Loud. Loud.

Q: Did the people appear to be pleading for their lives?

A: Yes.

Q: How long did the screaming continue?

A: Oh, it seemed like forever, infinite. I don't know.

Q: What did you do when you heard these screams?

A: I started to run towards the house.

Q: Why did you do that?

A: Because I wanted to stop, because I knew what they had done to this man, that they were killing these people.

Q: What happened after you ran toward the house?

A: There was a man (Voityk Frykowski) just entering out of the door and he had blood all over his face and he was standing by a post, and we looked into each other's eyes for a minute (The witness paused here to control herself) I don't know however long, and I said, "Oh God I am so sorry. Please make it stop." And then he just fell to the ground into the bushes.

And then Sadie came running out of the house, and I said "Sadie, please make it stop." and she said, "It's too late." And then she told me that she left her knife and she couldn't find it.

And while this was going on, the man had gotten up, and I saw Tex on top of him, hitting him on the head and stabbing him, and the man was struggling, and then I saw Katie in the background with the girl (presumably Abigail Folger) chasing after her with an upraised knife, and I just turned and ran to the car down at the bottom of the hill.

Q: You said you saw Katie. That is Patricia Krenwinkel?

A: Yes.

Q: Was she chasing someone?

A: A woman in a white gown.

Q: When Tex was stabbing this man, was the man on the ground?

A: Yes.

Q: Was he screaming?

A: Yes.

Q: Was he struggling with Tex?

A: Yes.

Q: And you say you saw Tex hit him over the head?

A: Yes.

Q: How many times did Tex stab this man?

A: I don't know. He just kept doing it and doing it and doing it.

Q: When the man was screaming, do you know what he was screaming?

A: There were no words, it was beyond words, it was just screams. Please.

No objections from Irving Kanarek. No grimaces from the girls. No sly smirks from Manson. Paul Fitzgerald sat slumped in his chair at the defense table, staring at his feet, looking like a man who would rather be somewhere else. The entire court was silent as time hung suspended for sec-

FITZGERALD CONCENTRATES

onds until reality took over and the press leaped to their feet
and dashed for the special battery of twenty-six phones in-
stalled outside the courtroom door.

Linda Kasabian began dutifully to examine pictures and
diagrams of the Tate residence, marking "X" here and circling
something there, but it was all over. As Aaron Stovitz told
me later: "I've seen them all up there, the Sarah Bernhardts
and the Ingrid Bergmans, but I've never seen anything like
this. This girl told the truth."

Few who sat in Judge Older's court that day could find
fault with the Head of Trial's evaluation.

Chapter XI

DAY
FORTY-THREE

It is difficult to convey Irving Kanarek's irritative capabilities to someone not actually present in the courtroom during the trial. He is like an itch that, once scratched for momentary relief, immediately returns to give even greater discomfort. It would be fair to say that Judge Older had scratched to the point where he was about to seek relief from the Kanarek itch by invoking some external medicative agent.

Judge Older was under a dual pressure relating to Kanarek's compulsive objections to the prosecution's questions. The irritant — the itch — of the continuous interruptions was in itself a nerve-jangling experience. In addition to that, Older had to restrain a natural inclination to respond to the objections in the spirit in which they were made, cavalierly and without regard to due process of law. Older, after listening to seven or eight spurious challenges might well have been forgiven, even applauded, for overruling number nine or ten; to his lasting credit, he did not do so. Each objection, no matter how haphazardly worded or inappropriately presented, was weighed on its merits and, in a number of instances, sustained.

The double burden of having to listen to Kanarek and then sort out the trivia from the germane objections, continued to take their toll on Judge Older's patience. On July 29, in the midst of Linda Kasabian's vital testimony, it should have been apparent to the defense counsel that his Honor was, to use the defendants' own jargon, coming on uptight; not only did he have Kanarek to contend with but now, since the attorney substitution, he had Ronald Hughes. That morning, at the bench before testimony began in open court, Hughes started a small itch of his own. After declaring in the presence of the jury that his investigator, Mr. Swinney, was being discriminated against, Hughes asked for, and was granted, permission to approach the bench. The following dialogue took place out of the hearing of the jury and press:

HUGHES: Your honor, I believe that this is a matter for the jury because it shows that we are being denied the equal protection . . .

OLDER: It is not a matter for the jury, Mr. Hughes, and I am warning you now that I do not want these things brought up in the presence of the jury. You take them up with the court first out of the presence of the jury until I find out what it is you are talking about.

HUGHES: Okay.

OLDER: And don't address the court as okay.

HUGHES: I am making a motion that you direct the sheriff to allow my investigator, Mr. William Swinney, to enter the courtroom.

OLDER: If you have some motions that are collateral to what is going on in the trial, as I indicated to other counsel, you prepare a written motion supported by some kind of declaration, and serve it on the opposing side, and we will consider it.

HUGHES: Your Honor, the opposition has two investigators inside the rail. Yesterday you saw fit not to allow my investigator to come inside the rail. He was forced to sit out in the courtroom itself. It makes it very difficult for me to communicate with this investigator.

I believe that it is gross prejudice on your part against the defendants in this case. It shows favoritism toward the prosecution, against the defendants.

OLDER: You are coming close to making contemptuous remarks, Mr. Hughes, and I suggest you watch your language very carefully and consider what you are saying.

HUGHES: Your Honor, I feel . . .

OLDER: I don't want to hear any more on that subject, Mr. Hughes.

Linda Kasabian resumed her testimony in open court and Irving Kanarek, who should have felt the hot winds of judicial wrath burning on his burly neck, resumed his obstructionist tactics. Over his repeated objections, Vincent Bugliosi took his witness back to the scene of the crime:

Q: This woman whom Katie was chasing, do you have any physical description of her?

A: I only saw the back of her and she had a long white gown, and I believe she had long, dark hair, possibly brown, I'm not positive.

Q: After Sadie told you that she had lost her knife inside the house, what did Sadie do, if you recall?

A: I believe she started to run back into the house.

Q: Is that about the time then you ran back down to your car?

A: Yes.

Q: What was your state of mind at that point?

A: I was in a total state of shock.

Q: Did you think of running to a nearby home or calling the police or anything like that?

A: Yes, that was my first thought.

Q: Then why didn't you do it?

Kanarek objected and Judge Older sustained the objection on the grounds of hearsay. Bugliosi then asked to make an offer of proof, that is, to show the judge and the other attorneys in private why he is taking this line of questioning. He was asked to approach the bench to do so.

BUGLIOSI: I think her answer would be, as an offer of proof, that the reason she did not call the police or go to a neighbor's house is because she thought of Tanya, her daughter Tanya, back at the Spahn Ranch, and also she thought of Manson at Spahn Ranch with Tanya, so she was frightened.
Again this goes towards the issue of her relationship with Manson and also the issue of whether or not she was an accomplice.

Judge Older, after some further discussion, could not see the relevancy of the argument and sustained Kanarek's objection. The trial resumed in open court with Vincent Bugliosi inquiring:

Q: Did Tex, Sadie and Katie eventually come to the car?

A: Yes.

Q: What happened then?

A: Well, I had started the car, and Tex came over and told me to turn the car off and to push over, and he seemed really up-tight because I had run to the car.

Q: Did Tex then drive off?

A: Yes, he did.

Q: Did Katie and Sadie say anything as you were driving off from the residence?

A: Yes. They complained about their heads, that the people were pulling their hair, and that their heads hurt. And Sadie even came out and said that when she was struggling with a big man, that he hit her in the head. And also Katie complained of her hand, that it hurt.

Q: Did she say why her hand hurt?

A: She said when she stabbed that there were bones in the way and she couldn't get the knife through all the way, and that it took too much energy or whatever, I don't know her exact words, but it hurt her hand.

Q: Did Katie say anything about one of the girls inside the residence?

A: Yes, she did. She said that one of the girls was crying for her mother and for God.

Mrs. Kasabian then described how Tex, Sadie and Katie changed from their bloody clothes to the spare sets they had brought with them and how they drove around looking for a place to hose the blood from their bodies. They found a house with a hose in front of it, parked the car, and Tex, Katie and Sadie started to wash themselves off.

A YOUNG GIRL'S STORY OF BIZARRE MURDERS

Q: Would you relate what happened, Linda?

A: An older woman came running out of the house.

Q: What happened next?

A: I don't remember her exact words but she said, "Who is there?" or "Who is that, what are you doing?" And Tex said, "We're getting a drink of water."
     Then she got sort of hysterical and she said, "My husband is a policeman; he is a deputy," or something like that. And then her husband came out and he said, "Is that your car?" And we said, "No, we are walking." And then we started walking to the car.

Q: All four of you?

A: Yes. And the man was behind us.

Q: Did the man follow you all the way down to the car?

A: Yes.

Q: Did all four of you get into the car?

A: Yes.

Q: What is the next thing that happened?

A: The man was right behind us and he came to the driver's seat and he started to put his hand in the car to reach for the keys, and Tex blocked him, grabbed his hand and just jammed, you know. So I thought the man's arm was going to go with him.

Q: Now, when you say Tex jammed, what do you mean by that?

A: He drove off fast.

    The Fates, if they were not with Charles Manson that

night, must surely have bestowed their protection upon the man who chased Tex away. Given the circumstances, it was nothing less than a miracle that the outraged citizen was not killed on the spot. Two of the knives used to commit the murders were still in the car, their blades wet with blood. (The third had been left behind by Susan Atkins.) And the murder gun was in the car. The homeowner, later to testify for the prosecution, must have had a number of occasions for sober reflection when he learned the identity of his intruders.

The witness then told of how Tex directed her to bundle up the bloody clothing and throw it from the car, which she did. He then told her to wipe any fingerprints from the knives and to throw them out; she complied but was not very efficient. One knife landed in some brush but the other bounced off a curb and lay exposed in the road as they drove away. They stopped at a gas station where Tex told the girls to go into the restroom and wash off, then they drove right back to the Spahn Ranch where Manson awaited them in the parking lot.

Q: What happened after you pulled the car into the parking area and parked the car?

A: Sadie said she saw a spot of blood on the outside of the car when we were at the gas station.

Q: What is the next thing that happened?

A: Charlie told us to go into the kitchen, get a sponge, wipe the blood off, and he also instructed Katie and I to go all through the car and wipe off the blood spots.

Q: What is the next thing that happened?

A: Charlie told us to go into the bunkroom and wait, which we did.

Q: Where is the bunkroom located?

A: It was called the gun room, also, which Danny DeCarlo had a side bed.

Q: Did you and Katie and Sadie enter the bunkroom?

A: Yes.

Q: Who was there?

A: Clem and Brenda.

Q: Is he also known as Clem Tufts?

A: I just knew him as Clem.

Q: Did Mr. Manson eventually enter the bunkroom?

A: Yes.

Q: Was he with anyone?

A: Yes, he was. With Tex.

Q: Did Tex say anything after you were all in the bunkroom?

A: He said, "I am the devil here to do the devil's work."

It should be remembered that the objections by Irving Kanarek were coming thick and fast through the above quoted testimony. A veritable cacophony of sound enveloped the defense table as Manson's attorney objected three and four times on different grounds to the same question. Interrupting the witness, ignoring orderly procedures, Kanarek was, legally speaking, pushing his luck. Aaron Stovitz addressed the court:

STOVITZ: Your Honor, may we ask your Honor to ask counsel to make his objection and then to allow the witness to continue? We are having great difficulty keeping the continuity of her testimony going with these constant objections.

I know the record reflects the objections because I have gone through the record, but I think the continuous interruption is made for one obvious purpose, to interrupt the witness's train of thought and interrupt Mr. Bugliosi's train of thought.

OLDER: Let's proceed. Bear in mind, Mr. Kanarek, what has been said by the court before regarding this subject.

Q: (By Vincent Bugliosi) Would you repeat what Tex said?

A: That "I am the devil here to do the devil's work."

Q: He was telling the people in the room that he was the devil?

A: That is what he told the people at the house.

Q: Did Tex say anything else about the killings?

A: Yes. He said that there was a lot of panic, and that it was real messy and bodies were laying all over the place, but they were all dead.

Q: Did Mr. Manson say anything in response to this?

A: Yes. He asked if we had any remorse.

Kanarek objected five times during the above testimony. Judge Older asked counsel to approach the bench in order to confer out of the hearing of the jury and press:

OLDER: Mr. Kanarek, you have directly violated my order not to interrupt repeatedly. You did it again.

I find you in contempt of court and I sentence you to one night in the County Jail starting immediately after this court adjourns this afternoon until 7:00 A.M. tomorrow morning.

The order will further provide that you are to be given free access to confer with your client, Mr. Manson, during the time you are in custody.

Proceed.

KANAREK: Your Honor, if I may, I will ask your Honor to read the record. I tried to object before.

OLDER: I don't have to read the record, sir. I was present. You have repeatedly, in spite of my warnings to you, interrupted. You just did it again in a flagrant disregard of the order.

KANAREK: Your Honor, that is not so. I beg the court to realize. If you will read the record, she answers so fast that I ask that you . . .

OLDER: You have been doing it continually, and you did it again after repeated warnings.

SHINN: Your Honor, may I be heard, your Honor?

OLDER: On what subject?

SHINN: On this same subject. I was present.

OLDER: You are not involved in this.

SHINN: But I want to make my observations, your Honor.

OLDER: I am not interested in your observations.

Clearly Judge Older was of a mind to keep his house in order.

In the afternoon session Linda Kasabian said that each of the four had answered "No" to Manson's question about remorse but that she, in fact, did feel great remorse but was afraid at the time to express her thoughts. She slept most of the day, August 9, 1969, then, after dinner in the evening, Manson again instructed her to get a change of clothing and her driver's license.

Vincent Bugliosi inquired:

Q: What did he say after that?

A: He said we were going out again tonight. Last night was too messy and he was going to show us how to do it. He told us that we were going to go to two different houses in two groups; that he would go in one group and leave another group off.

The witness then described what was, in many ways, the most chilling aspect of the whole affair. With Manson driving, Linda, Tex, Clem Tufts, Patricia Krenwinkel and Leslie Van Houten wandered at random around the city seeking, in military kill terms, targets of opportunity. They could have stopped at anyone's house to carry out their mission. At one point Manson spotted a man driving a white Volvo sport car. He told Linda, who was now driving, to pull up beside the car at the next light and he, Manson, would kill him. She did and Manson was out of the car, apparently ready to commit murder, when the light changed and the man drove off. The objective was quickly forgotten and Charlie next told her to stop at a church they happened to be passing. They parked in the parking area, Manson got out and tried the doors but they were locked. He got back in and they drove away.

The bizarre journey continued. They stopped at a house, Manson got out to scout the area but came back saying that he had looked in the windows and saw pictures of young children on the walls. He couldn't find it in his heart to indirectly harm them by killing the adult occupants.

Why did Linda Kasabian go on this second trip which she knew was for the specific purpose of committing murder? Vincent Bugliosi asked her:

Q: The second night did you know what was going to happen?

A: Yes.

Q: Why did you go along with Mr. Manson and the others?

A: Because Charlie asked me and I was afraid to say no.

The journey continued. They drove to an A-frame house on a hill and parked, but Charlie decided that the houses were too close together. They drove out along Sunset Boulevard toward the ocean and pulled up in front of another house on a dark road. Manson apparently thought that one over, decided against it and told Mrs. Kasabian to drive back along Sunset.

A number of people would have slept less easily that night if they had known that possible death sat just a few yards from their front doors.

Finally Manson gave the witness specific directions and they ended up outside of the home of Harold True, a neighbor of Rosemary and Leno La Bianca. Bugliosi inquired:

Q: Had you ever parked in front of that house before?

A: Yes, in the exact spot.

Q: When?

A: My husband and I and friends were on our way down from Seattle, Washington, to New Mexico and we stopped off in Los Angeles and this one particular person knew Harold True, so we went to his house and had a party.

Q: Now, when Manson directed you to stop in front of Harold True's place did you recognize the spot?

A: Yes I did. Right away.

Q: Did you say anything to Manson with respect to this?

A: Yes.

Q: What did you say?

A: Charlie, you are not going into that house, are you?

Q: Did he say anything to you?

A: Yes, he did, he said "No, I'm going next door."

Q: Then what happened?

A: He got out of the car. He disappeared up the walkway, the driveway, leading towards Harold's house, and I could not follow him any longer, he just disappeared.

Q: Did Mr. Manson eventually return to the car?

A: Yes, he did.

Q: How long after he left the car did he return to the car?

A: I remember we all lit up cigarettes, and we smoked about three-quarters of a Pall Mall cigarette, however long that takes.

Q: What happened after Mr. Manson returned to the car?

A: He called Leslie and Katie and Tex out of the car.

Q: What did you hear him say?

A: I heard him say that there was a man and a woman up in the house and that he had tied their hands, and that he told them not to be afraid, that he wasn't going to hurt them.

Q: Did he give any instructions to Tex, Katie and Leslie Van Houten? Did he give them any instructions at all?

A: I am not positive, but it keeps ringing in my head that he said, "Don't let them know that you are going to kill them."

Q: Did Manson say anything to Tex, Katie and Leslie about fear or panic?

A: Yes. I think I heard him say not to cause fear and panic in these people.

Q: What happened then?

A: Charlie got back into the car and handed me a woman's wallet, and he proceeded to drive off.

The witness then described how Manson told her to go into the women's restroom of a gas station and hide the wallet, later identified as belonging to Mrs. La Bianca, where it wouldn't be found for a long time. During this period, unknown to Linda Kasabian, the murders of Rosemary and Leno La Bianca allegedly were taking place.

Another incident occurred at the bench that provided yet another improbable twist in the already crazy quilt pattern of Tate/La Bianca. Vincent Bugliosi introduced a picture of a dune buggy into the court for identification by Linda Kasabian. By court order all evidence in the possession of the prosecution should have been made known to the defense. The picture had not been shown to any of the defense attorneys. Bugliosi later claimed that this was a last minute decision to show the picture, that it had been summoned hastily from the Los Angeles Police Department, and that it had arrived in court only moments before in company with a broken sword, that the defense *had* seen, and which was shown in the picture to be mounted on the dune buggy.

Bugliosi's last minute decision to show the picture as well as the sword had unfortunate repercussions for Ronald Hughes. Hughes objected when the picture was introduced and counsel approached the bench.

HUGHES: Your Honor, the objection that I am making is that this photograph has never been produced for us by way of discovery. This is just indicative of the complete disregard that the district attorney's office has had to various discovery motions and various discovery orders that this court has made.

OLDER: Statements like that aren't going to help you, Mr. Hughes. Just state the facts.

HUGHES: Okay. The district attorney's office is withholding evidence from us.

OLDER: Is that what you came up to say?

KANAREK: I make a motion to suppress.

BUGLIOSI: For the record, I just saw it for the first time a few minutes ago myself.

HUGHES: That is a lot of shit, Mr. Bugliosi.

RONALD HUGHES FOR THE DEFENSE: "THAT IS A LOT OF SHIT!"

OLDER: I hold you in direct contempt of court for that statement. I will take the matter up at 4:15 this afternoon.
The motion to suppress is denied.

That afternoon, after court had recessed for the day, Judge
Older remanded Irving Kanarek to custody and found Hughes
in direct contempt for "disorderly, disruptive, vulgar and unprofessional" conduct. He gave Hughes an opportunity to bail
himself out by sentencing him to a fine of seventy-five dollars,
payable immediately. When Hughes informed the court that
he was "a pauper" Older sentenced him to one night in the
county jail. Hughes giving the clenched fist salute of the mili-
tant left and uttering their rallying cry, "Right on," joined
Kanarek; with television film cameras grinding away they were
led off to jail where, Kanarek said next morning, his cellmate,
an unfrocked agent for the Bureau of Internal Revenue, was
a "very nice man."

Another day ended in the trial of Charles Manson, et al,
for first degree murder.

Chapter XII

DAY FORTY-FOUR

A murder that did not occur provided what might have been, in the eyes of the jury, the most damning denunciation of Charles Manson personally. After dropping Tex, Katie and Leslie Van Houten off at the La Bianca residence Manson drove to the beach with Linda, Clem and Sadie. With Vincent Bugliosi inquiring Mrs. Kasabian tells what happened:

Q: What happened when you stopped the car?

A: We all got out of the car, started walking towards the beach.

We got down to the beach, walked on the sand, and Charlie told Clem and Sadie to stay a little bit behind us, and Charlie and I started walking hand in hand on the beach, and it was sort of nice, you know.

We were just talking and I gave him some peanuts, and he just sort of made me forget about everything, and just made me feel good.

I told him I was pregnant and started walking. We got to a side street, a corner, and a police car came by and stopped, and asked us what we were doing, and Charlie said we were just going for a walk.

And Charlie said something like "Don't you know who I am?" or "Don't you remember my name?" As if the policemen were supposed to know him. They just said no. It was a friendly conversation. It just lasted for a minute.

Then we walked back to the car.

Q: You say you told Mr. Manson that you were pregnant. Were you pregnant by him?

A: No.

Q: What is the next thing that happened?

A: I took over driving, still, we just pulled out of the parking spot, drove down the hill, got back the same way we had come in, and Charlie asked us if we knew any people at the beach. We all said "No."

Then he looked at me and said "What about that man you and Sandy met?"

He said, "Isn't he a Piggy?"

I said, "Yes, he is an actor."

And then he further questioned me and he asked me if the man would let him in.

And I said, "Yes."

And he asked me if the man would let my friends in, Sadie and Clem.

And I said, "Yes."

And he said, "Okay, I want you to kill him," and he gave me a small pocketknife.

And at this point, I said, "Charlie, I am not you. I cannot kill anybody."

And I don't know what took place at that moment, but I was very much afraid.

And then he started to tell me how to go about doing it, and I remember I had a knife in my hand, and I asked him, "With this?"

And he said, "Yes," and he showed me how to do it. (Here

Linda raised her hand and drew the edge of her palm across her throat.)

He said, "As soon as you enter the residence, the house, as soon as you see the man, slit his throat right away." And he told Clem to shoot him.

And then, also, he said if anything went wrong, you know, not to do it.

At this point Irving Kanarek asked to approach the bench. The following private exchange between judge and counsel ensued:

KANAREK: I ask for a mistrial.

OLDER: Motion is denied.

KANAREK: And also your Honor, then I ask the testimony to be excluded on the grounds it is incompetent, irrelevant and immaterial. It is hearsay. It is a conclusion, and furthermore, your Honor, it is violative of the prosecution's representation that they were not going to put before the jury any crimes that were not set out as they indicated. This is a solicitation to murder.

OLDER: Have you completed your argument, Mr. Kanarek? I want you to complete your argument and I will rule once and for all.

KANAREK: It is not just to make a record. It is to try to convince the court.

OLDER: Have you completed your argument?

KANAREK: Yes, your Honor.

OLDER: The motion is denied, let's proceed.

In open court Mrs. Kasabian described how the intended murder victim had once given Sandra Good and herself a ride, had taken them to his apartment, let them take a shower, fed them and then had intercourse with the witness. Manson asked Linda to show him where the man's apartment was located; she took him there, led him up to the wrong floor and indicated a door other than that belonging to the actor's apartment. Bugliosi inquired:

Q: What is the next thing that happened?

A: Then we walked back downstairs to the car, and he gave Clem a gun.

Q: Charlie Manson gave him a gun?

A: Yes. At this point he said something . . . he said that if anything went wrong, you know, just hang it up, don't do it; and of course, to hitchhike back to the ranch, and for Sadie to go to the waterfall.
     And then he drove off.

Q: Before he drove off did Mr. Manson tell Clem and Sadie anything?

A: Yes.

Q: What did he tell them?

A: While I knocked on the door, for them to wait around the corner until I entered, and then to ask the man if they could come in.

The witness described how, with Sadie and Clem hiding around the corner, she knocked on the wrong door, identified herself as Linda, caught a brief glimpse of a male occupant through a partially opened door, said "Oh, excuse me, wrong door," and led the other two back downstairs. Bugliosi inquired:

Q: Why did you knock on the wrong door, Linda?

A: Because I didn't want to kill anybody.

Q: What is the next thing that happened?

A: Sadie went to the bathroom.

Q: Where did she go to the bathroom?

A: As we were walking downstairs.

The witness told how the three of them, she, Sadie and Clem began walking along the beach looking for a place for Clem to stash the gun. Sadie and Clem were singing.

Q: (By Bugliosi) What, if anything, were Sadie and Clem singing?

A: I remember one song that everybody always sang, but this day I remember them singing the Beatle song about piggies and forks and knives, and eating your bacon.

Mrs. Kasabian told how Clem finally stashed the gun in or near a sand dune, how three of them hitchhiked along Pacific Coast Highway to a house near an establishment named the Malibu Feed Bin where they "smoked some pot" with a man and girl acquaintance in the house. Then they hitchhiked over Topanga Canyon and through the San Fernando Valley back to the Spahn Ranch where Clem and she went to the main ranch and Sadie stayed with the man who had given them a ride and "presumably" went to the waterfall as directed by Manson.

The prosecutor then anticipated the defense's case by going into the subject of drugs.

Q: Do you know what LSD is?

A: Yes.

Q: Have you ever taken LSD?

A: Yes. I'd say approximately fifty times.

Q: Over how long a period of time have you taken LSD?

A: Over an approximately four year period.

Q: A four year period, off and on?

A: Yes.

Q: Have you seen other people take LSD?

A: Yes.

Bugliosi asked her whether she attempted to leave the Spahn Ranch after the two nights of murder.

A: Yes. On the morning after the second night I packed a sleeping bag with some of Tanya's clothes and planted it by the road in some bushes.

Q: Why did you plant the sleeping bag by the road?

A: I had to hide it. He wouldn't let me walk out of there knowing that I'd seen what I'd seen.

After one unsuccessful attempt the next day, Linda Kasabian finally slipped away from the Spahn Ranch in a borrowed car, leaving her daughter Tanya behind. "Confident that Tanya would be all right," she found her husband Robert at Ojosarco, a commune near Taos, New Mexico. Guilt-ridden, she told Robert and a friend named Joe Sage who ran a Zen Buddhist macrobiotic retreat in Taos, the essential facts of the multiple murders. Sage phoned Charlie Manson at the Spahn Ranch to check the story and Manson told him that she had flipped out and that her ego wasn't ready to die.

Mrs. Kasabian then spoke to Patricia Krenwinkel at the ranch to ask about Tanya and Miss Krenwinkel said, "You just couldn't wait to open your big mouth, could you?"

Sage gave Linda money to return to Los Angeles to retrieve Tanya which, after one more trip back to Taos because of a legal complication, she finally did. She set out with Tanya to see her father, Rosaire Drouin, in Miami, Florida, stayed there approximately one month and eventually wound up at her mother's home in Boston where she surrendered to police after learning she was wanted in connection with the Tate slayings. Bugliosi asked her some final questions on direct examination:

Q: Why didn't you do something about your guilt feelings before you were arrested?

A: I was afraid, I was pregnant again, I had Tanya and I had this thing about going to the police.

Q: You were brought back, then, to Los Angeles by the authorities in early December, 1969?

A: Yes, that is correct.

Q: You have been in custody ever since?

A: Yes, I have.

Q: And you had your child Angel while you were in custody?

A: Yes, I did.

Q: No further questions. The defense may inquire.

Linda Kasabian, hands folded in the lap of her embroidered peasant dress, a relieved smile playing across her face, appeared at peace with herself and ready to face the harrowing experience of a vigorous cross-examination. She had told the court a great deal about what had happened on those two fateful nights but she had said something more, perhaps without fully realizing it herself. Her matter-of-fact descriptions of Charles Manson's whimsical excursions to commit murder, of his neurotic shifting of moods, of his frighteningly helter skelter orders to his followers to drive here or there, to do this or that, of his childlike rambling selections of various widely-spaced locations as possible objects of his ill-defined, vaguely expressed wrath, confirmed, if it needed confirmation, psychologist Nathaniel Branden's evaluation of Manson, given in a previous chapter. And she did it in the best possible way: ingenuously.

The longer she sat on the witness stand the more that word ingenuous seemed to the observer to characterize Linda Kasabian's testimony. It is an odd word to use in her connection; a self-admitted hedonist, given to drugs and sex in the pursuit of her licentiousness, accused of seven counts of murder and one of conspiracy in a series of ghoulish killings, the witness would seem a poor candidate for the candor implied in a sympathetic description of her testimony. Yes candid she was, disconcertingly so, as Paul Fitzgerald, the first attorney to cross-examine for the defense, was soon to learn.

From the outset it was obvious that Fitzgerald was attempting to discredit the witness personally rather than break down her account of the events of August 8, 9 and 10, 1969. Fitzgerald's first question set the tone of his cross-examination.

Q: You testified this morning, did you not, that you had taken LSD fifty times, is that correct?

A: Approximately, yes.

Q: Do you recall when you first ingested LSD?

A: Yes. It was in Boston, it was Christmas Eve of '65.

PAUL FITZGERALD HEADS THE DEFENSE TEAM

Q: And is there some way to describe the experiences that you would experience each time you ingested the LSD?

A: I would call it a realization.

Q: Did it appear to you that when you took LSD it affected your normal thought processes?

A: No, not really.

Q: How long does it usually take when you ingest LSD for it to take effect?

A: It depends on the acid.

Q: It also depends on the dosage?

A: Yes.

Q: Have you taken LSD in different dosages?

A: I never knew the exact dosage, no.

Q: Was there some reason you never knew the exact dosage?

A: Well, the dosage was not usually inscribed on the capsule or tablet, so I don't know.

There it is; the pretty young girl in the pigtails from your home town talking about some dresses she bought the other day on a mild shopping spree. "Well, gee, some had the sizes on them but most of them didn't." It came across that way to many of the spectators in the courtroom and Fitzgerald appeared to be aware of it. Perhaps he sensed the slight rustling behind him as the press reacted to the witness's frankness; in any case he quickly attempted to break the spell.

Q: It is usually obtained through illegal sources, isn't that correct?

A: I suppose.

Q: Well, I am asking you about your experience.

A: I never obtained it illegally.

Q: Did you ever obtain it legally?

A: Well, I'm not quite sure what you mean by legal or illegal.

Q: Well, for example if you go to a doctor or drugstore and you have prescribed dosage, or frequently one knows what dosage or tablet or drug one has taken.

A: Yes.

Q: Do you know the unit of measure to describe the dosage of LSD?

A: No.

Q: For example, does it come in milligrams, micrograms, grams?

A: I think micrograms sounds right.

Q: Now, how were you able to arrive at the approximate figure of fifty LSD experiences?

A: Because I can usually remember the exact trips.

It was an answer that the witness would have cause to regret. As her attorney Robert Goldman confided to me later, "She brought it on herself. If she had just kept her mouth shut it would never have happened."

"It," was Irving Kanarek's cross-examination which was to seize on that one statement and very nearly bring the trial to a full stop.

But Paul Fitzgerald is still inquiring.

Q: You have also ingested peyote, have you not?

A: Yes, I have.

Q: What is peyote?

A: It is a form of cactus and it looks like a button, and it grows in southern Texas.

Q: Is it a hallucinogenic drug?

A: Yeah, I guess you could call it that.

Q: Is LSD a hallucinogenic drug?

A: Yes.

Q: Would it be fair to say that in LSD states you have had hallucinations?

A: Yes.

Q: Would it be fair to say that while taking peyote you have had hallucinations?

A: Yes. But they are different.

Q: Can you describe them?

A: Well, my sole purpose for taking it was for realization, God realization.

Q: That was to discover God?

A: Yes.

Q: Were you successful in your endeavor?

A: I realized you don't have to take peyote or LSD to discover God.

The simple direct answer; she admits her sins then draws an honest conclusion. Linda Kasabian may have been a bad girl, one suspects the jury might be thinking, but she is telling the truth now. After she gets through this she will probably straighten out and start a new life. That, in any case, was the opinion that this writer got from different women in the court-room polled through the days of the cross-examination. There was no reason to believe that the women seated in the spec-tator section were very much different from the women seated in the jury box.

Paul Fitzgerald, his voice rising slightly, becoming overtly belligerent so that no one would have the slightest doubt that *he* thought the witness was prevaricating, continued:

Q: Is it possible, in your experience, to take dosages of LSD that render you not in control of your mental faculties?

A: Yes, you could take an overdose.

Q: How much would be an overdose?

A: I never took an overdose so I don't know.

Q: Were the hallucinations you experienced while taking the drug, LSD, vivid in character?

A: Sometimes there would be colors that might not be there.

Q: You would see things moving that were actually stationary, is that correct?

A: Yes.

Q: Have you ever seen God under LSD?

A: No, I have not.

Q: Have you ever had delusions under the influence of LSD?

A: I don't quite understand what you mean.

Q: A delusion is a false belief.

A: False belief. Yes, I believe I have.

Q: What sort of false belief did you have?

A: For one thing, I believed that I could see God through acid.

Q: Were you able to see God through acid?

A: Yes, the acid told me it was God.

Q: Are you familiar with the term "acid trip?"

A: Yes.

Q: What is an acid trip?

A: What I have been doing the last fifty times.

Q: Has LSD altered your personality? If you are able to answer that question.

A: Altered my personality? It showed me parts of myself, yes, it has altered, I believe, to a certain extent.

Q: Is taking LSD like having a dream?

A: Yes, sort of, yes.

Q: Let's say on Monday you ingested some LSD and you see and experience something correct?

A: Okay, yes.

Q: On Wednesday you are not ingesting any LSD.

A: Uh-huh.

Q: And you are seeing and hearing things, but the things you see and hear on Wednesday are as real as the things you heard and saw on Monday?

A: Usually the things I saw and heard on Monday were in my own head, and they were not real.
But the things on Wednesday when I was not under the drug were real, were stationary.

It was a trick question, going to the very heart of the suspect's credibility as a witness. And it failed. Fitzgerald tried another tack.

Q: Have you ever had conversations with a person by the name of Katherine Share?

A: Is that Gypsy? (A long-time Family member and, at one time, Charlie's favorite.)

Q: Also known as Gypsy.

A: Yes, I have had conversations with her.

Q: Have you had LSD experiences with Gypsy?

A: No.

Q: Did you ever tell Katherine Share that you completely died under the influence of LSD and you were reborn again?

A: I don't recall that phrase, no.

Q: Do you recall ever having any experience under LSD in which you experienced death?

A: It was death of values, of thoughts, something was put into me that died, that I rejected.

Q: Did you ever experience an actual physical death of your own self?

A: (Smiles) No.

Q: Have you ever had the experience of your body melting under LSD?

A: (Laughing) No.

Q: Have you ever looked at your hand or some other portion of your body while you had been under the influence of LSD?

A: Yes.

Q: Have you ever seen a part of your body dissolve under the influence of LSD?

A: (Incredulous) Dissolve?

Q: Dissolve, melt.

A: No.

Q: What was your mental state during the month of July, 1969? (The month prior to the murders)

A: I was extremely impressionistic. I was — I can't think of the words — to describe it.

"I WAS EXTREMELY IMPRESSIONISTIC"

Q: Can you give us an example of your impressionistic aspects?

A: Well, somebody would tell me something, and at first something within myself would say that is not right, and then this person would further, you know, just keep, you know, putting it into me and putting it into me, and finally, you know, I would just give up.

Q: You were very angry with your husband, were you not?

A: Angry? (She smiles) No, I was just rejected. I felt hurt.

Fitzgerald then questioned her about a number of other drugs, mescaline, psilocybin, methydrine hydrochloride or "speed," all of which she admitted taking, and STP and bella-donna, which she did not take. Abruptly, the defense counsel changed the subject.

Q: You referred during your direct testimony to the hanging of little items from trees near your campsite in Devil's Canyon during the month of July, 1969.

A: Yes, that is correct.

Q: Little pieces of string, little pieces of wire, little pieces of paper?

A: Yes.

Q: And those things had a purpose?

A: Yes. So that we could find our way to the campsite.

Q: Weren't those also witchy things? (Here Fitzgerald's voice projected a suggestion of sinister things to come; of unplumbed depths about to be plumbed.)

A: Yes, that is what they were called.

Q: Do you know why they were called witchy things?

A: No, not particularly.

Q: Didn't you feel that you were a witch during the month of July, 1969?

A: I was made to feel I was a witch, yes.

Q: Did you refer to yourself as a witch?

A: While I was there, yes, and at one point, once when I left, I referred to myself as a witch.

Q: You are familiar with the name Yana, the witch?

A: Yes.

Q: Is that what you used to refer to yourself as?

A: Well, when I first entered the ranch, Gypsy told me that they all assumed different names, and if I would like to pick out a name? And the name just came to me, so I assumed that name, which I was called Yana maybe once or twice. Which just, you know, sort of went down, and they called me Linda.

Q: Did you profess to have magical powers?

A: (Smiles) No, I didn't.

Q: Do you feel you were a witch?

A: I think I tried to make myself believe I was a witch.

Q: Did you act like a witch?

A: No. I acted like myself.

Q: Were you a good witch or a bad witch?

A: (Smiles) I was a good witch, at the time when I was referring to myself as a witch.

Q: During the month of July and early August, 1969 were you preoccupied with the devil and witchcraft?

A: No. No.

Q: Didn't you attempt to practice the art of witchcraft?

A: No. I don't even know what witchcraft is. I don't know rituals.

Q: Well, was this whole thing about calling yourself a witch just a joke? (Very indignant now; clearly this is not a joke to defense counsel.)

A: I don't know. When I came into the ranch they told me I was a witch and that they were witches, so they made me believe that I was a witch, too.

Q: Did you ever see any ceremonial witchcraft at the Spahn Ranch?

A: (Puzzled) Ceremonial witchcraft? Not that I can recall, no.

Q: You didn't see any black magic rites or anything like that, did you?

A: No. No.

Q: (Very intense) You never saw anybody at the Spahn Ranch do anything a real witch would do, did you?

Whereupon Aaron Stovitz, seated at the prosecution table near Fitzgerald, threw his arms in the air and exclaimed loudly, "What would a real witch do, your Honor?" The courtroom erupted in a burst of laughter in which his Honor joined heartily. Fitzgerald, his point lost and several minutes of cross-examination possibly rendered ineffective, smiled ruefully and, wisely, left witch enough alone.

Q: Is the term "Family" your word, your term?

A: I consider them a Family and I considered myself part of the Family while I was there because we were a Family.

Q: Is it fair to say that you coined the word Family?

A: That I coined the word Family?

Q: Yes.

A: I don't understand what you mean.

Q: What did one have to do, if anything, to become a member of the Family you are referring to?

A: I don't know. I don't know if there was any special thing you had to do.

Fitzgerald then went to some lengths in an attempt to disprove the theory of a Family in the sense of an established gathering of people bound by some continuous set of rules. He then made reference to the group love scene in the back house described during the direct examination.

Q: Were you forced in any fashion to participate in love making?

A: No.

Q: Did you make love with somebody?

A: Yes.

Q: Did you make love with more than one person?

A: Yes, I did.

Q: How many persons did you make love to?

A: (Very factual and unemotional) Well, I remember I made love with Leslie and Tex, the three of us together, and then Snake made love to me, and then Clem was there and then Clem made love. That is all I recall.

Q: When you made love with the people you have just described, can you say you wanted to?

A: Yes.

Q: I take it during the period of time you were making love to them you were unaware of what other persons were making love with whom?

A: Sometimes I looked up, you know, but . . . (Titters from the spectators)

Q: And was this a pleasant experience for you?

A: Well, it was a different experience.

Q: Did you enjoy it?

A: Yeah, I guess I did. I will have to say I did.

Court adjourned for the day in anticipation of defense counsel's more closely pursuing the witness's sexual experiences on the following morning. Mention, however, should first be made of some of the unnoticed, weird connotations implicit in the introduction of drug ingestion into the defense's cross-examination.

Chapter XIII

A FASHION NOTE

"By 'Erotic symbolism'," Havelock Ellis wrote in his *Studies In The Psychology of Sex,* "I mean that tendency whereby the lover's attention is diverted from the central focus of sexual attraction to some object or process which is on the periphery of that focus."

From the beginning there was endless speculation among the press, spectators and court bailiffs concerning the Family's behavior during the trial. They simply did not act like four defendants in a multiple murder case. We can dismiss the turning of their backs on the court and the standing in the crucifixion position, as planned theatrics; whenever they tried those tactics they were removed from the courtroom and ceased to be the center of attention. Since that kind of enforced anonymity obviously did not suit their purpose they soon returned to their best behavior and were reseated at the defense table.

It was their best behavior that confounded courtroom observers. The defense table was "L" shaped and the usual seating arrangement had Charlie sitting at the extreme end of the

short bevel, Kanarek next to him, with Shinn, Fitzgerald, the
three girls and Reiner (later Hughes) filling out the rest of
the table.

Manson, watching the other defendants diagonally across
the table, constantly communicated with them verbally or
through facial expressions. He would make faces at them the
way a father might attempt to amuse or distract a younger
child. A long, sad expression switched abruptly to an idiotic
grin switched again to mock solemnity invariably drew giggles
and gasps of appreciation from his audience.

Frequently, when the girls were talking among themselves
or to their attorneys, Manson would stare fixedly at one of
them for as long as one minute until she turned and met his
gaze; everytime this happened he would break out in a pleased
smile, apparently certain in his own mind that he had cap-

MANSON PRACTICES HIS "HYPNOTIC STARE"

tured her attention through force of will. Occasionally he would select someone in the press section and fix he or she with what was quickly dubbed a "whammy." Usually the whammy's recipient was one of the more comely female reporters who would, not unnaturally, turn away from being stared at; this reaction always pleased Charlie immensely, possibly as another successful demonstration of his hypnotic powers.

Manson, at various times, tried out his stare on Judge Older who, although he refused to be whammied in court did order a twenty-four-hour guard placed on himself and his family, and on different members of the jury; whatever satisfaction he derived from this latter exercise might well have been self-defeating but it became increasingly obvious as the trial progressed that the defendants' (and their attorneys') behavior had little to do with accepted reasoning processes.

The staring pattern did not go unnoticed by the prosecution. Exploring every angle, Aaron Stovitz, in order to avoid speculation in the press of any undue influence on the already sworn jury, questioned Miss Donna Melinkoff, one of the prospective six alternate jurors, in chambers.

Q: You have been in this courtroom for, what? Three weeks?

A: Four weeks.

Q: I take it that you were on the second panel that came over; is that correct?

A: I was.

Q: You have, from time to time, looked at Mr. Manson; is that right?

A: Yes.

Q: And he has looked at you?

A: Yes.

Q: Has there been anything that he has portrayed in his eyes that has refreshed your memory as to the contents of that article? (Susan Atkins's published confession.)

A: No.

Q: And did he give you the appearance that he was smiling at you?

A: On occasion.

Q: And did you give him the impression that you were smiling back at him?

A: I believe I have.

Q: Did any of that conduct refresh your memory as to the contents of the article you read? Anything about his powers from his eyes or anything like that?

A: No.

Miss Melinkoff was excused.

During the pretrial and jury selection portions of the trial, before the first prosecution witnesses began their testimony, the news-hungry press, like an aging spinster peeking out from under her drawn blind, read significance into everything they could see and into a lot of things they could not. If Charlie shaved off his beard, as he did on numerous occasions, that became a signal to the Family, both in custody and at liberty, that they were to adopt a docile, "soft" line; when he let his whiskers grow back he was supposedly signaling the emergence of a fierce, lion-like attitude that might result in his acting-up in court and the Family engaging in some act of defiance on the outside.

When the well-endowed Miss Atkins appeared in court bra-less, one breast noticeably lower than the other, rumor had it that she had suffered some vengeful mistreatment as a result of her later-recanted published confession. "Naw," she told someone who asked her about it. "My tit got that way from nursing the kid (Manson's child)."

One aspect of daily Family court life that received, in this writer's opinion, justifiable attention, concerned their mode of dress. At the beginning both Charlie and the girls wore only Family-made clothes; garish mini-dresses of some satiny material on the girls and gypsy-style wide sleeved satiny shirts and buckskin trousers on the leader.

The girls on the outside, led by Sandra Good and Lynne Fromme, sewed the clothes at the Spahn Ranch where they continued to live in exchange for helping out with the general housekeeping and looking after the fifty-three horses. They brought clothes into the Los Angeles County Jail where Manson was held prior to being moved into the lockup in the Hall of Justice, and to the Sybil Brand Institute that housed the three girls; they took away clothing that needed cleaning or repair. One day the female defendants appeared in court all wearing cloaks of the same blue satiny material. While Charlie beamed approvingly, they took their seats looking for all the world like three long-haired supermen, fresh from the pages of the Sunday comics. The cloaks, if a theory held by this writer and presented here for the first time has any validity, were anything but comical but had a sinister symbolism. The garments could, as did Superman's cloak, send the wearers sky-high on a trip, a vastly different journey than that embarked on by the redoubtable Clark Kent.

The drug d-Lysergic acid diethylamide, tartrate 25 is color-less, odorless and tasteless. (The d means that this compound bends polarized light to the right, the lysergic acid diethyla-mide is the main nucleus of the compound which is also called acid or "L" by users, tartrate means that it's water soluble and the 25 means that it was synthesized in the 25th series of experiments in 1938 by a Swiss scientist named Hoff-man.) Although one dose theoretically consists of 100 micro-grams, or "Mikes," it is more usual for a would-be tripper to begin with 40 "Mikes," or about enough to cover the head of a pin.

Acid, undetectable after ingestion, is detectable at any time only with expensive equipment. It can be taken in any number of ways, in sugar cubes, in a glass of liquid, baked into brownies or cookies, and in a dozen other equally obvious means of ingestion.

There are other, more devious means. No less an authority than Dr. Thomas Ungerleider, Assistant Professor, Depart-ment of Psychiatry, University of California, Los Angeles Center for the Health Sciences, suggests some of them: "(Acid) can be concealed on the back of an envelope or stamp," he points out, "or soaked into a suit or sweater. Thus, it is possible to 'take a trip' (have an LSD experience) merely by licking the envelope or stamp, or sucking or chewing on the coat or sweater."

Or on a Superman cloak.

Sandra Good tells a story that Charlie liked to recount about his youth. One time, he said, he suddenly felt that he was as powerful and free as Superman. He acquired a make-shift cloak, climbed up to a roof, spread his arms and sailed through the air. It was a great feeling, comparable to the or-gasm, and one that he never forgot. When Sandy tells it there

THE SINISTER CLOAKS

is the strong implication that Charlie really did fly. No matter. The point here is that the cloak and Superman and the *feeling* are part of the Family's Manson legend.

In this context the cloaks that the female defendants sported in Judge Older's court represented, in addition to erotic symbolism, a gesture of loyalty and defiance; but, in one observer's opinion, they may have represented much more: a series of trips to sustain them through the ordeal of the trial.

LSD has few objective, observable effects; after watching them closely for weeks in the courtroom it is my feeling that the girls and, to a lesser extent, Manson exhibited unmistakable signs of having been, if not on a lengthy acid journey, at least on a modest excursion on more than one occasion.

Dr. Ungerleider, who has treated as many as seventy "bad trips" in the U.C.L.A. psychiatric clinic over one seven-month period, comments on some of the less serious, more commonplace reactions that he has observed. "We have seen them look around the room, apparently hallucinating, exhibit motor restlessness and approach being combative." At times the girls could hardly sit still in their seats, stared around the courtroom grinning seemingly at nothing, and stood and turned their backs on the judge. Their behavior prompted more than one comment that they looked as though they were "on" something and many discussions as to the security arrangements at Sybil Brand.

Dr. Ungerleider, again: "We have seen some previously rational persons become suspicious and withdrawn, with grimacing and inappropriate effects." Charlie's frequent changes of mood are a matter of observable record. At times he would sit staring morosely at the defense table, pulling at his long hair; other days he would make faces; still other times he was in the best of spirits, laughing and clowning with the girls. The significant fact is that there appeared to be no correlation between these changes in behavioral pattern and the progress of the case. Manson and the girls could have been experiencing "flashbacks," a phenomenon in which the original effects when taking acid recur without further ingestion anywhere from one week to one year after the first trip, or they could have been chewing on their clothes.

"We might speculate," Dr. Ungerleider continued, "that people who have a great deal of difficulty tolerating the anxiety and stress of everyday living are provided, in a sense, with a psychotic defense by LSD. They hope to experience an estrangement from reality with the drug that prevents them from having to experience any anxiety or depression. Many LSD users seem to reject the concept of working with an organized society."

Although meant as a generalization, the U.C.L.A. psychiatrist's observations read like a clinical analysis of the Family in court. Manson's estrangement from reality and his rejection of working within an organized society was no more apparent than during an episode in chambers after one of his outbursts had resulted in his being removed, struggling, from the courtroom. Judge Older made the observation that if the defendants (the girls had followed Charlie's example) were to reconsider their reliance on disorderly behavior he would let them back into the trial.

MANSON: Your Honor, you mentioned . . . you mentioned "Reconsider." Then you could possibly reconsider, if you can ask me to reconsider. Let me ask you to reconsider. I have a position as well as your Honor has a position.

My position is still as strong as it was the first day I was arrested. The position that I hold is as follows.

The confusion that has been created around the situation can be eliminated if your Honor would allow me to have my own voice in court. I am not here to use dilatory tactics or cause confusion. I am not here to shout in your courtroom. I am not here to fight with your bailiffs, and I am not here to go against my brother.

I am just here to try to explain what these two gentlemen, even though sincere as they may be, they have no idea of what is going on. They are still in the dark about the whole situation. They have a bunch of facts; they have a bunch of things —

OLDER: What two gentlemen are you talking about?

MANSON: The district attorneys, they are very good at what they do, but they are way out, they are on the edge of town, you know, like it's . . .

OLDER: Are you making some kind of a motion, Mr. Manson?

MANSON: Yes, I'm making a motion, if I can finish. I listened to you.

OLDER: Just tell me what the motion is.

MANSON: It is my opinion that the court is not supposed to think, but supposed to administer the laws that go into the book, Manson vs. the United States. You give me a case . . .

OLDER: Mr. Manson I don't want to hear a speech. If you have a motion or a request, state it to the court so I would know what you want.

MANSON: I would like to associate in with Mr. Kanarek as my own counsel.

OLDER: I have already ruled on that several times. Your motion will be denied.

MANSON: Yeah, okay, then you leave me nothing, you know, there is nothing else I can do. You can kill me now.

OLDER: All right.

MANSON: You understand what I am saying to you? Do you understand what I am saying to you?

OLDER: Is there anything further, gentlemen, before we resume in the courtroom?

It should be remembered, when speculating on the Family's courtroom deportment, that wildly eccentric behavior need not accompany an acid trip. The use of the term hallucinogenic in connection with LSD is misleading; hallucinogenic suggests imagined experience and, while this sometimes does occur, most acid trips deal with the heightened awareness of real phenomena. Sounds are "seen," pictures are "heard," faces appear to be melting away and skin might seem to be falling off, but even in "bad trips" what is seen and heard are more illusions — that is distortions of the real — than true hallucinations.

I asked Dr. Ungerleider if, in a hypothetical case, the heightened awareness of a "good trip" could in any way facilitate the commission of a crime such as murder. "It is possible," he said, "that the heightened awareness also results in a change in moral values wherein the person on the trip sees more clearly the need to commit murder in order to rectify supposed wrongs."

My thoughts went back to my conversation with Paul Fitzgerald. " . . . the tripper loses all contact with learned upbringing and becomes ripe for conscious manipulation by the right person," he had said.

Or by the wrong person.

Chapter XIV

DAY FORTY-FIVE

As expected, the next morning, Friday, July 31, 1970, Paul Fitzgerald tried to discredit the witness by stressing her sex life. The demand for seats in the spectator section was especially heavy this morning as the public, anxious to make certain that the finer points of law governing Linda Kasabian's legal position were scrupulously adhered to, exercised their right to know. Mrs. Kasabian, dressed in a fetching white and orange dress with black embroidery, appeared at ease as the defense attorney established that she had left home at sixteen, married, had a child and that the marriage hadn't worked out. She then began drifting from what Fitzgerald referred to as "one group situation to another."

First to Venice, California in 1967, then across country to Miami Beach, then to Greenwich Village in New York, then to Boston for a short time and on to the Haight-Ashbury district of San Francisco. Following that the peripatetic young lady met her husband in what she termed a "Psychedelic circus," an abortive plan to combine an animal show with a light show in the manner of the then popular *discotheques*.

The two of them traveled in a "drug-oriented" situation to a commune in Taos, New Mexico, returned to California and split up; Linda finally ended up at the Spahn Ranch on July 4, 1969 with her baby Tanya, but without her husband Bob.

It was difficult to evaluate the effect of the witness's story of her travels on the jury. She spoke, as she had done from the beginning, in a straightforward manner, acknowledging her use of drugs and the implied promiscuity brought out by Fitzgerald's questioning. It is, as any trial attorney knows, very hazardous to attempt to "read" a jury; this one, however, seemed undisturbed by Mrs. Kasabian's unorthodox lifestyle. It was Paul Fitzgerald's aim to leave the jury disturbed or, at the very least, confused as to the character of the prosecution witness; before he proceeded to question her about her activities at the Spahn Ranch, he asked to approach the bench. In joining counsel at the bench we are privileged to catch a glimpse of the little understood but extremely important process of criminal law whereby an attorney as an ethical officer of the court is denied an opportunity to introduce evidence that would undoubtedly have an effect on the minds of the jury. The following exchange goes right to the heart of our judicial system and, as such, is reproduced below. Remember, the jury and press are unaware of this dialogue.

BUGLIOSI: He (Fitzgerald) at this point apparently wants to go into this $5,000 theft. I want to compliment Mr. Fitzgerald on the record for his professional and ethical attitude in coming here to discuss this before asking questions about it.

FITZGERALD: I have information, and as a result of the information I believe, and I intend to produce evidence on the defense case in chief that Linda Kasabian had other motives other than this motive she has stated for leaving her husband on or about July 4, 1969.

I intend to introduce evidence that she came to the Spahn Ranch about July 4 asking for some sort of amnesty or asking to be hidden, to be hidden out because she had stolen $5,000 from her husband's roommate, one Charles Melton.

We also intend to introduce evidence that she attempted to give the $5,000 to various people at the Spahn Ranch, including one Katherine Share (Gypsy), and Charles Manson.

Now I think that the evidentiary import of this evidence is that it impeaches her in terms of her stated motives, for becoming involved at the Spahn Ranch. Number two, it impeaches her statements, or rather, her altruistic statement about her innocence, her being impressionistic and her naiveté.

OLDER: What question do you propose to ask?

FITZGERALD: I propose to ask her if she went to the Spahn Ranch for motives other than what she stated. If she says "No," I would ask her, "Isn't it a fact you went to the Spahn Ranch because you stole the money from your husband's roommate?

OLDER: I think that is clearly objectionable, Mr. Fitzgerald.

BUGLIOSI: There are many crimes, your Honor, that we would like to introduce at this trial against Mr. Manson, and we are not going into them because we just cannot do it. The law is clear that you cannot introduce evidence of other crimes.

OLDER: Let's proceed, gentlemen.

It may not be entirely clear to the layman why Paul Fitzgerald could not ask his question (Kanarek later would be less scrupulous) but the fact is that, under the law, he could not. His behavior is in contrast as we have seen, especially when Linda Kasabian first took the stand, to that of Kanarek.

The flagrancy of Kanarek's indecorous legal behavior may be judged better by having an appreciation of the fastidiousness of some of the other attorneys when dealing with points of law. Now, in open court, Fitzgerald resumes his cross-examination of Mrs. Kasabian, dealing with her first days and nights at the Spahn Ranch.

Q: You slept in a cave on the evening of July 5; correct?

A: Yes.

Q: Where did you sleep July 6?

A: In the cave.

Q: Who did you sleep with in the cave, if anybody, on July 6?

A: Let me see. I am not sure if it was that night or the night before. I slept with Charlie that night.

Q: Did you sleep with anybody on the 7th?

A: I don't know. I can't go back there and remember exactly, you know, dates and who.

Q: Do you remember who you slept with, if anyone, on the 8th?

A: No.

Q: The 10th?

A: No. But eventually I slept with all the men. So, I don't know the dates.

Once again, the ingenuousness; "Gee, I danced with *all* the boys at the party; so I can't remember each specific dance." She used the tone of a young, twenty-year-old girl recounting some social event to her mother. To the courtroom observer the fascinating thing about her testimony is that it came across exactly that way, the casual admission of a series of, at worst, indiscreet encounters.

After an interruption at the bench at which Vincent Bugliosi protested Manson's loud instructions to Fitzgerald to "Ask her about the $5,000," (Manson's exact words, according to another source: "Ask her about the Goddamn money.") which may or may not have been heard by the jury, Fitzgerald resumed:

Q: What sort of activity did you engage in during the day of July 5th?
A: Well, first I will have to explain to you the night of July 4th.

Q: You may do so.
A: Okay. I met Tex, and Tex took me into a dark shed, shack, whatever you want to call it, and he made love to me, which was an experience that I had never had before.

Q: You had never had sexual intercourse before?
A: No. I am saying that the experience I had in making love with Tex was a total experience, it was different.

Q: In what respect?
A: That my hands were clenched when it was all over and I had absolutely no will power to open my own hands, and I was very much afraid, I didn't understand it.
(Lady juror is observed with her gloved hands tightly clenched.)
And I questioned Gypsy about it later and she told me it was my ego that was dying. And I told him that I was on my way to South America, and we had all this money, and we were going to do these things.

A TOTAL EXPERIENCE WITH TEX

Q: You had all what money?

A: We had some money that Charlie Melton had inherited.

BUGLIOSI: Your Honor, may we approach the bench.

OLDER: You may approach the bench.

Had the witness inadvertently opened the door to testimony that would be damaging to herself or was she simply telling the truth, displaying the same apparent frankness that had characterized her other answers? The frustration of the press, if not the jury, may be imagined as the subject was debated in private.

BUGLIOSI: The way it developed is that apparently Tex told her to go steal $5,000, whereupon she did go and steal the $5,000, and gave it to Leslie, I believe. She didn't keep it for herself.

She is about to testify to this. And I think the defense is now bringing in through the back door what the court indicated it could not do.

OLDER: I don't see it that way. She is now relating a conversation that she had with Tex, one of the defendants in this case. I think it is permissible.

After the morning recess Fitzgerald inquired:

Q: Would you continue with the conversation you had with Tex Watson?

A: Yes. I told him that we and these people were going to go to South America by boat and sail around the world. And we had this money, and it seemed to me as soon as I mentioned money he started going on this trip, and telling me that it wasn't their money; that it was everybody's money and it was just there to take, and that there was no right and wrong. It was just theirs, ours.

I said, "Hey" —

He told me, you know, that I should go and take this money.

I said, "Hey, I can't do that, he's my brother."

He said, "But there is no wrong." And he just kept going on and on. And I accepted it and that was about the conversation.

Fitzgerald succeeded in causing the witness to admit that she had gone to see her husband Bob and his friend Charles

Melton and that she had retrieved a pouch of acid (pills) that she had left with them but the attorney was not able to bring out an account of the theft of the $5,000. He went on to establish that Linda did not have a memory for dates or time or even, in some circumstances, faces. This line of inquiry brought about, from the spectator's point of view, one of the high spots of the day. Throughout Paul Fitzgerald's cross-examination something had been missing and its very absence, like a continuous background noise that abruptly ceases, appeared to be, in itself, audible. The absent background noise was Irving Kanarek objecting, or, in this case, not objecting to the questions. Speculation was rampant among the press as to how long Manson's attorney could keep it up. Fitzgerald finally asked the question that, fuse-like, triggered Kanarek's mechanism.

FITZGERALD: Didn't you have a philosophy or organized set of thoughts that time was irrelevant, made no sense?

KANAREK: I object on the grounds the word organized — I don't think this witness — I object on the ground it is assuming facts not in evidence that she has an organized thought.

When the laughter died down Judge Older overruled the objection and the questioning, centering around the witness's understanding of Manson's philosophies, continued.

Q: Were you interested in those philosophies?

A: I remember the first — up in the cave, the first thing he said, he started to talk to me and I said that I already knew the truth, because I didn't know what he was going to say. And he said "Don't you want to hear it?" So he started talking to me about it.

Q: What would Charlie do with you when he spent this time with you?

A: He would talk to me, he would make love to me.

Q: How many times did he make love to you?

A: Let me think. (Frowns and puts her fingers to her forehead, a characteristic gesture when she was concentrating.) The cave, the waterfall, the trailer and the house; four times.

Q: Did you disagree with his philosophy in some respects?

A: Yes, I did.

Q: And you told him that you disagreed with it when he told you?

A: No. Because I was always told, "Never ask why."

Q: Were you also told that you couldn't disagree?

A: The girls used to always tell me that. "We never question Charlie. We know that what he is doing is right."

Q: Were you afraid?

A: Yes.

Q: What were you afraid of?

A: I was just afraid. He is a heavy dude — man. (Some laughter in the courtroom)

Q: What is a heavy dude?

A: A dude is a man. Heavy. He just had something, you know, that could hold you. He was a heavyweight, you know. He is just heavy, period.

Q: Did you love Charlie?

A: Yes, I did. To be truthful I felt . . . I felt that he was the Messiah come again; you know, the second coming of Christ.

(Manson, his long hair in disarray, his beard unevenly trimmed, stares down at the defense table during this testimony. He appears to be doodling and he does not look up at the witness.)

Q: You thought he was God?

A: No.

Q: You thought he was a God-man?

A: Yes.

Q: You thought he was a deity in human form?

A: Well, I thought he was the Messiah.

Q: A second Jesus Christ?

A: Yes.

Q: You used the term — or I believe my notes are correct — but I believe on your direct examination you said, "No sense makes sense."

A: Yes.

Q: What did you mean by "No sense makes sense?"

A: I don't know. That is what Charlie told me.

Fitzgerald then got to the heart of the matter: the murder testimony itself.

Q: Why are you testifying?

A: You want me to tell you?

Q: I asked you the question.

A: Well, from the moment it happened I knew that I would be the one to tell the truth; I knew I would be the one to tell it, and I never had immunity in my mind. I never knew this was going to happen. This is something that to me I look at as a miracle. I just know I have to do this, whether it's immunity or not, it doesn't matter.

The witness spoke very convincingly in a soft, matter-of-fact voice that projected emotion by the very absence of it; she sat composed, hands folded in her lap. Fitzgerald then read her the immunity agreement that was explained to her by Vincent Bugliosi in direct examination, ". . . that if you testify to everything you know about the Tate/La Bianca murders, the district attorney's office will petition the court to grant you immunity from prosecution and dismiss all charges against you." The defense counsel asked her about it:

Q: Is it your understanding of that immunity agreement that if you say these defendants are innocent you are granted immunity?

A: I just have been told that as long as I tell the truth I will be granted immunity.

No matter how he tried, Paul Fitzgerald could not shake the witness's expressed belief that all she wanted was to tell the truth and to "tell it like it was."

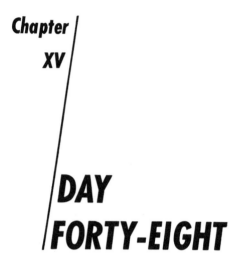

Chapter
XV

DAY
FORTY-EIGHT

The problem of violations of the gag order continued to plague Judge Older. On August 3, before court convened, he called the attorneys into his chambers.

OLDER: The reason I asked you to come in, gentlemen, was because there was some reference to what was apparently a recorded statement by Mr. Fitzgerald. I heard it on the way to work this morning on the radio, and it appeared to me it was a violation of the publicity order.

Now, the particular remarks that I referred to were remarks which related to the testimony of Mrs. Kasabian, which was characterized, it sounded like your voice . . .

FITZGERALD: I am sure it was.

OLDER: . . . you characterized them as being unbelievable and some other things. It was said rather quickly and I don't purport to quote you exactly. But it would appear to me that it comes within that order and I just wanted to call it to your attention.

KANAREK: In that regard, your Honor, I heard Mr. Stovitz make a statement in which he said that the reason Linda

Kasabian is telling the truth, or words to that effect, or one of the reasons that proves it — and I am synopsizing — is that she said the same thing Susan Atkins said.

STOVITZ: I never made that statement. You will never find a recording of my voice on it whatsoever that made that statement.

KANAREK: I am synopsizing. What she said is the same thing that Susan Atkins said:

STOVITZ: I never made that statement.

OLDER: I didn't hear it so I don't know.

The irritations set up in these private meetings between defense and prosecution counsel make their behavior in open court more understandable. To read in the newspapers that Kanarek said this and Stovitz said that was to know only part of the story. Irving Kanarek had occasion to rue his baiting of the Head of Trials when he called a conditional witness for the defense, the first such witness to appear in the trial. Supposedly, a conditional witness is one who is called and interrogated out of the hearing of the jury so that her testimony may be preserved should she not be able to testify when the defense puts on its case. In reality such a witness is often called so that the defense may observe how she stands up under direct and cross-examination without having to take the risk of unfavorable exposure to the jury. In the case of Mrs. June Emmer, now called to testify in open court but with the jury excluded, Kanarek had good reason to test the credibility of his first witness.

Mrs. Emmer, a plump, thirtyish woman who spoke and, except for her dark hair, physically resembled the character

JUNE EMMER HEARD STORIES IN FLORIDA

"Maisie" played so successfully by actress Ann Sothern, was sworn and took her place in the witness box. After establishing that Mrs. Emmer and her late husband had owned a bar and package store — the J & J Liquor Bar and Package — in Miami, Florida, that she now owned the bar and employed Linda Kasabian's father, Rosaire Drouin, as a bartender, Kanarek, in the following significant portion of the testimony, inquired.

Q: How long have you known Miss Kasabian?

A: She stayed a month with me at my house between the middle of October and the middle of November. (Following the Tate/La Bianca slayings when Mrs. Kasabian, after retrieving her daughter Tanya in Los Angeles, hitch-hiked across the country.)

Q: Now, while she stayed at your house did Linda Kasabian discuss with you LSD?

A: Yes.

Q: Now, directing your attention to the matter of acid and LSD, would you please tell us whether or not Linda Kasabian told you that she had consumed acid or LSD?

A: Yes. She told me when she was carrying her baby, Tanya, she took it, and for me not to believe everything I see in the papers about taking LSD as far as having a child.

Q: What did she tell you concerning her stay in California?

A: She had a ball there and really enjoyed it.

Q: Did she tell you that she had been in a $250,000 house?

A: Yes.

Q: And did Mrs. Kasabian state words to you, anything, as to her state of mind towards other people when she went on trips?

A: She did not care what happened when she went on trips.

Q: Do you have in your mind a meaning for the word trance?

A: Yes.

Q: Now, directing your attention to Linda Kasabian, would you state that what you observed concerning her, as to whether or not she appeared to be in a trance?

A: Yes, she . . .
   (The witness responded before an objection by Vincent Bugliosi had been sustained. It was ordered stricken from the record.)

Q: Would you indicate to us, Mrs. Emmer, what her manner appeared to be to you?

A: Hippie-type.

Q: And when you say hippie-type, what do you mean, Mrs. Emmer?

A: The way she dressed.

Q: Did she wear shoes?

A: No.

Q: Mrs. Emmer, at one time while you were discussing a $250,000 home with Mrs. Kasabian, did you ask her why she was at this house?

(Bugliosi objected and asked for an offer of proof as to the validity of the question.)

KANAREK: Well, I believe the Sharon Tate home, your Honor, is worth about $250,000. And it is our belief that Linda Kasabian was in that house, that Linda Kasabian had a participation in these murders that is far and much greater than Linda Kasabian has testified to.

(Judge Older overruled Bugliosi's objection and permitted the question.)

A: Yes.

Q: What did she tell you?

A: She told me she couldn't tell me. I said, "Why not?" I said, "What kind of people do you know with that kind of money?" She said, "I just cannot tell you."

Q: Do you have an opinion, Mrs. Emmer, as to the truth, honesty and integrity of Linda Kasabian?

A: I know she lies.

STOVITZ: May that be stricken your Honor, as pure specula-
lation, pure conjecture, and pure malarkey?

OLDER: It is non-responsive. The answer is stricken.

A note here on "stricken" questions and answers. The implication is that when something is stricken it is expunged
from the record, that it is physically removed from the court
transcript. (During Tate/La Bianca, in order to provide all
counsel with a daily written record of everything that transpired, two court reporters worked in alternate fifteen minute
shifts, taking their mechanically recorded notes out to a typist
who converted them into a typewritten official transcript as
the trial progressed.) In fact the "stricken" words remain in
the transcript with the notation that they are stricken. Since,
presumably, the words, once uttered, are not stricken from
the jury's minds even though so directed by the court, the
use of "stricken" has a practical value only in the appeal stage
where a judge, versed in the ways of the law, may supposedly
strike from his consciousness anything that is officially stricken
or, having noted it, may take into account its impact on the
jury and allow for that when evaluating the verdict.

Q: (By Kanarek) Well, you lived with her for a whole
month?

A: Yes.

Q: Did her father tell you what his opinion was concerning
her reputation?

A: Yes.

Q: You had occasion to observe her, and among other
people besides yourself?

A: Yes.

Q: All right, would you tell us what, then, her reputation for truth, honesty and integrity was in the fall of 1969 in the community in which she lived in Miami?

A: She was a liar.

Q: What was her reputation, was it good, bad?

A: All I can say is she just lied, that is all.

Q: What is her reputation for truth, honesty and integrity, good or bad?

A: It was bad. (The witness paused perceptibly before she said this and it was duly noted in the record.)

Q: Did she ever state to you — did she ever state to you anything concerning the taking of any other drugs other than LSD or acid?

A: She told me she took them all.

The court then invited the prosecution to cross-examine and Aaron Stovitz accepted.

Q: (By Stovitz) Mrs. Emmer, when Linda Kasabian first came to Florida, she first moved in with her father, is that right?

A: No.

Q: Whom did she move in with?

A: She arrived on a Saturday and spent Saturday night, her and the baby, upstairs over the liquor bar. Her father could not be found.

Q: Was there any particular reason her father could not be found?

A: He has weekends off and sometimes he goes out in his boat or goes here or there.

After establishing that the witness's late husband was an ailing sixty-two at the time under discussion and that the witness herself was twenty-nine, Stovitz, his voice rising, began aggressively questioning Mrs. Emmer. Gone was the cigar-smoking, reflective Head of Trials who obligingly carried cups of water to his junior partner in the courtroom.

Q: When Linda came to live with you she was more or less like a young person to you and you and Linda started to talk, is that right?

A: Yes.

Q: One of the things that you and Linda got to talk about was your drinking habits, isn't that right?

KANAREK: I object your Honor, on the grounds that it is immaterial, irrelevant.

OLDER: Sustained.

(Throughout the following dialogue Kanarek repeatedly objected to the line of questioning. These are omitted here in the interest of clarity.)

Q: (By Stovitz) All right now, do you imbibe a little? Do you partake of alcoholic beverages from time to time?

A: Yes.

Q: And do you find that as the occasion arises, when you have taken too many alcoholic beverages, your memory becomes a little bad at times?

A: Yes.

A "Maisie," but, according to the prosecutor, a boozy Maisie.

Q: This weekend, for instance, you have not taken an excess of alcohol, have you?

A: I have four or five drinks a night.

Q: What about this morning, did you have four or five drinks this morning?

A: (Silent)

Q: (Voice rising) The shaking of your hand, especially when you took the oath, is that because you were nervous or the four or five drinks?

A: My shaking has nothing to do with my drinking whatsoever.

Q: Do you drink to stop your shaking?

A: No. When I drink I shake more.

Q: All right, now, did you ever see Linda drink?

A: Once.

Q: When was that?

A: All I seen her, during the month, was take one beer, that is all.

Q: Now, when did your husband pass away?

A: November 22nd.

Q: 1969?

A: Right.

Q: And following your husband's demise did you increase your drinking habits or did you decrease your drinking habits?
    (Objected to and sustained.)

Q: All right now, was your husband ill at the time Linda left Miami?

A: He was under a doctor's care.

Q: And when Linda left Miami, when was the last day before that that she lived with you?

A: The same day. She left from my house to go to the airport.

Q: Now you like Linda's father, Mr. Drouin, right?

A: Yes.

Q: Do you have any matrimonial plans?

A: No.

Q: Do you feel that Linda's affection for her father or her father's affection for Linda in any way interferes with your relationship with Mr. Drouin?

KANAREK: This is assuming facts not in evidence. In fact the contrary is true, the father feels Linda is a liar.

OLDER: Overruled.

STOVITZ: (To Kanarek) I suggest you stand next to your witness if you want to coach her. It's very disconcerting your standing over there.

A: (By witness to last question) All he does is work for me.

Q: How long has he worked for you?

A: For my husband fourteen years.

Q: How long has he worked for you?

A: Four years.

Q: In other words you were only married to your husband four years?

A: Three years.

Q: Three years?

A: Three.

After establishing that Kanarek had flown back to Miami to talk with Mrs. Emmer and was paying all her expenses on her trip to Los Angeles the prosecutor continued:

Q: Did you ever discuss the term "reputation" with Mr. Kanarek?

A: Yes.

Q: What do you understand the word "reputation" to mean?

A: What she is known as.

Q: Now, besides Mr. Drouin, did you know anyone else that knew Linda Kasabian at Miami Beach, Florida?

A: Her father's girl friend.

Q: What is her name?

A: Judy. Judy Short.

Q: Is Judy here in California now?

A: No.

Q: Where have you last seen her?

A: She helps Rosy at the bar. Rosy is Linda's father.

Q: And did you discuss Linda Kasabian with anyone else besides her father and Judy?

A: Yes. A neighbor across the street.

Q: What is that neighbor's name?

A: A Mrs. Frye.

Q: Do you like Linda Kasabian?

A: She never did anything to me.

Q: Mrs. Emmer, would you like a drink of water?

A: No, thank you.

Q: Your mouth is still not dry?

(Kanarek's objection was overruled.)

Q: Mrs. Emmer, you stated that you had about five drinks last night, is that right?

A: Not last night, no.

Q: The night before?

A: (No answer)

Q: Now, what about one occasion in Miami Beach, Florida, when Linda Kasabian was telling you all of these things about California, how many drinks did you have on that occasion?

A: I never drink in the daytime. I have a couple of drinks at night as most people do.

Q: Was this conversation in the daytime or the nighttime?

A: Daytime.

Q: All right. Now, one of the things that she said to you about California was that she was in a house with beautiful chandeliers, is that right?

A: Yes.

Q: Did she describe what type of chandeliers, whether they were French Provincial, or the Spanish type, or whether the early American chandelier?

A: No.

Q: Did she show it to you in a book?

A: No.

Q: Tell us everything you remember about the chandelier and about the house.

A: She told me she was in several homes worth over $250,-000, with chandeliers. That is all she told me.

Q.   Linda told you that she was using acid when she was carrying Tanya, is that right?

A: Right. She told me not to believe everything I read in the papers. Because she was taking a lot of it when she carried Tanya, and she said "Look at that baby; there is nothing the matter with it."

Q: How old was Tanya when you saw her?

A: Two and a half.

Q: Did she walk?

A: Yes.

Q: Was she saying words? Did she say anything like "Mommy" or "Daddy" or "Charlie" or anything like that?

KANAREK: Or "Aaron?"

A: She used the word "Mama" and "love."

Q: And aside from going around barefooted and being a little hippie-ish, did Linda appear to be a normal girl?

A: Yes.

Q: As far as you are concerned, the amount of alcohol that you drank in no way affected your opinions whatsoever; is that right?

A: No.

Q: And the amount of alcohol you drank in no way affected your memory?

A: I told you I had a couple of drinks every night; but during the day, that is when we talked, because we were home alone.

Q: At the bar did you have a couple of drinks each night?

A: No. I wasn't at the bar. I was home with her.

Q: At night?

A: During the day.

Q: What about having a couple of drinks; when did you have a couple of drinks?

A: At night. I never drank in the daytime.

Q: At the bar or at the house?

A: At the house.

Q: Was Linda there when you were having a couple of drinks?

A: Yes.

Q: And didn't she, on one of those times, ask you, "Judy" — she called you Judy, didn't she?

A: Right.

Q: Didn't she say, "Judy, why do you drink so much?"

(Kanarek objected and it was sustained.)

After further questioning elicited the fact that Mrs. Emmer had only spoken to three people about Linda Kasabian and that two of those had expressed doubts as to her character Judge Older found that "There is no evidence that Mrs. Emmer is familiar with the general reputation of Linda Kasabian in the community for truth, honesty and veracity. Therefore her testimony regarding reputation as to Mrs. Kasabian will be stricken."

Privately, the prosecution was delighted with Kanarek's move to bring Mrs. Emmer all the way from Florida. She turned out to be a fine witness for their cause. The fact that the defense attorney, having interviewed Mrs. Emmer at length in Miami, had brought her out at all was the subject of considerable speculation. That she turned out to be a liability was due, in no small measure, to Stovitz's well-informed cross-examination during which he managed to turn the whole procedure around and cause the defense's witness to be suspect rather than, as was originally intended, Linda Kasabian. It was apparent that bad judgment had been exercised in bringing so potentially vulnerable a witness to testify even though it was done prudently out of the hearing of the jury. Such was Irving Kanarek's reputation for unpredictability that neither of the prosecution team would hazard a guess as to whether or not Kanarek would bring Mrs. Emmer back when the defense presented its case. The prospect of the *prosecution* calling her was suggested only half-facetiously.

The trial continued in open court with Paul Fitzgerald cross-examining Linda Kasabian. The attorney took her through all of her previous testimony, attempting to show that she could have reported the murders on several occasions but chose not to; he then brought up the matter of a book being written about her life.

Q: Is it your understanding that upon the publication of your book you will be quote famous unquote?

A: I don't care. I don't care if I am famous or not. It doesn't matter.

Q: The purpose of the book is to secure money, isn't that right?

A: Actually the purpose for the book is so that younger people can relate to me and see that this road I went down is not the way, and they will go another way. That is my purpose.

Q: They will profit from the mistakes you have made in the past, is that right?

A: Yes.

Q: I have no further questions.

Mrs. Kasabian's stated purpose came through with a great deal of sincerity. Cynics will scoff (she is to realize twenty-five per cent of the sales) and perhaps rightly so; the reading of her words, however, fails to convey the simple eloquence with which they were delivered. By almost any standards the prosecution's "star witness" scored points for herself with the jury at the conclusion of Fitzgerald's cross-examination. "She crapped all over him," was the way one of the attorneys put it.

Occasionally it appeared that Tate/La Bianca was being defended by a used car salesman or the manager of a rock group rather than a member of the bar, so gauche were some of their maneuvers. This was, in fact, the case. Daye Shinn, attorney for Susan Atkins, worked his way through law school at the age of forty-three by selling used cars (he is now a youthful-appearing fifty-three); thirty-five-year-old Ronald

DAYE SHINN, REPRESENTING SUSAN ATKINS

Hughes, representing Leslie Van Houten, managed a rock and roll music group named the United States Government before passing the California bar examination. Both men are to be commended for making it the hard way but, as is sometimes the case, industry may, in the minds of some people, erroneously be substituted for talent. Shinn, who had built up a lucrative personal injury practice did not seem to be trying hard enough: Hughes was involved in his first criminal case, Gary Fleischman, Mrs. Kasabian's co-counsel, told me he thought Hughes was "Crazy" to take on the case with his lack of experience. "I've tried over two hundred cases," Fleischman said, "and I don't know whether I'd have taken that one."

As happened so frequently during the trial, an unforeseeable event — truly the *deus ex machina* so reviled by fiction editors — made truth appear stranger than fiction as Daye Shinn rose to cross-examine the witness. Paul Fitzgerald and Aaron Stovitz, in a rare display of harmony respectively asked to approach the bench and to appear in chambers. Counsel approached the bench where Fitzgerald informed Judge Older that the President of the United States, that very morning, Monday, August 3, 1970, had made certain statements in regard to the guilt of Charles Manson.

Before we follow the private dialogue that ensued we should go back to 1:50 P.M., ten minutes before court convened that day following the luncheon recess. Fitzgerald, after an exhausting morning getting nowhere in a cross-examination capped by Linda Kasabian's effective declaration, was riding in the company of this writer and several members of the press (all of whom had partaken of a relaxing lunch), in the elevator to Judge Older's court on the eighth floor of the Hall of Justice. Somewhere between the sixth and the eighth floors a reporter asked Fitzgerald if he had heard about the Nixon statement. The attorney had not. At that moment the elevaor doors opened and the glare of television lights flooded the interior, causing the passengers to squint and shield their eyes.

Clearly, something was up. Fitzgerald had time only to learn that the President had publicly declared Manson guilty, before the media were shoving microphones into his face and, as the first defense counsel to arrive from lunch, ply him with a verbal barrage of questions. What followed was, to one observer at least, an outstanding example of an intelligent man thinking fast on his feet.

Patricia Krenwinkel's counsel did, to use a show business term, five minutes on television and radio unsurpassed as a display of outrageous indignation. Phrases fell freely, and grammatically, from his lips as he waxed indignant at "The *faux pas* of American jurisprudence." (Had Paul been given more time for reflection he probably would not have used expressions like *faux pas;* it was a trifle high-toned for the audience he was trying to reach.) Nevertheless, he did extremely well. Learning from the questions, he tackled each section of the President's statement as it came up. "He sets out," Fitzgerald proclaimed, "to condemn the news media for glorifying Charles Manson. What does he think is going to happen when the most important man in the world . . . " (he paused, savored the phrase, and repeated it) " . . . the most important man in the world makes a statement like this. I think it's shocking. I think it's unbelievable. I think it's un-American."

Did Manson have any comment to make? By golly, he did. "Here is a man," Manson reportedly said, "who is accused of hundreds of thousands of murders, accusing me."

The crusading young attorney pushed grimly past his interrogators, bent on seeing that justice was done in the courtroom.

At the bench Paul Fitzgerald pressed his case.

FITZGERALD: I have been handed what purports to be a Western Union telegram, a telegraphic copy of an AP Wire Service that was handed to all the news media wherein the President of the United States is quoted as saying that a man who is guilty, directly or indirectly, of eight murders without reason — and he is referring to Charles Manson — I am a little emotional perhaps, but I think it would absolutely be grounds for a mistrial.

OLDER: Well, if true it is a perfect example of why I insisted the jury be sequestered.

FITZGERALD: Yes, it was a wise thing, no question about it. Everyone is entitled to change his opinion.

Judge Older ruled that, solely on the basis of a wire service report, he felt it was premature to consider any motions, denied a motion for mistrial by Irving Kanarek, and returned the trial to open court.

Daye Shinn went to some lengths to establish that Linda Kasabian had a number of conversations with Aaron Stovitz, Vincent Bugliosi, her attorneys and miscellaneous police officers while she was in custody, hardly surprising information. Shinn has developed a courtroom habit of asking questions while walking away from the witness, then waiting, usually with his back turned and ostensibly examining important documents, for an answer. This led to an exchange that was indicative of the general level of his cross-examination. Mr. Shinn inquires about the witness's meetings with Vincent Bugliosi:

Q: Do you recall what Mr. Bugliosi said to you at the first meeting?

A: What he said to me?

Q: Yes. (Back to witness, apparently examining the contents of a file folder)

A: Well, he always stressed for me to tell the truth.

Q: Besides the truth I'm talking about.
   (Broad smiles from Stovitz and Bugliosi as the witness looks puzzled)

SHINN: (Looking over his shoulder at the court) Did she answer the question, your Honor?

KASABIAN: I was waiting for you. I thought you were busy.

SHINN: You can answer the question, I'm sorry.

KASABIAN: I have no question to answer.

(Some of the confusion stemmed from the fact that Shinn, although a natural born United States citizen of Korean ancestry, spoke chop-chop English, clipping his words sometimes to the point of unintelligibility.)

SHINN: I did not get the last answer, your Honor.

STOVITZ: She was waiting for you, she did not want to be discourteous and answer your questions while you had your back turned.

OLDER: I would suggest you put the question to her again, Mr. Shinn.

SHINN: I forgot the question.

(Laughter)

OLDER: Let's go back and read the record.

(The question was read back by the court reporter and declared to be ambiguous by the judge.)

Mr. Shinn appeared to be fascinated by the fact that an attorney would consult with a client or potential witness. He spent over a half-hour on the subject. Shinn did get into an area of testimony that her attorney, Gary Fleischmann, later told me made him somewhat uneasy. Defense counsel, however, appeared not to feel that he was in a sensitive area. Shinn inquires:

Q: I believe you also stated that you have hallucinations sometimes?

A: Under the drug?

Q: Under the drug or not under the drug; hallucinations?

A: Well, sitting here right now, when I look at all those holes, they just sort of seem to all go together. I don't know if that is hallucination.

Q: What holes?

A: Excuse me. The holes in the tiles on the walls. (Acoustical tile)

Q: What else do you see?

A: I see a clock, and I see wood, and I see people.

Q: Do you believe in Santa Claus?

STOVITZ: Then or now, counsel?

Laughter in the courtroom broke Shinn's line of questioning. Stovitz, sensing that talk about seeing little holes come together was getting on dangerous ground, apparently seized the first opportunity to distract counsel's attention. If it was a ruse, it succeeded. Mr. Shinn went on to other things, mostly concerning Mrs. Kasabian's reasons for not telling the truth about the murders in the three months between their commission and her subsequent arrest, then yielded the cross-examination to Irving Kanarek. Vincent Bugliosi told me that he considered Shinn to be *"Amicus curiae* for the prosecution."

To say that, in the days following, Mr. Kanarek lived up to the direst predictions of the district attorney's office is still not to excuse the early attempts to have him barred from the case. During Kanarek's cross-examination of the witness, Aaron Stovitz's characterization of the defense attorney's appointment as counsel for Charles Manson as "A disaster of major proportions," assumed great validity. As it turned out, however, the disaster was not so much to the trial itself, although the disruption was certainly evident, but to the defense.

If Irving Kanarek's incessant interruptions and objections during the direct examination could be described as an itch that Judge Older felt the need to scratch with increasing vigor, the defense counsel's cross-examination of Linda Kasabian can perhaps be compared to watching a modern day Sisyphus push his rock uphill only to have it roll back down again *ad nauseam* with the added frustration that today's penitent keeps *voir diring* the rock to explain why it always rolls back down. As we watch we experience an overwhelming urge to rush over to Sisyphus, pummel him about his perspiring face and shoulders, and shout "Because it *does,* that's all. It's *obvious."*

To which the Tate/La Bianca Sisyphus would reply; "What do you mean by obvious?" and begin pushing the rock back up again.

Plodding, bullheaded, stubborn, stupid (which he is not), aggravating (which he is), any number of frustration-inspired adjectives were applied to Irving Kanarek as, polite to a fault, seemingly puzzled by the simplest explanations of the most rudimentary phenomena, he conducted his cross-examination.

Chapter XVI

DAY FORTY-NINE

If all four defense attorneys could be characterized as displaying one common emotional state that condition must certainly have been paranoia. Each had his bogeyman to which, in greater or lesser measure, he attached suspicion of persecution most foul.

Paul Fitzgerald had a thing about the establishment. The defendants, Fitzgerald repeatedly declared, could not possibly get a fair trial. The term "fair," used here by the astute lawyer in his own context, implied that the Family members should be tried somehow outside the social structure in which the murders were committed; that the members of the establishment, the piggies, should abdicate the right to sit in judgment on someone who had allegedly killed in their midst. To give him his due Paul Fitzgerald privately understood the difficult philosophical gymnastics implicit in this so-called denial of a fair trial but, in public, he left no doubt but that "they" were out to do his client in.

Daye Shinn appeared to fear the demands of logic. Much of his questioning betrayed an either feigned or real ignorance of previous testimony and reestablished facts already in evidence without any particular thrust to his examination. One is tempted to invoke the specter of the unfathomable reasoning processes of the Asiatic mind, but Shinn passed the California Bar, not the Seoul, so his wandering inquiries may be put down to at best, disinterest and at worst, laziness.

Irving Kanarek's persecution complex was most publicly manifested in the person of Evelle J. Younger, District Attorney of California's Los Angeles County and, at the time, candidate for election to Attorney General of that state on the Republican ticket. Kanarek never lost an opportunity to denounce Younger for his alleged use of Tate/La Bianca to gain publicity in order to further his political ambitions. Manson's attorney's paranoia was to reach, as we shall soon see, astronomical proportions.

Ronald Hughes worried that his pants would rip.

And with good cause. Hughes, a man of large stature and considerable girth, wore the same suit, a large tent-like pinstripe, every day during the first month and a half of the trial. True to his declaration of pauper status to Judge Older, Leslie Van Houten's second attorney of trial record trailed Irving Kanarek in sartorial inelegance only because he possessed but a single suit. After weeks of reaching across tables, standing to voice objections, and waving documents, the inevitable happened: the seams of his jacket gave way.

Jacketless, Hughes showed up at the beginning of the day's trial and joined the other attorneys in chambers from which he was promptly ejected by Judge Older as being improperly dressed. Hughes, standing at the rail that separates the bench, jury and prosecution-defense tables from the spectator section, issued an appeal to anyone in the court to provide him with a jacket so that he might properly represent his client. Mike

McGovern, reporting for the *New York Daily News,* made the grand gesture and Hughes returned to chambers.

McGovern should have known better; nothing was simple during Tate/La Bianca. Within minutes after lending his jacket, the reporter received an urgent call from his bureau dispatching him to a fast breaking story in northern California involving the shooting of a judge outside his courtroom and the death of three suspects in an escape attempt. McGovern, his plane scheduled to leave in thirty-five minutes, began furiously petitioning everyone from the court clerk to the female bailiffs to go into chambers and ask Hughes for his jacket. Such was the temper of the times that he had difficulty finding anyone who would break in on Judge Older's private deliberations; someone finally did, only to be told by Hughes that he would give him the jacket when he got out of chambers. Coatless, McGovern, adding still another chapter to the saga of dedicated American journalism, raced off to the airport on the way to cover his story.

Hughes, on being apprised of the crisis when he finally came out of the chambers, said that he did not understand the urgency of the situation. Next day he appeared in court with his jacket neatly sewn back together but, presumably, with other threads straining because of daily use.

It was Kanarek, however, who was presented with an opportunity to refine and embellish his neurosis on August 4, 1970. On that day President Richard M. Nixon, fresh from a working vacation at San Clemente that put him within the daily reach of Los Angeles newspapers, television and radio stations, observed, in part, at a Denver, Colorado press conference:

"I noted, for example, the coverage of the Charles Manson

case when I was in Los Angeles. Front page every day in the papers. It usually got a couple of minutes in the evening news. Here is a man who was guilty, directly or indirectly, of eight murders without reason. Here is a man who, as far as the coverage was concerned, appeared to be rather a glamorous figure, glamorous to the young people whom he had brought into his operations, and also another thing that was noted was the fact that two lawyers in the case, two lawyers who were, as anyone who could read any of the stories could tell, who were guilty of the most outrageous, contemptuous actions in the courtroom, and who were ordered to jail overnight by the judge, seem to be more the oppressed and the judge seemed to be the villain."

There was something there for everybody. Despite the fact that the President was speaking in the context of the general crime picture and that his press secretary Ronald Ziegler issued a statement to the effect that the word "alleged" had been omitted from the statement, the Tate/La Bianca defense reacted with a uniform display of outraged indignation. After offering the *Los Angeles Times* banner headline "Manson Guilty, Nixon Declares," as a special court exhibit, Paul Fitzgerald asked, out of the jury's presence, that each juror be examined separately to determine whether or not he or she had been exposed to the story.

Judge Older, after informing the attorneys that he had already taken special precautions — such as rendering opaque with Bon Ami the windows of the bus that transports the jury from the courthouse to the Ambassador Hotel so that they might not see the headlines on a newsstand — remarked that he thought the sequestration of the jury should act as an adequate shield between themselves and the President's statement. Refusing to *voir dire* the jurors on their possible exposure to the publicity, Older made, in the light of subsequent events, a significant order.

OLDER: I want to direct all counsel to remove from counsel table any news containing any of this material so that they will not inadvertently be displayed to the jury when the jury comes in.

Irving Kanarek then asked for the floor.

KANAREK: I believe that this jury, with the facts of life being what they are, this jury, I would believe it without being able to prove it, that this jury knows what President Nixon said, the substance of what he said, and the retraction (by Press Secretary Ziegler) is inadequate. The bell has rung; the Presidency of the United States has been invoked and the President has declared that Mr. Manson is guilty.

And I say something else, without being able to prove it. The district attorney of Los Angeles County is running for attorney general. I say it without being able to prove it, that Evelle Younger and the President got together to do this.

It was not exactly Mr. Kanarek's finest hour. Why, one was attempted to ask, would Younger and Nixon conspire to pull a boner that might well have resulted in a mistrial, making the President look like a fool and Younger absorbing, at least peripherally, some of the blame? Ronald Hughes asked that the judge censure President Nixon and was turned down; Kanarek moved for a mistrial and this was denied. Charles Manson then asked to make a motion and was granted permission.

MANSON: Your Honor, in view of the publicity, and it doesn't look like it is going to stop, I request this court, as provided in the Constitution, to be able to confront and cross-examine witnesses, to be able to take part in these proceedings in order for the court, the jury, the spectators and the world that is misinformed so badly, to take a look at what they are judging.

It is easy to sit and be quiet and have someone else speak, but they are not my words, they are not my philosophy that you speak of, they are not my Family's that you talk of. All the things that the court seems to be confused about, I might be able to assist and help you straighten this mess out, because you have certainly got a mess, you have made a mess of the whole thing. You have made a mess of it.

All things considered, Judge Older took it rather well, merely confining himself to asking Manson if he was making a motion. The defendant replied:

MANSON: Yes, I am making a motion to be allowed to move as my own counsel and have movement of the courtroom to cross-examine and to be confronted and confront witnesses, with the assistance of an attorney who can help me in the legal matters.

Your Honor, each man has a reality, each man knows what he knows to be true. For me to communicate to you, I have to use my reality because I don't know your reality. I know you are a pilot and I know you have been through wars . . .

OLDER: Mr. Manson, . . . I am not going to let you continue unless you get back on the track. Tell me precisely what relief you are seeking and you may argue in support of that.

MANSON: This is the problem. The track that you are on and the track that I am on is two different tracks. You judge me from a slanted view. I ask this court if I may stand up and be a man and maintain my voice in the courtroom to cross-examine witnesses that I am confronted with.

Manson then made a motion that he be allowed to proceed as his own attorney. Judge Older, after recapitulating previous discussions on the same subject, ruled that "It would be a miscarriage of justice to permit you to represent yourself in a case having the complications that this case has," and denied the motion. As the jury was being led in, Manson leaned toward the bench and said: "Mr. Older, I can't accept you as being a good judge. A pilot maybe. The inadequacy is a reflection of your own." The judge merely ordered him to be quiet and the trial proceeded. One could not help but speculate with some apprehension what would happen if Defense Attorney Irving Kanarek ever examined Defendant Charles Manson on the stand.

For the moment Kanarek's, and the court's, only concern was Linda Kasabian's testimony. The attorney asked her about a conversation she had with one of two hitch-hikers she picked up on her way to Taos, New Mexico after the murders. The resulting dialogue provides a good example of Kanarek's cross-examination technique.

Q: Now, did you tell this person that your name, at that time, when you spoke with him, was Yana, but that your name used to be Linda?

A: Maybe.

Q: Well, would you reflect upon that for a moment and tell us whether, in fact, you did state that your name was Yana and it used to be Linda? (The attorney gives this question, as he does all others, the benefit of a studied scowl that carries the strong implication that this question is going to break the case wide open. The observer, after finding himself brought to the edge of his seat dozens of times over a period of days, only to be greeted with the kind of exchange that follows, begins to substitute exasperation for expectation.)

A: Yes, I probably said that.

Q: Pardon? Excuse me?

A: I probably said that.

Q: Well, did you, in fact, say that?

A: Well, I can't remember if I did say it.

Q: Well, what makes you think you probably said it?

A: It just sounds right.

Q: May I ask you what sounds right about it?

A: That I would say my name is Yana but it used to be Linda. It just sounds right.

Q: Well, may I ask you why it sounds right?

A: I don't understand.

Q: You don't understand what?

A: Didn't I answer it the way I am supposed to answer it?

Q: Well, has anyone told you that you are supposed to answer questions a certain way?

A: No, but I thought I answered your question, but you keep asking.

Q: Well, my question is — may that question be read back, your Honor?

STOVITZ: Which question, counsel?

OLDER: Reframe the question, Mr. Kanarek. We have long since gone by it.

KANAREK: Very well.

Q: Why, Mrs. Kasabian, why did you say it sounds right that Yana was your name at that time rather than Linda?

A: I still don't understand.

Q: Well, may I ask you — you don't understand the last question?

A: No, I don't.

Q: Well, did you in fact, Mrs. Kasabian, say "My name is Yana, but my name used to be Linda?" Did you in fact say that?

A: I probably did, yes.

Q: Then may I ask you, then, why do you say "probably?" Is there any doubt in your mind as to whether you said "My name is Yana but it used to be Linda?"

STOVITZ: Objected to as argumentative, your Honor. She answered the question three or four times.

KANAREK: I submit she hasn't, your Honor.

STOVITZ: I submit the record speaks for itself, your Honor.

OLDER: You may answer.

A: I remember telling them my name was Yana and I just might have said "It used to be Linda," but I'm not sure.

Q: May I ask you then, now, would you listen to this carefully, Mrs. Kasabian: Why aren't you sure as to whether or not you said that your name used to be Linda?

STOVITZ: To which we object as being argumentative, your Honor.

OLDER: Sustained.

So began a cross-examination that was to last eight days,

one that, in the opinion of veteran courtroom observers, was one of the most tedious and repetitious they had ever heard. But even that statement should be qualified. It was the most tedious and repetitious only to those who previously had never seen Irving Kanarek in action; to the veteran "Kanarek watchers" he put on only a moderately circumlocutious performance.

There was no question, however, but that there *was* method in his peculiar madness. The constant pressure, never letting a chance remark or phrase by the witness pass unnoticed, asking for detailed explanations of the most obvious events and opinions, the steady flow of questions began to visibly rattle the witness. Where she had been calm and sure with Paul Fitzgerald and Daye Shinn, Linda Kasabian began to back off and hesitate under Irving Kanarek's relentless cross-examination. It did not matter that she had been on the stand for seven days, and that even the most composed person who had not been through her drug and jail experience, would feel the strain; what mattered to the prosecution was that their witness was, for the first time, showing fatigue and some uncertainty. The jury, themselves undoubtedly sensing the same tension, might make allowance for her, true, but the fact remained that Kanarek's type of interrogation was, for the first time in the defense's cross-examination, getting some results.

After the noon recess counsel approached the bench to discuss a procedural matter regarding records subpoenaed by the defense. All counsel were facing the bench with their backs to the defendants except Aaron Stovitz who stood, as was his habit, facing the defendants, jury and spectators, one ear cocked toward what was happening to his left. Suddenly in the midst of the discussion Stovitz cried out "Your Honor — your Honor — Mr. Manson just held up the *Times* edition and showed it to the jury!"

THE PRESIDENT EXPRESSES AN OPINION

Manson, who sat directly opposite from the jury, had reached under a pile of books and documents, fished out a copy of the newspaper and held up the glaring headline "Manson Guilty, Nixon Declares," for approximately three seconds facing full toward the jury box, before court bailiff William Murray, standing behind and to his left, snatched it away. There was consternation in the courtroom — many of the press believed that this signified an automatic mistrial — and, from Judge Older, barely suppressed anger at the bench. Immediately after Stovitz's cry Older asked:

OLDER: Where did he get it? Who left that on counsel's table?

KANAREK: The sheriff was supposed to sequester it.

STOVITZ: It was in Mr. Kanarek's books. They are right with Mr. Kanarek's books.

OLDER: Was it on the counsel table?

STOVITZ: It was on the counsel table, right under Mr. Kanarek's law books.

OLDER: Bring it up here. I want to see what it was.

BUGLIOSI: It was the *L.A. Times.*
(The newspaper is handed to the court by Stovitz)

STOVITZ: The bailiff observed him doing it and he tried to stop him.

OLDER: What did he do with it?

STOVITZ: He picked it up from counsel table, the bailiff tried to stop him, and then he held it up and showed it to the jury so the jury could see the headlines of the Tuesday morning August 4 edition.

OLDER: I directed you this morning, all counsel, to get the newspapers off the table.

KANAREK: Your Honor, to my knowledge, every newspaper was off the table.

OLDER: Where did he get it?

KANAREK: I don't know, your Honor.

OLDER: I want to know where that paper came from that Mr. Manson held up. Where did it come from, Mr. Kanarek?

KANAREK: I don't know, your Honor.

OLDER: Are you saying it wasn't yours?

KANAREK: To my knowledge, it certainly was not mine.

OLDER: Where did he get it?

KANAREK: I don't know, your Honor.

OLDER: (To Bailiff Murray) Where did he get that newspaper?

MURRAY: I saw him pick the paper up. He got it right off the bench there where there are other newspapers.

OLDER: What do you mean, bench?

MURRAY: The counsel table. I came over after lunch and there were no papers with the headlines on it. Counsel told me that they took the papers away. They said there was nothing with the headlines on it. That has just gotten here in the last couple of minutes.

OLDER: I hold Mr. Kanarek totally and directly responsible for that.

KANAREK: Your Honor, I did not bring any papers into the courtroom.

Judge Older, after telling counsel that he wanted to see them in chambers, left the bench with an uncharacteristically brusque, "This court is now in recess," that stirred speculation among the spectators. It was a dramatic moment. Few doubted that some of the jurors had seen the headline. Almost everyone had an opinion as to the incident's impact. It was pointed out that a defendant cannot "invite error," that is, deliberately hold up a damaging piece of evidence and then declare that he is not getting a fair trial. But what about the three female defendants? Their case was linked inextricably with Manson's yet they had not held up the newspaper (although they all laughed and indicated their appreciation of the "coup" when the leader grinned broadly, savoring the pandemonium he had caused). Were they to be held responsible and have their trial unfairly prejudiced, if indeed it had been, by Manson's irresponsible actions?

At least one wire service began writing two "leads" for the story that would follow the results of the deliberation in chambers, one announcing a sensational mistrial and the other explaining why one had not been declared. In chambers, Judge Older was even then deciding to personally *voir dire* each juror to ascertain what they had seen and, if they had seen anything, how it had affected their attitude toward the trial. At first he opted to do the questioning in chambers but, at the suggestion of both defense and prosecution (Aaron Stovitz pointed out that having them sit, one at a time in open court, would be tantamount to their visiting the scene of the disputed event and would provide a better perspective to both court and witness), he agreed to have the jury removed from the courtroom and then have them brought back in, one by one, and take the witness stand.

As each juror was brought into open court Judge Older had the clerk swear them in as a witness, an unusual procedure as each had already taken a juror's oath. After each had declared "I do solemnly swear, that the testimony I may give in the cause now pending before this court shall be the truth, the whole truth and nothing but the truth, so help me God," the judge asked them what, if anything, they had seen and, in the event they had noticed the headline, what effect it would have on their ability to fairly and impartially judge the case.

Of the twelve regular and six alternates so questioned eleven admitted seeing the entire headline "Manson Guilty, Nixon Declares," five said they saw the word "Manson" but were not sure of the remaining words, and two declared that all they witnessed was Bailiff Murray grabbing a newspaper from Manson's hand. All stated that the incident would in no way affect their ability to decide the case on its merits. Their individual comments ranged from Larry D. Sheely's, "It should sell newspapers," to Ken Daut's response that evoked a burst of laughter from those in the courtroom with Judge

Older heartily joining it; Mr. Daut observed, "I didn't vote for Nixon in the first place."

After each juror had been interrogated Judge Older took an unprecedented step. The juror's oath, already given collectively before the prosecution's opening statement, was again administered. "Do you swear on your oath as a juror," Judge Older asked each in turn, "that you can and will act impartially and fairly in the matters to be submitted to you and that you can and will base your verdict solely on the evidence presented in this trial and in accordance with the court's instructions?" It was an indication of the seriousness with which the jurist viewed the entire episode.

After a brief recess Older assumed the bench in open court with the jury excluded.

OLDER: It appears to the court that Mr. Kanarek is in direct contempt of court for disobeying the court's order made this morning to all counsel to remove from counsel table all newspapers, news and material referring to Mr. Nixon's statement regarding this case.

Daye Shinn, Susan Atkins's attorney, asked to take the stand under oath and testified:

SHINN: During the lunch period I believe I came back to court approximately 1:45 or 1:40, and I saw some newspapers on top of the file cabinet.

Now, I believe those were the newspapers that we took from the counsel table after removing all the front pages, and I put it on the counsel table during the recess to read the sports page, and I had no idea that the front page or any part of the front page was in that part of it. And Mr. Kanarek had nothing to do with it.

As so frequently happens in real life drama, virtue, in the form of Daye Shinn's noble declaration, had to be content in being its own reward. Judge Older clearly felt that *someone* put that front page there for Manson to pick up and he wasn't of a mind to let the potentially damaging incident pass by unpunished.

OLDER: It appears that the court was in error with respect to the violation of the order by Mr. Kanarek. However, it does appear that there was a violation of the order by Mr. Shinn which would constitute a direct contempt of court.
Do you wish to be heard, Mr. Shinn?

SHINN: Yes, your Honor. I had no intent to violate the court's order, your Honor. I felt that most of the front pages were removed, and unconsciously I brought the paper to counsel table and started reading.

But Judge Older wasn't having any. He found Shinn in direct contempt of court, sentencing him to spend three nights in the County Jail, starting with court adjournment each day and ending at 7:00 A.M. the following morning. He was to have full attorney privileges and access to his client. Older concluded by saying: "And so that the record will be perfectly clear, my finding is that this was a wilful and deliberate violation of the order with full knowledge of its content."

Shinn asked for time to get a toothbrush and attend to his car but this was denied. Court adjourned and Daye Shinn joined the defendants in custody.

A local television station, KABC-TV, owned and operated by the American Broadcasting Company, decided to make an issue of the incident. Taking its cue from President Nixon's repeated denunciation of those who would flaunt the dignity of the law, the station broadcast an editorial which stated, in part:

"Attorney Shinn was sentenced to three nights in jail by the trial judge.

"But such reprehensible conduct by a member of the bar deserves more severe censure, Channel 7 feels.

"In our opinion, Shinn should be called before the California Bar Association for disciplinary action and possible disbarment procedures.

"The legal practice has an honored and dignified heritage. If it is allowed to become a laughingstock our entire society must suffer."

The television station then urged its viewers to write to the bar association making known their displeasure; the station also offered Shinn equal time.

The incident points up the distorted sense of values that threatened to engulf anyone subjected to long and intimate association with Tate/La Bianca. In the first place no one saw Daye Shinn do anything wrong; the media cried out for fair play and due process yet, in the case of the defense attorney, denied him both. True, Judge Older characterized the incident as a "wilful and deliberate violation of the order," and held Shinn in contempt. The fact that Older first thought that Kanarek had violated the order and then, denied that tempting target by Shinn's statement, switched the penalty to Susan Atkins's attorney, constituted nothing more than the jurist's *opinion* which, because of the circumstances, he was able to back up with legal action. The evidence was entirely circumstantial and, in another situation, might well have been disallowed by the jurist.

No one would suggest that Daye Shinn was conducting his share of the defense with anything approaching the expertise expected of an attorney in a capital case, yet it is difficult to comprehend how KABC-TV, whose reporters had daily witnessed the peregrinations of Irving Kanarek and Ronald Hughes could blithely pass them over and indict Daye Shinn for conduct that would result in the legal profession becoming "a laughingstock of our entire society . . . "

The KABC-TV indictment awarded first prize to the man who was running an inarticulate third in the competition.

Chapter XVII

DAY FIFTY

The drug issue made its presence felt in a surprising way before the court convened on Wednesday, August 5. Judge Older called counsel into chambers and told them he had received a letter from one of the regular jurors, Walter A. Vitzelio, that he felt should be brought to their attention. Mr. Vitzelio, complaining of stomach trouble, had been examined by the medical doctor from the sheriff's department. The doctor had prescribed medication and Mr. Vitzelio was concerned. His letter said, in part:

"Is it permissible to be under the influence of drugs while being in the jury box? (The doctor) prescribed 13 bottles of medicine. What I'm concerned with was one bottle of Belladonna and Phenobarbital. I took a dose last night and it made me dizzy and dulled my senses and I don't like to take it, as it's habit forming and I don't want to become addicted to it."

After a discussion in which the defense argued for replacing Mr. Vitzelio and the prosecution against, the judge decided to give it a try for a little while longer to see if the juror's health improved. It did not; a few days later he was excused to be replaced as Juror Number 11 by Larry D. Sheely, chosen by lot from the six alternates and who, of course, had been in attendance throughout the course of the trial.

A few minutes later, in open court but still without the presence of the jury, Daye Shinn, having spent his first night in custody, made a motion that he was to repeat on the succeeding two mornings. He asked for a continuance because he had not been able to sleep in jail, was presently tired and dizzy as a result of his sleeplessness, and was not in a position to properly represent his client. The motion, then and on the two succeeding days, was denied, Judge Older suggesting that Shinn take a nap during the two-hour noon recess.

Outside the court Shinn aired his complaints to a sympathetic listener. "They've got me on this top bunk, you see," the attorney explained. "It's about this wide (indicating about eighteen inches with his hands). At home I sleep in a big double bed and I toss and turn. I had to stay awake all night because I was afraid if I fell asleep I'd fall out of that thing. They have a concrete floor up there, you know. I could break my neck.

"My wife doesn't read or understand English," he continued. "She doesn't believe I'm in jail, she thinks I'm stepping out on her. I've got domestic problems."

Such are the wages of virtue.

Paul Fitzgerald made a formal motion for mistrial on the basis of the jury's exposure to the Nixon headline; after considerable argument on both sides it was denied. Judge Older asked that the jury be brought into court. As they were filing into the box the three female defendants, Susan Atkins, Patricia Krenwinkel and Leslie Van Houten stood up and recited, in unison: "Your Honor, the President said we are guilty, so why go on with the trial?" The judge told them to sit down and the trial resumed with Irving Kanarek cross-examining Linda Kasabian in the following typical exchange.

Q: Mrs. Kasabian, on the night, on the second night that you left the Spahn Ranch, did you know that you had participated with three other people who, all together, you and the three other people together, had killed five people?

A: No.

Q: Directing your attention, Mrs. Kasabian, to the second night and your state of mind, your thinking as you left the Spahn Ranch on the second night, did you know that what you and three other people had done the night before caused the killing of five people?

A: I don't understand the question.

Q: You don't understand that question?

A: Right.

Q: What about the question don't you understand?

A: Well, I don't know what the answer is.

Q: You mean you don't know what answer Mr. Bugliosi wants you to give?

BUGLIOSI: (On his feet, shouting) Your Honor, I object to this. These are unbelievably outrageous remarks.

OLDER: Mr. Kanarek, if you repeat that I will have to take some action against you. The jury is admonished to disregard this colloquy between counsel.

They *were* outrageous remarks. Indefensible legally, they could have been spoken only to influence the jury. The question arose in the observer's mind, as it did so many times during Kanarek's cross-examination: did that kind of blunt, shock-effect approach do the defense more harm than good? On balance it would seem that Manson's lawyer's manner and the ponderousness with which he dropped his dubious bombshells more than offset any legitimate reasons he may have had for introducing them.

Kanarek was achieving one purpose, however. He was bringing notice to himself, often at the expense of his client.

Manson became increasingly aware that his attorney's behavior might be hurting his case. The bearded defendant, according to a copyrighted story by Mary Neiswender, resourceful reporter for the *Long Beach Independent, Press-Telegram,* threatened to stab Kanarek if he persisted in his obstructionist tactics. Mrs. Neiswender, who daily covered the trial, became the subject of admiring and, in some cases envious, comment among her press corps colleagues. Consistently scooping her larger circulation rivals, she was afforded a near-magical access to Charles Manson in his prison cell. A rumored romance between the happily married Mrs. Neiswender and Irving Kanarek proved to be utterly without foundation.

After spending nearly the entire morning unsuccessfully trying to trace Linda Kasabian's street route when she left the Spahn Ranch two days after the murders and drove to New Mexico, endeavoring to show that she had intended to stop and retrieve Mrs. Leno La Bianca's wallet stashed in a Standard service station the night of the second murders, Kanarek resumed his attempt, with the aid of a road map, to refresh the witness's astonishing ignorance of street names.

An interesting sidelight: defense, prosecution and Judge Older all received a continuous trickle of letters and telegrams from different parts of the world concerning the case. Many were patently the work of deranged minds, some offered constructive suggestions and some, and these were of the greatest interest, fell somewhere in between. They probably had no substance but, on the other hand, they contained enough solid information to, as Older characterized the following letter, "raise the eyebrows." The writer's name is omitted in the interests of privacy.

> Dear Judge:
>
> I am writing to you in the hopes that I can be of some help in the Sharon Tate murder case.
>
> You see, I believe the same as President Nixon that this man might lose his life just for the sake of newspaper reporters want for a story.
>
> I played Sharon Tate with a blonde wig on and also Patti Duke and Barbara Perkins in "Valley of the Dolls."
>
> I was supposed to have had a wedding in England with Roman Polanski because he was the director of the picture. After the picture I was told I was going to be murdered in 1969 and they had an ambulance come to the Garden City Hotel where the picture was made and lay me on a stretcher and covered me up to be shown being wheeled out of the house as one of the murder victims.
>
> I was never pregnant and am still alive. So I thought I should stick in and tell you what I know about the case.
>
> I was given the name Tate after Mr. Fred Tate, the acting director of the U.S. Mint. Those newspaper reporters would do anything for a story.

Now back to open court where Irving Kanarek, after an-

KANAREK SHOWS LINDA THE MURDER PICTURES

other fruitless half hour of trying to pin Mrs. Kasabian down to her route out of Los Angeles, came back to the subject of the first night, the night of the Tate murders. He approached the witness with an 8½ x 11 inch picture of Steven Parent, slumped over in the front seat of his automobile after being shot three times in the chest and once in the face by Tex Watson. Mrs. Kasabian recoiled at the sight of the picture and Kanarek, standing next to her by the witness box, kept thrusting it at her, urging her to hold it in her hands. The defense attorney was to do this with other, even more gruesome photographs of murdered bodies at the Tate residence and the witness was to respond even more dramatically.

The defense attorney pressing these pictures upon an obviously distraught young woman, pressing them to a point that suggested sadistic intent, had an effect on the jury that was inimical to the defense's cause. Linda Kasabian's response to the pictured mayhem was so genuinely spontaneous that whatever Irving Kanarek might have accomplished in rattling her or making her hesitate in her answers was nullified by his insensitive tactics. Judge Older finally told Manson's attorney to turn the picture face down on the witness box ledge, to return to his place behind the defense table and to conduct his cross-examination from there. (In California courts custom dictates that the attorneys conduct their examination of a witness from behind the defense or prosecution tables. Permission to approach the witness is asked as a matter of courtesy. Long usage has afforded this procedure the status of a *de facto* statute.)

Kanarek continued asking questions about the first night at the Tate residence, then, with another picture tucked in a folder under his arm, he asked once again to approach the witness. Permission was granted and Kanarek asked:

Q: Mrs. Kasabian, you looked through the window, didn't you, in that house?
   (She had previously testified that she looked inside and saw a table and a bowl of flowers.)

A: Yes.

Q: (Thrusting the picture in front of the witness) Mrs. Kasabian, I ask you . . .

He got no further. Linda Kasabian, shown a large color photograph of the body of Sharon Tate, clad only in bikini pajama tops and bottoms, lying on her side with her full pregnancy revealed, her body perforated by sixteen stab wounds, caused the witness to pull away from the scowling attorney. She pressed both hands over her face, gasped, "Oh,

God," and squeezed herself toward Judge Older as though seeking protection from the awful thing even now being moved closer to her face. A ten minute recess was declared and, in chambers, Ronald Goldman, co-counsel for Linda Kasabian, spoke his mind.

GOLDMAN:　In the first place, your Honor, I want to make an objection to the court to the tactics that are being employed by Mr. Kanarek at this time in exhibiting certain photographs in connection with this case where there has been no evidence introduced concerning my client's percipient testimony, or the fact that she was a witness in or to the matters that were being shown.

　　The evidence has shown that she was not a witness nor did she see the scenes depicted in that photograph, No. 87 (Sharon Tate's body), and I imagine that there are other photos concerning others who were inside that residence.

　　I submit, your Honor, it is improper courtroom decorum, improper tactics of counsel unless he lays a foundation that they have some relevancy to her testimony.

After rebuttal by both Kanarek and Fitzgerald, Judge Older said that he thought that the defense had a right to show Linda Kasabian the picture and to ask her if she saw it. "It may well be," his Honor declared, "that the shock of that alone would cause her to change her story, if she were lying, and admit it. I agree that the photographs should not be displayed until after the question has been put to the witness and the court has had a chance to rule on any objection.

"I agree," Older continued, "it is improper to stand up there with a photograph in your hand for five minutes, and put it in her hand and have her hold it, while you go through a series of questions that have nothing to do with the photograph."

Irving Kanarek went back into court with the Judge's approval to show pictures of the murder victims to the witness. The jury, of course, was not aware of the conference in chambers. They may have assumed, since the defense attorney had possession of the pictures, that he was free to show them: what might have given them cause for reasonable doubt was the propriety of his showing them to Linda Kasabian in the manner in which he subsequently did.

The whole picture incident is indicative of the continuing enigma that was Irving Kanarek. Observers attempting to give him an identity, stupid or smart, good or bad, dull or quick-witted, failed to come up with a definitive term. His plodding repetitious, bullheaded questioning wore down the witness to the point where she was behaving indecisively and giving answers that, if they were not actually contradictory, could have sown seeds of doubt as to her reliability in at least some of the jurors' minds.

Once having rattled Mrs. Kasabian (she admitted on the third day of his cross-examination that she was close to exhaustion) Manson's attorney would then do something, such as showing her a gory picture that had little to do with his examination, that would draw the jurors' minds away from the serious business at hand and possibly render all his previous work ineffective. Linda Kasabian was a very convincing witness; incredibly so when one considers her limited educational background, her admitted years of indiscriminate sexual activity and drug use, and her unstable emotional relationship to her stepfather and her husband. A so-called normal, one-hundred-percent American girl would have been hard put to face Irving Kanarek for eight days and not admit to *something* damaging. Although Mrs. Kasabian admitted to many things she never once, in most spectators' minds, cast the slightest doubt on her basic testimony as to her own and the defendants' participation in the Tate and La Bianca murders. Kanarek went back to one of the defense's favorite topics.

Q: Now, Mrs. Kasabian, on how many instances, Mrs. Kasabian, did you have sexual relations with Mr. Watson?

A: Two or three times.

Q: Two or three times?

A: Yes.

Q: Now, could it have been more than that?

A: Not that I can remember.

Q: You mean it might possibly be more than that?

A: It could be, yes, but I remember just two specific instances, and possibly a third.

Q: Is it a fair statement that while you were at the Spahn Ranch you had sexual relations with many people?

A: Yes.

Q: With many men?

A: With the men at the ranch, yes.

Q: All of the men at the ranch; right?

A: Not all of the men, no.

Q: Well, will you tell us those with whom you had sexual relations?

A: Charlie, Tex, Bruce, a guy named Chuck, Bobbie. That is all. (Afterthought) And Clem.

Q: Anyone else?

A: No, not that I can remember.

Q: And it is a fair statement, is it, that you enjoyed sexual relations?

BUGLIOSI: That is immaterial. Object.

OLDER: Sustained.

Jumping around from place to place and time to time constitutes, one theory has it, good cross-examination. Abruptly leaving one topic or scene tends to throw the witness off-balance, to confuse and disorient her, and, presumably, get her to make damaging admissions or contradictions. By that standard Irving Kanarek was a master cross-examiner. He took the witness back to the murder scene at the Tate house.

Q: Well, Mrs. Kasabian, I am now asking you: At the time that you state that you ran toward the house with the thought that you were going into the house, at that time — at that time — were you in a state of shock?

A: Yes, I guess so.

Q: And so, being in a state of shock, you don't know whether you went into the house or not; is that correct?

A: I know I didn't go into that house.

Q: You know you didn't?

A: Yes.

Q: Or is it a fair statement to say that you wish you didn't?

STOVITZ: That is objected to as argumentative, your Honor.

OLDER: Sustained.

KANAREK: Your Honor, may I approach the witness in connection with a photograph?

Judge Older granted permission and Kanarek, after an elaborate display of selecting a photograph from a file folder, began walking toward the witness. Half-way there he dropped the folder in front of the jury box. Amidst muttered apologies and protestations, the defense attorney, with the aid of an obviously skeptical Aaron Stovitz, gathered up the gruesome photographs and, holding one in his left hand, leaned toward Linda Kasabian.

Q: Mrs. Kasabian, I show you this picture.

Kanarek thrust a picture of the body of Voityck Frykowski, stabbed fifty-one times, shot twice, his head bashed in by the butt of a revolver, in front of the witness. She recoiled, exclaimed "Oh, God," looked over at the defense table, said "How could you do that?" then kept her eyes averted from the picture being held at her eye level. Kanarek, doggedly oblivious of her emotional display, stared uncomprehendingly at the picture as though he was trying to decipher what was contained in the photograph that was the least bit objectionable.

BUGLIOSI: She has already looked at it, your Honor. Is there any necessity for him to continue flashing it in front of her face?

KANAREK: Your Honor, it seems like I am the one that is always the villain.

OLDER: Just a moment. Mrs. Kasabian, did you see the photograph?

A: Yes, I did. (She is sobbing openly, now)

OLDER: Did you see it well enough to identify the person in the photograph?

A: He was the man I saw at the door. (Of the Tate residence the night of the murders).

OLDER: All right. (To Kanarek) You may return.

KANAREK: Thank you, your Honor.

Scrupulously polite, as always, to the judge, the defense attorney turned his back on the sobbing witness and returned to the defense table. He stood facing the witness and began a line of questioning that betrayed his lack of sensitivity to the impact that the witness might be having on the jury. Here was a sobbing young girl, eminently believable in her consternation at seeing the picture, confronted by the self-declared "villain."

Q: Mrs. Kasabian, why are you crying right now?

A: Because I can't believe it. It is just — I don't know.

Q: You can't believe what, Mrs. Kasabian?

A: (Composing herself) That they could do that.

Q: That they could do that?

A: Yes.

Q: I see. Not that *you* could do that, but that *they* could do that.

A: I know I didn't do that.

Q: You were in a state of shock, weren't you?

A: That's right.

Q: Then how do you know?

A: Because I know it. I do not have that kind of thing in me to do such an animalistic thing.

Q: And you are basing it upon the fact that you don't have it in you to do that kind of an animalistic thing?

A: Right.

Q: Is that why you are saying you didn't do it, right?

A: Right.

Q: Is that why you are saying you didn't do it, right.

A: (Makes an obvious attempt to pull herself together, breathes deeply, then says quietly): I just know I didn't do it, Mr. Kanarek.

In addition to doing himself and the defense a disservice in showing Linda Kasabian the picture (he could not have wanted the reaction he got) Manson's attorney was actually helping the prosecution's case. An argument could have been made, Paul Fitzgerald told me, that the picture of the bodies were so gruesome that the shock effect of showing them to the jury far outweighed their probative value; their function as evidence was far overbalanced by the prejudice that merely seeing them would put in the jurors' minds. The defense might have been able to block the prosecution from showing them to the jury, but now, with each one being introduced so dramatically, the jurors were going to see them and, presumably, be influenced by what they saw.

A bone of contention that stuck in the defense's collective craw through most of Mrs. Kasabian's testimony was the fact that she was acting in a dual capacity, as a defendant and as a prosecution witness. As a defendant she had not been granted immunity; in the eyes of the defense she was not free to recant her story because she would be prosecuted for the seven counts of murder and one of conspiracy if she did. Despite the fact that Judge Older repeatedly, in chambers, voiced the opinion that she already had immunity as a matter of law, the defense wanted very much to have the immunity formalized for two reasons: first to make certain that Linda understood that *no matter what she said* she could not be prosecuted and, second, so that as a declared witness the defense might have access to whatever records of conversations that existed between herself and the deputy district attorneys. The defense also wanted to speak with her directly but this was all but precluded by the advice of her own counsel.

"Why don't you want to talk to me?" Kanarek asked her in open court.

"Because I was told you couldn't be trusted," Linda answered, to the amusement of those present.

Judge Older finally signed a grant of immunity to be followed, a few days later, by the dismissal of all charges in the Tate/La Bianca case against Linda Kasabian. This, however, did not mean immediate freedom for the witness. She was retained in custody until a secret hideout could be arranged, rumored to be located in the San Fernando Valley, where she would live guarded constantly by a policewoman and two male officers of the Los Angeles Police Department. She was immediately subpoenaed as a witness by the defense, which meant that she had to be produced in court within forty-eight hours, if she was called. At the conclusion of her testimony she returned east to her mother's home in Milford, New Hampshire and resumed the care of her two children. A police guard had been requested at that location, as well, but her attorneys feared for her safety once out of the Los Angeles area.

The implied threat to her life and the seriousness with which the authorities viewed it, suggested a continuing Family operation with the power to order people killed. Bruce Davis, wanted for murder in connection with the slaying of Gary Hinman, was considered by many to be the chief candidate for the job of Family enforcer; the suggestion that a conscious will existed on a collective basis to carry on the Family tradition by the revenge killing of Mrs. Kasabian was difficult to accept if one watched the daily comings and goings of the likes of Sandra Pugh or Lynne Fromme, who remained dedicated to preserving life at the Spahn Ranch but who seemingly lacked the physical resources to execute anyone for Charlie.

According to Squeaky (Lynne Fromme), whom I talked with just after Linda had been granted immunity and who showed up at the Hall of Justice on a near daily basis, the authorities thought otherwise and maintained a constant harassing pressure on the five or six hard-core Family members still at liberty, living at the Spahn Ranch.

Squeaky, a little wisp of a thing with her face covered with freckles, wrinkled her small button nose and told me about the Family's relationship to the police. "They come around looking for a piece of ass," the soiled gamine explained. "They park up on the highway (that runs past the Spahn Ranch) and wait 'til they see someone come in on a bike (motorcycle). Then they drive in and, you know, they give the guy a hard time."

I asked in what way.

"Well they check all his I.D.'s then they take his colors (some motorcycle clubs have small strips of colored ribbon attached to their handlebars; these colors identify the owner's group and are a source of special pride), and they, you know, stomp them in the dust and spit on them. Then if the guy makes a move to stop them and the cops cuff his hands behind him and, you know, make him lay face down in the dirt."

Do the police approach the girls sexually?

"Not like that," Squeaky said, smiling. "They come in and look around, you know, and pretend they're searching for strays (underage youngsters whose parents may be looking for them). But we know what they want. They think we're a bunch of kids."

Squeaky, small and undernourished, does not look her twenty-six years. It would be an especially unobservant person however who, after speaking with her for any length of time, would invest her with the innocence implied in her reference to being mistaken for "a bunch of kids."

Chapter XVIII

DAY FIFTY-SIX

Aaron Harris Stovitz, forty-three mission World War II radar/bombardier, holder of the Distinguished Flying Cross ("They figured anybody who had flown that many missions had to have done *something* that deserved a medal,") chief prosecutor in one of the nation's most sensational murder trials, gave vent to song on the morning of August 12, 1970. Sitting over a cup of coffee in the district attorney's private lunchroom on the sixth floor of the Hall of Justice, he went through a full verse of "It Was Just One of Those Things," with good projection if modest tone, to the smiling approval of his colleagues. That Wednesday marked the day that Irving Kanarek was programmed to wind up his cross-examination of Linda Kasabian.

The information had been fed into Kanarek by Judge Older the afternoon before after a particularly trying exchange in which counsel seemed to be losing his ability to ask a coherent question. This is how it went, with Kanarek inquiring:

Q: Compare your idea of time, Mrs. Kasabian, before you

first took, let us say, LSD, compare that meaning of time, whatever it was in your mind, to the meaning of time between let us say, the first time you took LSD and the date of your arrest.

BUGLIOSI: Ambiguous, your Honor.

KANAREK: I haven't finished the question, your Honor.

BUGLIOSI: My apologies.

KANAREK: Were your ideas of time the same before you started taking drugs as they were after you started taking drugs but before the date of your arrest?

A: I don't understand your question. You have got so many words, I am not following you.

OLDER: Will counsel approach the bench, please?

Viewed from the spectator section of the courtroom Judge

"WILL COUNSEL APPROACH THE BENCH, PLEASE?"

Older did not appear to be more or less upset by the questioning than he had been during the previous days on which Kanarek had conducted his cross-examination. At the bench, however, his private feelings were made manifest in the following dialogue held out of the hearing of jury and press.

OLDER: Mr. Kanarek, it is apparent to me that you are now simply being very, very repetitious and going nowhere. I think you had better be prepared to wind up your cross-examination.

KANAREK: I am, your Honor. The point is that when we have a witness on the stand, all of us —

OLDER: That is not the point I made. Did you understand what I said?

KANAREK: Yes, I understand what your Honor said, yes. What I am saying is that when we have a witness of this type, some of our ordinary ground rules don't apply; otherwise we are in danger of going off completely.

OLDER: What ground rules are you talking about?

KANAREK: What I am talking about, we have previously asked this court to appoint doctors to examine this witness. We asked for it before this trial started.

OLDER: Let's not get off into that subject.

KANAREK: Well, this witness's ideas, her meanings —

OLDER: I have told you what I thought, Mr. Kanarek. Now, we are going to adjourn for the day. I suggest that if you have anything important, that you arrange your thoughts and examination so that you can complete it tomorrow morning. Apparently you have simply run out of examination.

That day, before Judge Older directed him to wind up his cross-examination, Irving Kanarek succeeded in accomplishing one of his most cherished goals: the witness's theft of $5,000, so scrupulously skirted by Paul Fitzgerald, was finally brought out before the jury. Its emergence demonstrated both the best and worst about the defense counsel's tactics. He got the information out through a slogging application of questions and answers in a bench conference as to its admissibility, then proceeded to worry it to death. Having paraded before the jury the potentially damning information that she was a thief, he proceeded to turn her, as he had done with the pictures, into a badgered witness, a near-martyr to his seemingly inexhaustible capacity for formulating different approaches to the same question. His repeated references to the money took up most of the afternoon of August 11. Finally, on the following day, Wednesday, August 12, 1970 at precisely 11:26 A.M., Irving Kanarek disclosed that he "had no further questions *at this time.*" With that sinister proviso, after eight and a half days of cross-examination, Manson's defense counsel sat down.

As was so often the case during Tate/La Bianca, events that were not public knowledge were making for considerable drama. While the public read about what was going on in the courtroom or watched and listened to endless interviews with various counsel, a behind-the-scenes confrontation was taking place that went unreported simply because the press had no knowledge of its existence. Judge Older learned about it first on the morning of August 12 in his chambers before the trial began. (The trial day extended from 9:45 each morning to 12:00 noon and from 2:00 until 4:15 P.M., with a fifteen minute break morning and afternoon at the discretion of Judge Older).

OLDER: (With counsel present) Now, it has come to my attention that it was necessary to carry Mr. Manson down from upstairs (the jail) this morning. In other words, he refused to come down without being carried. Apparently he did not put up any resistance, but he just would not come down by himself. According to the bailiff Manson said that he would not voluntarily walk out into the courtroom either. He would have to be carried out there.

After being informed that the prisoner was protesting the conditions under which he was being held captive Judge Older agreed to see Manson in chambers with all counsel present and the other defendants excluded. The defendant, so often critical of the court's denying him the right to speak with his own words, exercised that right. What he said is most enlightening as both a social and psychological document pertaining, as the legal phrase has it, to the prisoner's "state of mind."

MANSON: Your Honor, I think you are probably more capable of understanding this than most people because you have been in the military; you understand procedure. You understand the necessity for it.

But sometimes it gets to be so strenuous and so stiff, that the personality of the human being does not get a chance to make a decision, and the ego of the personality of the human being wants to make decisions, and looks to make a decision, you know, and — am I making sense?

OLDER: I would suggest you get to the point, Mr. Manson.

MANSON: I am trying to as rapidly as possible. This is the same problem that arose in the other county jail about pro per (when he represented himself *in propria persona* as his own attorney), the reason I was considered a messenger boy to the courtroom is the procedure and the rules that are set down in one circumstance may not be apropos in using them in another circumstance.

A man says "Stand up," and you feel, well, he says stand up, so you should stand up. And he says "Sit there," and — his insecurity becomes your motion.

"Don't sit there because they're coming."

"Better not handcuff him because the jury is coming. There is the judge; put him there; stand him in that corner."

Then they stand like that so the jury cannot see you, and you say, "That doesn't make sense because the jury just seen me in the jury room."

They say "Go on, take your clothes off." You take your clothes off and they go through the procedure of looking under your genitals, in your rectum, your mouth, your ears. I say that is understandable because there are things which get smuggled into the county jail. You go through another door. As soon as you go in the other door there's three officers standing right there with you for maybe three minutes; you go through the other door, the same thing happens in the other door, twenty-five, twenty-six shakedowns a day.

I am a reasonable human being, a reasonable person. I can see reason for procedure, and I can see reason for following procedure. You follow procedure to the point where it is ready to break you, and that is the point I have reached.

I am ready to be broke. I have been in jail all my life. I have been through beatings and kickings. I have been in the south; I have been in some of the roughest penitentiaries in the world. There's all kinds of punishment; there's physical punishment and there's mental punishment. Now, I can put up with both. Now, I just figure which is best. I am trying my best to get along.

I tried my best in the new county jail to get along. It seems every man says "There's Manson; he don't look so great to me. I don't like him, anyway. He shouldn't have done this and he shouldn't have done that."

I am in a television cell. Everyone goes by to look at

the freak. They get to look; they even bring their sons in on the week-ends to take a look at the freak, which is all right, I don't mind that, but it just keeps on. Every day it piles up a little more; I can't have visitors; I can't have letters; I cannot communicate with anyone on the street. Everyone in their fear, in their paranoia has made me their victim. I am not out to do anyone any harm in any direction, in any shape or form.

One of the things that Manson was seeking consisted of, in the absence of a better term, masturbation privileges. He could never be sure, day or night, that someone was not watching him. It might be argued (and *was* so argued in private by the deputy sheriffs) that anyone who had led his kind of life would not be disturbed by having someone watch him sexually relieve himself. According to sources with access to the prisoner, however, it appeared that the continuous surveillance was beginning to crack even his jail-oriented psyche. "Do it under the blanket, Charlie," as one jailer advised him, failed to allay the prisoner's anxieties.

One of Manson's earliest infractions of prison rules during the pretrial phase of Tate/La Bianca serves as an indicator both of his wiliness and of his convict philosophy. When he first represented himself *in propria persona* he was permitted to make outgoing telephone calls in connection with the preparation of his case. One of the first calls he made was to Roger Aldi, enterprising news reporter for KHJ, a Los Angeles radio station. He called Aldi, in defiance of the pro per ground rules, to set up a radio interview that he intended to conduct over the jail phone. The interview that finally was aired is of small interest here because it merely restated much of Manson's standard "I love everybody. No one can speak with my voice," declarations.

What *is* of interest is the recorded but not broadcast first conversation with Aldi, made available to this writer, in which Manson is conning his way into the reporter's confidence in the hope of doing the interview in exchange for much needed cash (payable, incidentally, to Gypsy, (Katherine Share) often described as Manson's female counterpart).

"Sincerity," Manson told the reporter, "is the best gimmick in the world. You can get anywhere with sincerity, man."

Aldi asked him what he meant.

"Be sincere," Manson repeated. "You're calling me because of your job. (Actually Manson made the call). You want a story. So you're sincere. I know you're not of my world. I'm a juvenile delinquent who never made the grade. You pat me on the back and call me brother. Hey, what's this? This guy's sincere because of his job."

Aldi then said that he wanted the story but that he wanted to give Charlie an opportunity to give his side of the case at the same time.

"What we've got here is trickeration," Manson told him. "It's a game between the defense and the D.A., between you and me. It's trickeration and if you're sincere you can win the game."

No simpler statement of Charles Manson's operating procedure can be found in all the circumlocution that he indulged in during the months that followed, leading up to and during the trial.

In the courtroom, after Manson had finished making his statement, Judge Older promised to hold a hearing to look into the charges and the trial resumed without incident. The hearing was subsequently held and Older, after a personal inspection of the jail facilities, found no substance to the defendant's allegations and the petition for relief was denied.

"WHAT WE'VE GOT HERE IS TRICKERATION"

If anyone connected with the trial thought that Irving Kanarek's temporary withdrawal from the scene meant a relief from tedium, they were soon disillusioned by his successor, Ronald Hughes. (Aaron Stovitz was heard loudly to declare at the conclusion of Hughes's first day of cross-examination, "Irving, come back!")

Although it is doubtful that the prosecution, had the option been granted, would have substituted Kanarek for Hughes, it was clear, early in Leslie Van Houten's attorney's cross-examination, that he had a flair for the irrelevant question. The courtroom observer could not help contrast the bushy-bearded balding lawyer and Miss Van Houten's first trial attorney, Ira Reiner. Not once since his appointment as attorney-of-record had Hughes attempted to separate his client, accused of two counts of murder and one of conspiracy as opposed to the other defendants seven counts of murder and one of conspiracy, from Charles Manson, Susan Atkins and Patricia Krenwinkel in the minds of the jury. Where Reiner had worked continuously to establish this independence, Hughes appeared deliberately to foster the impression that the Family members were on trial for all the crimes as a unit, an impression that could not but work against the best interests of his nominal client.

After first making a motion that Linda Kasabian be subjected to a psychiatric examination and having that motion denied, Hughes began his interrogation of the witness.

Q: What do you feel love is?

A: Well, there's different degrees of love. There is an earthly love between people, a physical love. There is also an important love where, you know, you feel love towards all living things, which is more of a universal love.

Q: How do you feel about the defendants in this case now, Mrs. Kasabian?

A: Well, I feel compassion for them. I wish they would be up here and do what I am doing, tell the truth.

Q: Let's take a situation, Mrs. Kasabian, where A talks to B; B comes and tells C what his interpretation of A's conversation was with him. Now C turns around and tells someone else what B said about A and B's conversation. Is it not a fact that all C heard was what B told him?

STOVITZ: I object to the question. It's improper algebra.

OLDER: (Joining in the courtroom laughter) Sustained.

It might be noted here that Judge Older, while still a model of judicial restraint, was loosening up in regard to some of counsels' actions. He laughed more easily and more frequently; whether this was due to a desire to relieve the sense of ennui that the lengthy cross-examination engendered or whether he simply began to find more amusing things happening before his bench, his Honor began to give freer reign to a natural sense of humor, a most desirable circumstance in a court that possessed more than its share of unwitting jesters.

Ronald Hughes displayed a peculiar vocal delivery during his interrogation. The questions would begin at a low pitch, rise to a modest crescendo half way through, then fall again at the end. He continues his cross-examination:

Q: In fact he never really talked to A, did he?

STOVITZ: Object to the question, your Honor.

OLDER: Sustained.

Q: (By Hughes) Mrs. Kasabian do you follow the truth you see or the truth you hear?

A: Both.

Q: What is truth to you, Mrs. Kasabian?

A: The reality, the actual reality.

Q: Do you judge others from your reality or from the reality you feel in someone else's mind?

BUGLIOSI: Ambiguous; it doesn't even make sense, your Honor.

OLDER: Sustained.

Q: (By Hughes) Now, directing your testimony — I believe it is proper to characterize that you referred to the defendants as "them" and to yourself as "me." At one time you considered yourself as part of this Family. What do you consider yourself now?

KANAREK: I will object to that question on the grounds that
there is no showing of any Family your Honor. It is assuming facts not in evidence. It is a matter of sheer and
absolute lifting by the bootstraps. I must object to the
question and also object on the grounds that it is calling
for a conclusion, hearsay.

OLDER: (Smiles at Kanarek) Sustained.

Q: (By Hughes) Mrs. Kasabian, do you cry with remorse
at the mutilated children in Biafra?

STOVITZ: That is objected to as being immaterial.

OLDER: Sustained.

With that, court broke for lunch.

Hughes's line of questioning was, at very least, unorthodox.
The beginning of the afternoon session presaged Hughes's ultimate downfall as Judge Older, a perplexed expression on his
face, began sustaining both prosecution and defense objections
to counsel's questions. Hughes inquires:

Q: Is God a reality to you?

A: Yes.

Q: Is your personal life as an individual important to you?

A: Yes.

Q: You said you did not understand what discontent means,
are you in such a state of mind now, Mrs. Kasabian, that you
could sit on a rock for the rest of your life?

(Objected to; sustained)

Q: If you believed that Mr. Manson was a messiah, would
you again doubt his word?

(Objected to; sustained)

Q: Would you again let public opinion crucify the truth?

(Objected to; sustained)

Q: Would you have enough faith to follow Christ to the cross?

(Objected to; sustained)

Q: Christ said, "To enter the kingdom of heaven you must be as a child," is that right?

A: Excuse me?

(Objected to; sustained)

Q: Are you going to send Angel (Mrs. Kasabian's son) to war when he is eighteen?

(Objected to; sustained)

Even when Mr. Hughes got on to less esoteric paths, his line of questioning appeared to have little bearing on the case at hand. An example:

Q: Do you smoke cigarettes?

A: Yes, I do.

Q: Did you ever smoke in the courtroom here?

A: Yes I have.

Q: But you never smoked in front of the jury?

A: Yes, I have.

Q: Have you?

A: Once.

Q: Was it a mistake that you smoked that one time in front of the jury?

BUGLIOSI: It is ridiculous, your Honor, and I object on that ground.

OLDER: Sustained.

Judge Older's sustaining the objection on the ground of its being "ridiculous" had a significance beyond the laughter that the exchange provoked at Ronald Hughes's expense. There is no such thing as "ridiculous" as a legal ground for an objection. Theoretically, to an appellate court, the sustension constitutes legal error and, as such, becomes part of grounds for a reversal of the verdict. Realistically, the fact that Judge Older did sustain the objection, as had others such as Aaron Stovitz's classic "Improper algebra," serves as an indication of how rambling and uncoordinated the defense position was becoming. The real test of a case being heard on appeal, and by this time everyone connected with Tate/La Bianca was thinking beyond the present, is whether or not the small legal errors, if eliminated from the transcript, would still result in the same verdict. Judge Older must clearly have felt that a few improper sustentions would not, in light of the overall case, prejudice the record of this trial.

Hughes's questioning, now being objected to by Irving Kanarek in addition to the prosecution, dragged on over familiar ground through the afternoon. There was one question, however, that Mr. Kanarek did not object to; Hughes is examining:

Q: When did Mr. Manson turn into a devil-like man?

A: Well, he was a devil-like man the whole time, but I saw him differently.

Q: You loved him then?

A: Yes.

Q: Do you love him now?

A: Yes.

Q: Do you love the girls now?

A: Sure, I love everybody.

Q: You don't love Mr. Kanarek, who you feel is dishonest, do you?

A: Sure I love him.

Irving Kanarek, rumored to be a ladies' man, beamed from his seat at the defense table. His craggy features lit up in a pleased glow as he gazed speculatively at the youthful witness. "He just wants to be loved," a female wire service reporter whispered as the spectators reacted with knowing grins to the defense attorney's pleased expression.

The courtroom, a high-ceilinged structure serviced by five laboring air conditioners stuck on the window ledges like dripping afterthoughts, became increasingly muggy and hot as each day progressed. Around three o'clock in the afternoon the over one hundred close-packed bodies thickened the atmosphere in Department 104, shortening tempers and generally causing the press to get the "Kanareks," a condition peculiar to that time and place that found expression in a barely suppressed desire to leap to one's feet, confess to all seven counts of murder and one of conspiracy, and plead with the court to make it all stop.

Ronald Hughes's nerve-jangling fatuities did little to alleviate the chronic phobia. The next morning, Thursday, August

13, when the courtroom temperatures had not yet touched eighty-five degrees and deodorants were still functioning as advertised, the defense attorney concluded his cross-examination and Aaron Stovitz began the prosecution's re-direct. The temperature did not appear to rise quite so much the afternoon of that day.

Chapter XIX

DAY FIFTY-SEVEN

Aaron Stovitz's re-direct examination brought forth a torrent of objections from Irving Kanarek; Judge Older occasionally took advantage of that circumstance to indulge himself at defense counsel's expense. This form of therapy probably afforded his Honor a certain satisfaction and it helped to relax the rest of the participants as well. A typical exchange:

OLDER: Mr. Kanarek, I told you before if you want to make an objection, state the grounds.

KANAREK: Yes, your Honor, I have enunciated grounds.

OLDER: If you think the argument is sufficiently important, you can ask to approach the bench.

KANAREK: (Eagerly) May I approach the bench, may I?

OLDER: No, you may not. (General laughter in the courtroom)

Again:

KANAREK: (Excitedly) Object, your Honor. Your Honor, I must object to that question.

OLDER: (Dryly) You *are* objecting.

Bearing in mind that the prime object of the defense was
to prove that Linda Kasabian was lying, Stovitz made a highly
pertinent point in his re-direct examination. On cross-examination she had stated that she did not completely understand
what the phrase "penalty of perjury" meant; the manner in
which this admission was elicited could have led some jurors
to believe that she might be lying without fear of legal retaliation. The Head of Trials wanted to set right any possible mis-
conception. Kanarek matched him objection for question, the
former omitted here in the interest of lucidity.

Q: Now, you stated that you did not particularly understand
the phrase "penalty of perjury," but you knew what perjury is.
Is that correct?

A: Yes.

Q: And if you testify falsely under oath there are certain
penalties attached to it.

A: Yes.

Q: Now has anyone ever told you what the specific penalty
for perjury in an ordinary case is?

A: No.

Q: Has anyone ever told you what the penalty for perjury in
a capital case is?

A: Yes.

Q: Do you have a state of mind as to what the penalty for
perjury in a capital case is?

A: Yes.

Q: What is that penalty?

A: The death penalty.

She said it as though she truly believed it and the vehemence of Kanarek's objections merely underscored the guilelessness of her answer. If she told a lie she would die; simple, to the point, and most effective.

After this last exchange Judge Older had a few words for Irving Kanarek at the bench. They are important words because they indicate, to use one of Kanarek's favorite expressions, his Honor's "state of mind" at this stage of the trial. Coming from Older, a man who was bending over backwards to be impartial, the statement carries added weight.

OLDER: There is no question about it, your objections are frivolous. They are obviously made, Mr. Kanarek, for the purpose of obstructing the proceedings.

Most of them are groundless. The manner in which they are made and the content of them indicate they are made without any thought whatever on your part, but simply to interpose something between the question and the answer.

They are not made in a way that a responsible lawyer makes an objection, that is, because of any apparent belief in the merit of his objection, but they are a trial device used by you to obstruct the proceedings and to distract the jury from concentrating on the questions and the answers.

I want the record to clearly reflect that.

If a semblance of decorum was being maintained by counsel in open court, in private defense and prosecution attorneys were getting on one another's nerves. In chambers Kanarek accused Stovitz of violating the gag order by giving prejudicial interviews to the media. To which the deputy district attorney replied.

STOVITZ: I will tell you what we will do. We will make a statement right now that Mr. Bugliosi and I will make no statement for radio, press, television or any other news media whatever, if you — I am not asking the other defense attorneys — if you agree to do the same. Because you can't control yourself. Your statements that you make here in chambers are enough to show me that you are completely unbalanced sometimes; and if you make a statement right now, Mr. Bugliosi and I, under oath, will say that we won't make any statements whatsoever.

BUGLIOSI: (To Kanarek) You got on television and said that Younger met with Nixon. That is what you said over T.V.

OLDER: He said that in court, too.

BUGLIOSI: He said it on television, too.

KANAREK: That is not so. I said, "I believe." There is a vast difference. I said, "I believe." There are many ways that people can slice baloney, your Honor. What I am saying is what I believe. I made it very clear that I believe that President Nixon is trying to foster the career of Mr. Younger.

OLDER: Mr. Kanarek, I couldn't care less what you believe on that subject; it is totally irrelevant to what we are talking about, and has nothing to do with this case.

BUGLIOSI: I would request that the court start holding Mr. Kanarek in contempt of court when he starts making absurd objections. What bothers me, the jury's job is to assimilate all these questions and answers. I think they are having a difficult time. If you look at the transcript, there is a question on one page and the answer doesn't come out until the next page, due to Mr. Kanarek.

KANAREK: I would ask that your Honor hold Mr. Bugliosi and Mr. Stovitz in contempt. They are deliberately — I hope it is deliberately — if those questions they asked are really thought out, they are incompetent as lawyers. Your Honor even himself has told Mr. Stovitz to sharpen his questions. The man doesn't know how to ask a proper question.

This man Mr. Bugliosi, he has some kind of a paranoia because he teaches some criminal law somewhere in some college (The deputy teaches criminal law in Los Angeles's small but prestigious Beverly School of Law.) that he is some God-given person to the legal profession or something.

STOVITZ: You are God-given, Mr. Kanarek.

OLDER: All right, that will be enough.

It is with no little amusement that the observer watches the same gentlemen perform in open court ten minutes later. Pencils and pens are courteously loaned; evidence is studied and discussed with a great show of mutual comprehension; one side defers to the other and is, in turn, deferred to; apologies are given for unwarranted interruptions and a general air, if not of bonhomie, at least of *laissez-faire,* prevails.

Following Aaron Stovitz's re-direct examination, Paul Fitzgerald, Daye Shinn and, to everyone's pleased surprise, Irving Kanarek conducted brief recross-examinations. Ronald Hughes, the last to take the floor, began bellowing his questions, apparently on the theory that volume somehow compensates for substance. After having his first eight questions objected to and the objections sustained, Hughes asked if the witness had taken any drugs at the Sybil Brand Institute, where she was being held in custody.

Q: Nobody brought you any marijuana?

A: No.

Q: Or hashish?

A: Somebody tried to give me hashish once, but I refused it.

Q: In the jail?

A: Yeah.

Q: So you turned to mysticism, to yoga in the jail?

Mrs. Kasabian told of how she had turned to yoga as a means of meditating and reaching what she called a "God awareness." Defense counsel obviously felt that he was onto something significant because his voice rose to a steady shout as he continued his inquiry:

LINDA KASABIAN, DRUGS BEHIND BARS

Q: What type of yoga do you practice?

(Objected to as being irrelevant; sustained.)

Q: What kind of yoga do you practice?

(Same objection; sustained.)

Q: Do you know of a form of yoga that deals with mysticism?

(Same objection; sustained.)

Q: Do you know of a form of yoga that deals with werewolves?

(Same objection; sustained.)

Q: Devils?

(Same objection; sustained.)

Q: Monsters?

(Same objection; sustained.)

Q: Is one of the purposes in using yoga to lose your mind?

(Same objection; sustained.)

Q: Is the purpose of yoga to have your mind leave your body through the third eye, to leave the body and travel effortlessly through space?

(Same objection; sustained.)

Q: Have you ever left your body through the third eye?

(Same objection; sustained.)

Judge Older, after cautioning the bearded attorney to

"modulate" his voice, suggested that he try some other line of approach.

OLDER: Mr. Hughes, you apparently have exhausted all legitimate avenues of recross-examination. If you continue in the same vein I am simply going to terminate your examination and get on with the trial. This has now reached the point of absurdity.

JUDGE OLDER TERMINATES THE CROSS-EXAMINATION

Ronald Hughes refused to heed the judge's warning. Leaving yoga, he turned to extra-sensory perception and Judge Older, obviously getting his own special emanations, terminated the recross-examination. As the defense counsel sat down after registering an objection, one could not help but reflect on the quality of Leslie Van Houten's defense. Her attorney when court recessed for lunch, continued his bombast in the corridors outside of the courtroom. In chambers, before the afternoon session, Judge Older took note of that behavior.

OLDER: It has come to my attention that Mr. Hughes, after this morning's session, was creating a rather loud disturbance in the hall outside, including some statements which, if the reports that I received are accurate, accused the court of being prejudiced against the defendant and I don't know what else.

But the reports that I received indicated that this was done in a voice that could be heard all the way down the hall, and apparently was stated in what amounted to a yell, this before the television media representatives.

I am not in a position to do anything about it until I know what it was that occurred. But I might remind you, Mr. Hughes, that you are not free to be contemptuous simply because you are outside the courtroom, and when you stand out in the hall outside of the courtroom in a criminal courts building and yell at the top of your voice things that may be attributed to you, it might very well be contemptuous conduct.

But his Honor was not saving all his shots for the defense. Aaron Stovitz then requested that Older renew an often violated order that photographers be kept away from the hallway immediately outside of the courtroom. He had witnesses, he explained, who did not want to be photographed and who did not want publicity and he, Stovitz, would appreciate it if his Honor would make sure that the media were kept back from the courtroom entrance. To which his Honor replied:

OLDER: I take it that Mr. Younger (Stovitz's superior) is no longer so vociferous in all the media about the desirability of having the public fully informed.

Touché!

The next morning, Tuesday, August 18, Judge Older called all counsel into chambers and read part of the transcript of an on-camera interview Ronald Hughes had given the day previously to Dick Hathcock, a reporter for KTLA, a Los Angeles television station.

Hughes: . . . you know, hundreds of years of Anglo-Saxon jurisprudence brought us in this point in time today so this judge can cut me off in such a way to frustrate the ends of justice.

Hathcock: Did you have more questions?

Hughes: Indeed I did. I had several more hours' questions for this witness.

Hathcock: Do you feel that he has . . .

Hughes: I feel it's just because he is tired. He's tired of seeing this witness up there for fourteen days. I think he is afraid to get to the truth. He is afraid to hear astrophysical or metaphysical things issue from the lips of the star prosecution witness, and I accuse that judge of being biased for the prosecution. I accuse him — I would file — were it the proper time I would file an affidavit of actual prejudice against Judge Older.

OLDER: That is the end of the transcript.
      Now apart from any questions as to whether those re-

marks constitute a contempt of court, which question will be investigated, I reprimand and censure Mr. Hughes for making such statements. By your own statements it is clear that your remarks are based solely on the rulings of this court during the course of these proceedings and upon no other facts.

You have demonstrated by your conduct a lack of professional qualifications and maturity as well as a lack of respect for the court, which the courts have a right to expect from lawyers appearing before them.

Your conduct has brought discredit upon yourself and has impugned the integrity of this court. It is conduct which should be brought to the attention of the state bar, and I intend to see that it is.

Hughes then asked to be represented by an attorney should the judge bring formal contempt charges against him and this request was granted.

The fact that Judge Older was using strong language in his private condemnation first of Irving Kanarek then of Ronald Hughes all the better illustrates the judicial restraint that he was exercising in public, on the bench. The trial had developed two separate "feels." The give-and-take in open court during which business, to the untutored eye, appeared to be proceeding as usual (or as much "as usual" as anything in Tate/La Bianca), and the sense of professional, perhaps personal, repugnance becoming increasingly implicit in the relationship between the jurist and at least two members of the defense team.

Hughes, loudly braying to the outside world that Older was prejudiced, created, rather than reported, that condition. In fact, the judge was making the greatest attempt to be fair to both sides, despite extreme provocation.

"He thinks he's being fair," Paul Fitzgerald acknowledged.

"He really thinks that he is being impartial. But they (the defendants) cannot possibly get a fair trial." Counsel once again made his point. "It's just impossible."

If Fitzgerald was right in his analysis, something esoteric, the establishment, the mood of the country, the tenor of the times, had affixed itself to Judge Older's subconscious without his knowledge so that he, or presumably any other educated, intelligent man (including Paul Fitzgerald), if he exercised his intellect and called upon his background in the law, could *under no circumstances* give Charles Manson, Patricia Krenwinkel, Susan Atkins and Leslie Van Houten a fair trial.

Another, possibly overly-simplistic way of putting it, might be that the defendants were guilty not only beyond all reasonable doubt but beyond any effort of rational men and women to give them the benefit of that doubt.

But, as Paul Fitzgerald would have been the first to admit in private conversation, the niceties of philosophical debate have no place in a court of law. Accordingly, Vincent Bugliosi, on redirect examination, took Linda Kasabian back through the, by now, celebrated orgy that took place at the Spahn Ranch.

Q: In addition to hugging and kissing that took place at the orgy, did any other type of sexual activity take place?

A: Yes.

Q: You had sexual intercourse with Tex and Clem?

A: No intercourse with Tex, with Clem I did, yes.

Q: But you did have some type of sexual activity with Tex also?

A: Yes.

Bugliosi left it at that and went on to other things but Fitzgerald, as he said later " . . . wasn't about to let Vince get away with that hugging and kissing stuff." On re-recross-examination he read the above testimony from the daily transcript and inquired of the witness:

Q: (By Fitzgerald) Were you asked those questions and did you give those answers?

A: Yes, but I think they are jumbled around.

Q: Would you like to explain that?

A: Yes.

Q: Please do. (He raised his eyes ceilingward and cocked his head, a mannerism that indicated to veteran Fitzgerald-watchers that he was setting up the witness before making a strong point.)

A: There was hugging and kissing between Tex and I, but there was intercourse between Clem and I.

Q: And what sort of sexual activity did you engage in with Snake? (Another Family member.)

A: Hugging and kissing.

Q: There was no other form of sexual activity that took place between you and any other participant, is that correct? (Watch out, Linda, here it comes.)

A: Yes.

Q: With the exception of sexual intercourse with them?

A: Right.

Q: There was no form of oral sexual activity, is that correct? (Matter of fact tone. Witness frowns. Jury shifts in their seats.)

No response from witness.

Q: (Voice rising) You did not orally copulate the penis of any male person present, is that correct?

BUGLIOSI: I object on the grounds of undue harassment and embarrassment, your Honor. There is a section of the evidence code to that effect.

OLDER: Overruled, you may answer.

KASABIAN: What was your question? (How, the observer wonders, could she forget *that?*)

Q: (Repeated) You did not orally copulate the penis of any male person present, is that correct?

A: (Puzzled frown) What does that mean?

Q: (After a pause) Mrs. Kasabian, are you familiar with oral-genital relations?

Bugliosi objected and was sustained. Paul Fitzgerald hesitated, thought it over and then switched the topic of his examination. After court adjourned he admitted that he was caught off stride by the witness's response. "Every other way I could think of to ask her the question was either more technical or," he grinned, "not technical enough." He had been bested and he knew it; Linda Kasabian's remarkable poise had, once again, held her in good stead.

Chapter XX

DAY SIXTY-THREE

As was so often the case in Tate/LaBianca, a significant development meant different things to different people. On Wednesday, August 19, 1970, at 11:58 A.M., after eighteen court days of testimony, Linda Kasabian was finally excused. It had been a marathon effort during which the former Family member had demonstrated amazing staying power in the face of hundreds of questions in direct, cross, redirect, recross, re-redirect and re-recross-examination. As Richard Seldeen, a deputy district attorney observed: "She had to be telling the truth; no one could remember lies through all that."

That fateful Wednesday also marked another milestone in the journey toward acquittal or conviction; the day that Irving Kanarek ran out of gas. The stocky, perpetually frowning defense attorney did not slow down gracefully. He approached the end of his re-recross-examination in a series of jerky stops and starts, as though, his propellant running close to "empty," he had some foreign residue stuck in his carburetion system. He would alternately come on in a quick burst of energy then grind to a full stop, staring at the floor perplexedly for as long as thirty seconds before asking his next question.

He began badly by referring to the witness as "Mrs. Bugliosi," a slip which he quickly identified as being Freudian in origin. (A monograph could be written on that comment alone; but on to the business at hand.) Kanarek began going over ground that had been covered a number of times and objections to his questions were being repeatedly sustained. He began a random fishing expedition that, even for him, took the examination somewhat far afield. For example, he asked Linda Kasabian:

Q: Is this a fact, Mrs. Kasabian; looking at your life since 1966, really, the only place, the only time you haven't been rejected is by the District Attorney of Los Angeles County?

BUGLIOSI: Oh, your Honor, that is ridiculous. There has to be an amendment to the evidence code. (To permit broader objections.)

OLDER: Sustained.

KANAREK: Your Honor . . .

OLDER: Sustained.

Manson's attorney, laboring to maintain the floor, began asking to approach the bench every time an objection to his question had been sustained. It was an old tactic of his, designed to take the jurors' minds off the testimony and to give himself time to think of another question. Once at the bench, as we have seen, his argument was usually meaningless and was intended as a stalling device. This time, however, it didn't work. Older, in addition to sustaining objections, routinely denied Kanarek access to the bench so that the defense attorney was hard put to switch topics without provoking an "asked and answered" objection.

Soon Paul Fitzgerald began objecting to his colleague's questions, a situation that must have appeared unusual to the jury. It had happened before but never to this extent; Fitzgerald consistently beat the prosecution to the punch, doing their work for them, and, just as consistently, his objections were sustained.

Another attorney may have been intimidated by this near-unanimous expression of displeasure but Kanarek merely dug in and used the only weapon left to him: silence while he formulated his next inquiry. Judge Older began directing him to "Ask your next question, Mr. Kanarek," and the attorney became increasingly hard put to respond. A regular cycle was established with Kanarek going back to the very start of the trial in an attempt to find something to ask Linda Kasabian.

KANAREK: Mrs. Kasabian how long did it take you to get to New Mexico after you left the Spahn Ranch?

FITZGERALD: Asked and answered.

OLDER: Sustained.

KANAREK: Your Honor, then I must approach the bench.

OLDER: Ask your next question.

It couldn't go on this way for very long. Older, privately at the bench, warned Manson's attorney several times that he would not permit him to go over ground already covered. Kanarek, in a final desperate gesture, seized upon these instructions to try to convey to the jury a suggestion that he was being gagged, that he had significant questions to ask (which he did not) but was being prevented from asking them by Judge Older. This constituted highly irregular legal practice and soon brought Kanarek his comeuppance. After an attempt to approach the bench on a constitutional point had been denied, Judge Older invited the defense attorney to state his constitutional ground in open court. Predictably, he did not do so.

KANAREK: I state that the court's orders are denying due process of law to Mr. Manson. He is being denied a fair trial, a fair hearing. And I allege to the court — your Honor is asking me to do this in open court so I am doing it that way. I allege . . .

BUGLIOSI: Your Honor, this type of stuff, this type of garbage . . . I call it that advisedly, should be at the bench, your Honor. It is a legal issue. It should not be within the earshot of the jury.

OLDER: Mr. Kanarek, either ask your next question or sit down, sir.

KANAREK: In view of your Honor's statements I want to obey the court's order.

OLDER: Then do so.

KANAREK: But I also wish to make the record.

OLDER: Mr. Kanarek, if you don't ask your next question I will terminate the examination and we will proceed to something else. You understand that, don't you, sir?

KANAREK: I understand that, your Honor.

OLDER: All right, then let's proceed.

KANAREK: Then I would ask your Honor to ask the jury to disregard the most unprofessional remark by Mr. Bugliosi.

OLDER: Don't compound it, Mr. Kanarek, by stating your remarks in front of the jury. Let's proceed, sir. Ask your next question or you will sit down and examination will be terminated.

KANAREK: I wish to obey the court's order so I must sit down.

OLDER: All right. (Irving Kanarek went to his seat and slowly sank into it, as though overwhelmed by the forces of oppression bent on making him adhere to the rules of law.) Mr. Hughes, do you care to examine?

HUGHES: Yes, I do, your Honor.

OLDER: All right, you may proceed.

The objections began flying thick and fast around Hughes's head. Of twenty-three objections made by the prosecution, only one was overruled by the court. Somewhat chastened, Hughes then asked the witness if she would be willing to be examined by a psychiatrist, had the question objected to and the objection sustained, then concluded his re-recross-examination. Linda Kasabian, without any outward change of expression or demeanor, stepped down from the witness stand, a free woman.

True, she was subject to recall as a defense witness but the major part of her ordeal was over. Her subpoena by the defense was a protective device; if anything should happen to her that made it impossible for her to appear when called, the defense could ask that all her testimony be stricken, that they had significant questions to ask her and that the fact that they were unable to do so prejudiced the case against them. If, on the other hand, they called her and she appeared there was always the possibility that her testimony would do the defense more harm than good.

Compared to the preceding nearly three weeks of Linda Kasabian's testimony during which it seemed that no other individual would ever be called, the prosecution began parading witnesses in and out of the courtroom at a lightning pace. Police officers came, were sworn, were asked questions that established their presence for various reasons at the Tate murder scene (the La Bianca testimony would follow), occasionally were briefly cross-examined but most often were not, and were quickly excused.

The first meaningful witness in the sense of offering corroborative testimony to Mrs. Kasabian's recitation of the events of August 8, 9 and 10 was Rudolf Weber the man who confronted Tex, Susan, Patricia and Linda when the first three stopped to wash the blood off themselves with a garden hose after leaving the Tate residence. A dignified, white-haired man who spoke with a European accent, Mr. Weber told of how he saw a man and three girls using the hose on his front lawn. Most importantly the witness had jotted down and subsequently recalled the car's license number GYY 435, the same license number that was frequently used on a 1959 Ford owned by John Harold Swartz, Jr., a ranch hand at the Spahn Ranch and borrowed the night before the Tate murders without his permission.

What surprised many observers including, as he remarked later, Deputy District Attorney Vincent Bugliosi, was the fact that the defense chose not to cross-examine Mr. Weber. "He was a key witness," Bugliosi told me. "If none of the jurors have read Susan Atkins's confession (published in 1969 in some newspapers and as a paperback book) then he was the only one who was telling them that what Linda said was true."

The defense appeared, by their lack of examination, to concede that Linda Kasabian had spoken the truth about the stop and, by extension, the reason for it being made.

A much anticipated return witness, Winnifred Chapman, the maid who first discovered the bodies at the Sharon Tate home proved to be something of a disappointment both as to her deportment and her testimony. Mrs. Chapman, a sepia *Camille,* described entering the front gate, going around the house by way of a sidewalk, entering the back door and seeing "too much." Whereupon, she said, she turned, ran back down the walk and along the street to a neighbor's house to summon the police. The witness, producing a cup from her purse, asked Aaron Stovitz to get her a drink of water as, hands wringing and palms flying to forehead, she indicated that the ordeal of testifying was making great demands on her physically and emotionally. She was excused.

A Los Angeles Police Department narcotics officer then described how he found 76.9 grams of marijuana in a cabinet in the Tate living-room, 30 grams on a nightstand in the room occupied by Abigail Folger and Voityck Frykowski, and 1 gram of cocaine and a two-inch roach (partially smoked marijuana cigarette), 6.3 grams of marijuana in Jay Sebring's car. In addition ten capsules of a drug called MDA — Methaline Dioxy Amphetamine, possession of which is not illegal in California — were found in the Folger-Frykowski bedroom. (Urinalysis of the two bodies later showed a 2.4 milligrams percentage and 0.6 milligrams percentage of MDA in their respective bodies.)

Prior to the testimony of Dr. Thomas T. Noguchi, Coroner for the County of Los Angeles, counsel met in chambers to discuss what photographs the prosecution could or could not show to the jury. It was here that Irving Kanarek, protesting the showing of a group of colored photographs of Voityck Frykowski's body, suffered from either a sudden loss of memory or the convenient pangs of remorse.

KANAREK: Some of these (pictures of the decedents), even from the prosecution's theory of the case, it is so obvious where Tex Watson is the perpetrator actually doing the act, it seems to me that the court can remove some of these pictures from any consideration whatsoever, because there gets to be . . .

OLDER: What are you referring to about Watson?

KANAREK: I am referring to some of these pictures of Mr. Frykowski which, according to the prosecution's own evidence, Mr. Watson is the actual actor. In other words I think Mr. Frykowski should be eliminated, these horrible pictures concerning him should be eliminated because the prosecution's theory of the case is that Mr. Watson did the overwhelming majority of it.

Those "horrible" pictures, the reader will recall, are similar to the ones that Kanarek repeatedly thrust before Linda Kasabian's face when she was on the witness stand.

SHARON TATE

ABIGAIL FOLGER

JAY SEBRING

VOITYK FRYKOWSKI

STEVEN PARENT

ROSEMARY LA BIANCA

LENO LA BIANCA

Chapter XXI

DAY SIXTY-FIVE

The four Family members sat pale and subdued as Dr. Thomas T. Noguchi, Coroner for the County of Los Angeles, took the witness stand on August 21 to provide a puncture-by-puncture account for the one hundred and two stab wounds suffered by the collective victims at the Tate residence. (Rosemary and Leno La Bianca, murdered on the second night and receiving a total of sixty-seven wounds, were described by Dr. Noguchi's assistant, Dr. David A. Katsuyama, on a subsequent day.)

Inflicted by a "strong, sharp instrument or instruments measuring not less than five inches in length, one to one-and-a-half inches in width and of a thickness of from one-eighth to one-quarter of an inch," the sixteen wounds in Sharon Tate, twenty-eight in Abigail Folger, seven in Jay Sebring, and fifty-one in Voityck Frykowski, were clinically described as to direction of thrust, penetration and size of surface laceration.

The oriental cadence of the medical examiner's voice describing in precise detail the abattoir-like condition of the

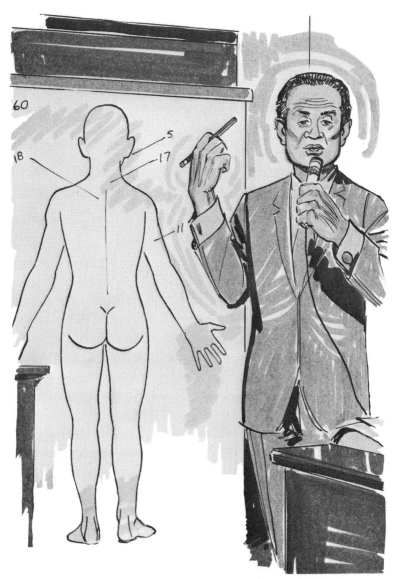

CORONER THOMAS NOGUCHI: " . . . STRONG, SHARP INSTRUMENTS"

"SUSPENSION DURING THE AGONAL STAGE"

murder scene suggested a gruesomeness that the most impassioned account could not have conveyed. The listener felt a mounting sense of shock as the savagery of the incident was hammered home more forcibly with the introduction into evidence of each new wound.

The general air of unreality was heightened when the coroner, describing the bodies of Sharon Tate and Jay Sebring as being joined by a rope pulled taut around their necks then looped over an overhead beam, expressed the opinion that they had, for a brief period, been hanged. A hushed courtroom listened to Dr. Noguchi's conclusions.

"I believe, based on wound findings on the left side of the cheek and the way the rope was tied at the scene and placed over the beam of the livingroom, I would form the opinion that Miss Sharon Tate had been suspended, perhaps for not too long a period, but perhaps a partial suspension for a short time . . . I believe that the suspension was caused during the agonal stage, the dying process."

The four defendents, usually animated or restless during periods of lengthy testimony, sat motionless, staring straight ahead or down at the defense table in front of them. Charles Manson, his long hair pulled forward like a tangled curtain on either side of his face, tugged occasionally at his beard, toyed with a pencil and made notes on a sheet of yellow foolscap paper.

The sallow, slightly-built Family leader tucked his bare feet up under him in the yoga lotus position on his chair as he listened to the chronicle of murder. He represented a living cliché.

If ever a man was literally born a loser, that man was Charles Miles Manson. The accidental son of Kathleen Maddox, a teen-age prostitute, and a casual client known only as a shadowy "Colonel Scott," Manson took the name of the man his mother married for a brief time to give him a semblance of legitimacy. It had been a long, arduous journey from his birthplace in Cincinnati on November 11, 1934 to Judge Older's court.

A biographer seeking to capture the life-style of his subject must, sooner or later, look to the record. Personal recollections of friends and enemies are important but what the subject actually accomplished or failed to accomplish must be a major factor in any final evaluation. This writer has conducted an extensive investigation into Charles Manson's background in order to better understand why, as he puts it, "Your life is not my life."

"WHAT TYPE OF YOGA DO YOU PRACTICE?"

Charles Miles Manson, also known as Charles Miller Manson, Charles M. Milles, Charles Deer, Charles Willis Manson, Charles William Manson and Charles Maddox, committed the first crime of a serious nature in Beaver, Utah on February 16, 1951 when, at the age of sixteen, he was arrested for violation of the Dyer Act, the interstate transport of a stolen vehicle, a felony. Prior to that he had been in and out of boys' correctional institutions and reformatories. In Utah, however, he made his initial bid for the "big time," and was subsequently sentenced to the National Training School for Boys in Washington, D.C. for four years, eight months and one day.

Manson served only a portion of that sentence and was paroled on May 8, 1954 from the Federal Reformatory at

Chillicothe, Ohio to which he had been transferred during his incarceration.

Charles Manson went west, but not to make good. He was arrested by the Los Angeles Police Department less than a year later on suspicion of Grand Theft, Auto. He received five years probation for that offense, registered as an ex-convict in Culver City, California, stole a car and was arrested in Indianapolis, Indiana for an offense against the Dyer Act and violation of parole. He was returned by U.S. Marshals to Los Angeles where he was sentenced to three years at Terminal Island, San Pedro. After an attempted escape he was released in 1957 and re-arrested on May 1, 1959 for mail theft and check forgery for which he was put on ten years probation.

Early in 1960 Manson was arrested in Laredo, Texas for the unlawful transportation of females in interstate commerce for the purpose of prostitution, returned to Los Angeles because of his parole violation and sentenced to ten years at the federal penitentiary on McNeil Island in the State of Washington. After being transferred to Terminal Island, San Pedro he was released on June 29, 1966. From that time until his capture at the Barker Ranch he was involved in a number of arrests for such offenses as possession of a forged driver's license, possession of marijuana, forcible rape and relatively minor traffic infractions.

In and out of penal institutions all of his life, Manson, during his last months of liberty when he lived as an aging, conniving pseudo-hippie, was different things to different people.

To his lackluster female followers, three of whom sat facing him as the coroner recited their alleged collective crimes, he was a lover, father-image and a stern disciplinarian who threatened them with mayhem, gave them drugs, alternately coaxed and forced them into sexual subservience and ended up, in the warped perspective of their simple minds, a Christ-figure.

To the employees of a Richfield service station on Topanga Canyon near the Spahn Ranch where Manson frequently bought gasoline or brought his dune buggies to be repaired, he was known simply as "Crazy Charlie," a bearded renegade. Manson performed something in the nature of a miracle during this period; he used a credit card stolen from the Tweedy Furniture Company to pay for his gas and repairs; despite the fact that the card was on the Richfield "hot sheet," Charlie successfully used it until an attempted purchase at another station caused it to be seized.

To Allan Adamson, a film producer, shooting on location near the Spahn Ranch, Charlie was a nuisance. "He's a little man," Adamson recalls. "We had to kick them off the set. They were bothering the actresses. They were literally little people. Dirty types. You see them all around Southern California and you don't think too much about it."

To Paul Watkins and Brooks Poston, working a mining claim in the Panamint near Death Valley not far from the Barker and Myers ranches where the Family was arrested after the murders, Charlie was bad medicine. "Shorty (Shorty Shea, a missing Spahn Ranch employee) was murdered," they revealed to investigating officers. A Family member allegedly told Watkins: "We killed Shorty (at the Spahn Ranch); he was bad mouthing the ranch."

Watkins and Poston then gave their version of the actual murder. "They got Shorty in his car," the miners reported. "They hit him in the head with a big wrench. They took him with them. They let him sweat. When he would come to, they would cut him some more. He was begging for his life. They finally had to cut his head off. He got to NOW, and they killed him."

Getting to NOW is a term employed by the Church of Scientology indicating a high state of self-awareness. Charles Manson reportedly learned something about the church in the federal penitentiary in Washington and was taken by its precepts.

"Shorty was buried under a full moon," the miners continued. "The girls scooped a grave out with their knives while the men sat around smoking a joint (marijuana)."

To Los Angeles County Deputy Sheriff S. Olmstead, Charlie was a potentially dangerous, possibly mentally unbalanced suspected car thief. Investigating two stolen cars found in the vicinity of Spahn Ranch, Olmstead came across Manson supposedly standing guard against a Black Panther raid.

"The motorcycle gangs and the police should join forces," Manson told the officer, "and attack the Negro community and wipe them out." The Family leader then calmly told Olmstead that there were hidden guns trained on him at that moment and that, on a command from Manson, he would be wiped out. In a subsequent search Olmstead and his fellow officers found three guns and "observed" ten to twelve knives and bayonets.

As the complex personality that was Charles Manson sat listening to Dr. Noguchi meticulously position the size and place of each wound on life-size human silhouettes, one of his co-defendants appeared to be exhibiting signs of nervous tension. Susan Atkins (who two days later would be hospitalized with what was officially diagnosed as an "impacted colon"), pale even by prison standards, began fidgeting noticeably and seemed loath to follow the testimony. Paul Fitzgerald turned his seat all the way around so that his back was to the court and began talking to her; he reached into a file folder and gave her a pile of documents to read. The conclusion was easily drawn that Fitzgerald, worried about her behavior, was attempting to distract her. She took the typewritten pages, thumbed through them, began reading but soon cast them aside. The press, by now an effluent source of black humor, diagnosed her unease as a reaction to listening to details of *other people's* stabbings; a recounting of her own transgressions, so the theory went, didn't disturb her, but listening to a description of her co-defendants' supposed criminal acts set her off her feed.

Susan Atkins's temporary disability which, according to testimony by an attending physician, was cleared up by the judicious administration of laxatives and enemas, served to point up that Judge Older was, to use Linda Kasabian's words in another context, a very heavy dude. The day after Miss Atkins's return to court she summarily stood up and, in a quavering voice, pleaded with his Honor to get her out of the courtroom because she "hurt too much." Judge Older recessed the court, had the defendant examined again and, next morning, ordered her brought into court in a wheelchair.

Out of the presence of the jury Dr. Margaret McCaron, in charge of the County Jail Medical Facility, carefully recounted the treatment given the prisoner and the examinations conducted by a team of medical experts. She concluded that, although Miss Atkins might have been suffering pain at the time of her original impacted colon diagnosis she now was either experiencing "anxiety pains" or, Dr. McCaron strongly implied, was faking the symptoms.

Susan Atkins was then wheeled over to the witness stand and sworn. Lesser men would have quailed at the sight of the pale, slight figure in the prison denim dress, supporting her

AN ENEMA CLEARS UP THE CASE

head on an arm propped up against the side of her wheelchair, handkerchief clutched to her tear-streaked face; Judge
Older merely inquired if there was any reason why the defendant could not step up into the witness box. No one, Miss Atkins included, could think of any, so she did.

Under Daye Shinn's sympathetic questioning, the defendant
began testifying in a whisper to the lack of consideration
shown her by both prison and hospital officials. When, for
example, she was reported as having rested comfortably, she
said, she was really curled up in pain, too frightened to move.
As her indignation rose so did her projection until, her little-
girl squeal gone, she was answering Shinn's inquiries with
scathing denunciations of her tormentors.

Aaron Stovitz, declining to cross-examine, merely noted that the witness appeared to grow stronger as she testified and that, contrary to her implication that she had been heavily sedated, answered all questions lucidly and with an obvious awareness. In the days following, Susan Atkins, after one or two sessions of burying her head in her hands on the counsel table, apparently grew weary of being ignored and gradually became her old giggling, gesticulating self.

The incident demonstrated the judge's capacity for decisive action in a situation that well could have rebounded to his and the trial's discredit. Although Judge Older did not begin the trial with a reputation for being overly familiar with the finer points of law, he was known as an impartial, no-nonsense jurist, a constructionist as the term currently in vogue would have it; his actions pleasantly surprised people on the first point and confirmed his record on the second.

Chapter XXII

DAY SEVENTY-NINE

Senior prosecutor Aaron Stovitz was taken off the case today, a move roughly comparable to the pilot of a jumbo jet being ordered back to a seat in economy during a landing approach. The passengers, concerned citizens reasonably certain that the co-pilot can bring the plane in safely, are nonetheless uneasy at the seeming irresponsibility implicit in the move.

It may well have been, as Chief Deputy District Attorney Joseph P. Busch remarked privately, that "The case is in," that the important prosecution witnesses had been heard from, and that, as was officially announced, the Head of Trials was needed back at his desk to resume his not inconsiderable duties involving the supervision of seventy-five deputy district attorneys assigned to his jurisdiction.

Thoughtful observers, however, were well aware that the office of the District Attorney of the County of Los Angeles consisted of a civil service pyramid upon the apex of which the only elected officeholder perched regally, exercising the absolute power vested in him by the people's mandate, yet sensitive to the tremors caused by the internecine warfare in the structure below. Which jostle dislodged Aaron Stovitz and how far that displacement was communicated through the power structure we leave to a future Stovitz biographer. Our concern here is Tate/La Bianca and of the Head of Trial's contribution to its ultimate resolution.

The senior member of the prosecution team brought stability and depth to the peoples' case. It was no accident that, on the day following his removal, Irving Kanarek had more of his objections sustained than he had during the previous five days of testimony. Vincent Bugliosi, possibly pressing, missed his partner's ability to ease tensions with remarks that quite often brought smiles to the faces of both judge and jury. A meticulous, seemingly tireless worker (he would regularly take a short nap at home after dinner then spend two or three hours preparing the next day's questions) Bugliosi openly began displaying his impatience with Judge Older's sustensions of defense objections, as well as engaging in shouting matches with Kanarek.

Despite the addition of two young deputy district attorneys, Donald Musich and Stephen Kay, to assist him in the background preparation of the case, Bugliosi of necessity had to carry the weight of the prosecution alone. How, for example, could either of the newcomers argue the credibility of past witnesses before the jury when neither man was present during the testimony? It was a burden that the now senior member of the prosecution accepted because, if the truth were known, he had long failed to understand his ex-partner's apparent lack of messianic zeal.

Way back at the beginning, before the jury had been selected but after some months of intensive preliminary investigation and interviewing of witnesses, an exchange in Stovitz's sixth-floor office pointed up the basic difference between the two men.

"Aaron," Vince Bugliosi employed his quietly controlled, I'm-trying-to-be-reasonable tone, "I know that I've probably gotten this wrong but I thought I heard you interviewed on radio last night and I thought you said that, to you, the Tate case is no different from any other homicide.

Stovitz pleaded guilty. This was in the days before multiple gag orders forbade public comment on the case.

"Aaron," Bugliosi, extending his arms in supplication, advanced on the seated man. "How could you say a thing like that?"

"Because it's the way I feel." Stovitz loosened his collar. It was first thing in the morning, he had a number of court appearances that day, his mother-in-law, whom he liked, was in the hospital and his fiery young associate was building up a head of steam. Well, his expression appeared to say, this too shall pass.

"I find it very difficult to believe, Aaron," Bugliosi began his opening statement, "that you really mean that. That you really mean that this is no different from any other murder case."

"Why?"

"Why?" The deputy district attorney turned his eyes heavenward. "I honestly don't understand you, Aaron. Why? Because this is unlike any other crime ever committed . . . perhaps the whole history of mankind. That's why. Calling this just another murder is . . . " his hands flailed the air helplessly " . . . I just can't believe that you really mean it."

"I didn't say 'just another murder.' What I said was that this office considers all homicide a grave offense and does not consider any murder as more special than any other."

"You said that?"

"I said that."

"And you *mean* that?"

"Of course."

It's hard to tell with Stovitz. His face goes deadpan and his eyes telegraph nothing. It could be the big needle or it could be a simple statement of principle. Or, what is more likely the latter automatically triggering the former.

"A guy gets a bunch of girls from middle-class families, puts the hex on them, and gets them to commit murder." The listener fills in "Ladies and gentlemen of the jury." *"Murder"* he emphasized, "while he's sitting in a desert cave somewhere flipping mental switches and you say that it's not different from any other case?" Bugliosi turned and shook his head in bewilderment. "This has got to be the biggest murder case that ever happened."

"What about the guy who got up in that Texas tower and shot all those people?"

"A crackpot with a gun." Bugliosi smiled condescendingly. "Crackpots with guns are nothing new."

"What about the guy who got into the nurses' house and killed them all except one?"

"Look Aaron, if what you're trying to say is that murder is bad, I agree with you. Killing people is wrong, but to say that the Tate case is just another homicide . . . " His voice trailed off as he placed his palms down flat on Stovitz's desk. "Aaron I hope you don't take that attitude into the courtroom with you." He frowns a gentle admonition and repeats, "I really hope that you don't take that attitude into the courtroom."

"This office would prosecute any capital offense with the same . . . "

"Come on, Aaron. I've been working seven days a week, day and night on this thing. I wouldn't be doing that if it were some other case."

"What time did you come in this morning?"

"Nine o'clock."

"Well," Stovitz made an elaborate ritual of examining his watch, "it is now nine thirty-five. You're wasting valuable time."

"Yes, *sir*." Bugliosi backed toward the door, bowing as he went. "Yes, sir, *sir*. This case is having international publicity on a fantastic scale. Hundreds of requests from all over the world for press coverage. But this office is handling it routinely." He bowed again. "I just hope that you change your attitude before we go into court, Aaron. That's all I hope."

The door closed behind Vincent Bugliosi and Stovitz stared at it thoughtfully. Moments later it opened and J. Miller Leavy who, as Director of Central Operations, oversees all of the trial attorneys, poked his head in.

"Vince getting excited?" Leavy asked.

Stovitz pointed to an acoustic tile in the ceiling, discolored by some past malfunction of the forty-five year old Hall of Justice plumbing. "He was just up there," he said.

"Sticking to the ceiling?"

"Like a pizza."

Leavy grinned his understanding as Stovitz shrugged noncommittally. Both men had a high regard for the young deputy's abilities but both knew of his low boiling point.

Vincent Bugliosi's explosive temperament was put to the test in the days following Aaron Stovitz's departure from the case, not only by the plodding, obstructionist tactics of Irving Kanarek but by the unpredictable nature of his own witnesses.

Danny DeCarlo, whose earthy testimony involving Robert

DANNY DE CARLO LOVED GUNS MORE THAN HIS "OLD LADY"

Beausoleil and, to a lesser extent Charles Manson in the Hinman case we noted earlier, was called by the prosecution to establish Manson's general dominance over the Family and his specific plans for Helter-Skelter. DeCarlo, Bugliosi admitted privately, rarely answered questions put to him on the stand in the way that the prosecutor had reason to expect from past interrogations; he was the first of a series of witnesses who, in less serious circumstances, would have provided all the ingredients of an old-fashioned vaudeville bill. Raunchy, candid to a fault, DeCarlo came through with a number of punch lines that kept the courtroom and, in some instances, Judge Older amused. Most importantly, the short, mustachioed sometime drifter, sometime gunsmith, sat well with the jury; polished he wasn't, frank he most certainly was.

On Manson's relationship to the girls: "He told them to take care of the men. He told them to take their clothes off."

BUGLIOSI: You liked that, eh Danny?

DE CARLO: (Big smile as he pulls reflectively on his mustache) Yeah, I dug it. (The court reporter looks up questioningly) I *liked* it (Danny obliged him, leaning over the witness stand)

The jury apparently liked it, too. Bugliosi asked him about Manson's use of the word "pigs."

"Charlie said pigs were police," DeCarlo said. "They were white collar workers, ones that work from eight to five."

And what should be done with pigs?

"They otta have their throats cut and be hung up by their feet."

This time the jury didn't smile.

On cross-examination Irving Kanarek played upon De-Carlo's self-admitted preoccupation with guns.

KANAREK: Would it be a fair statement Mr. DeCarlo to say that you like guns?

DE CARLO: I love guns.

KANAREK: What do you mean when you say you "love" guns?

DE CARLO: I love guns better than I love my old lady.

KANAREK: By your "old lady" Mr. DeCarlo, do I take it you mean your wife?

DE CARLO: Yeah.

KANAREK: Is it a fair statement to say that you love guns more than you love people?

DE CARLO: I didn't say that. I said that I loved them better than I loved my old lady.

Judge Older joined in the general laughter.

Manson, according to the witness, wanted "Blacks and whites (to go) against each other (as he) sat up on a hill and watched them shoot each other." The Family leader would voice these opinions when "Charlie would get us all together and we'd sit down and eat chow," according to De-Carlo. The defense sensed that the witness's unfeigned coarseness was working in the prosecution's favor and Irving Kanarek began objecting routinely to every prosecution question.

DeCarlo's "cool" was well demonstrated when the defense failed to register an objection to one of Vincent Bugliosi's queries. After waiting a few seconds for something to happen, DeCarlo turned to Judge Older, seated slightly above him and to his right.

DE CARLO: Ain't they objecting to that?

OLDER: I didn't hear anything.

KANAREK: Objection, your Honor. On the grounds of immateriality and improper foundation.

OLDER: Sustained.

DeCarlo, grinning at the defense table, folded his hands and awaited the next question.

It was a measure of the general air of unreality that increasingly pervaded Tate/LaBianca that the jury appeared to believe ex-Navy Gunner's Mate Danny DeCarlo. By his own admission "smashed" on beer ninety-nine per cent of the time that he spent at the Spahn Ranch, habitually in trouble because of his fondness for brandishing and discharging his great loves in the direction of police officers, with a child, Dennis, aged two years and four months of whom he seemed genuinely fond (DeCarlo's voice wavered and nearly broke when Judge Older ordered him to reveal his present address on the stand; he said later that he feared Family retribution against his son), the witness who called a broad a broad projected a curious credibility that communicated itself to the spectators.

So, too, did another sometime Family member, Barbara Hoyt, a shapely eighteen year old afflicted with a severe case of near-sightedness. (Irving Kanarek, in a typically disjointed attempt to impeach her hearing, asked her to remove her thick glasses and, displaying four fingers, advanced toward the witness so that his hand very nearly touched her face before she succeeded in identifying the number).

But there was nothing wrong with Miss Hoyt's hearing and her testimony, that she had overheard Susan Atkins (Family name Sadie Glutz) telling Ruth Morehouse (Family name Ouisch) about the Tate murders after the Family had moved up to the Barker and Myers Ranches in the Panamint Range near Death Valley, was especially damning. Specifically Miss Hoyt heard Miss Atkins tell Ouisch that "Sharon Tate was the last to go because she had to watch the others die," on the night of the slayings.

Attempts by the defense to shake his witness's testimony proving fruitless, Vincent Bugliosi decided to establish Charles Manson's personal hold over the female members of the Family. In some of the spiciest and, for Manson, most personally damaging testimony thus far, Miss Hoyt told of her sexual involvement with Juan Flynn, self-described "manure shoveler" at the Spahn Ranch and peripheral Family member.

BUGLIOSI: Now, Barbara, what did Mr. Manson tell you to do with Juan Flynn?

The witness, her hands folded in her miniskirted lap, stared silently out over the courtroom. She tossed her flowing hair back over her shoulders, appeared about to speak, then refrained from doing so.

BUGLIOSI: (Sympathetically) Would you rather not answer?

As Kanarek registered his violent objections to this dialogue between counsel and his witness the three girl defendants made a great show of nudging one another and tittering behind their hands. Clearly they wanted the jury to believe that Barbara Hoyt's reticence was feigned. Judge Older directed the prosecutor to re-ask his question.

BUGLIOSI: What did Mr. Manson tell you to do with Juan Flynn?

HOYT: (After another pause) That oral whatchmacallit.
(Smiles from the press section.)

BUGLIOSI: Orally copulate?

HOYT: Yes.

BUGLIOSI: Charlie told you to do that?

HOYT: Yes.

BUGLIOSI: Did you want to do it?

HOYT: No.

One could almost see the steam rising from Irving Kanarek's ears as he awaited the opportunity to recross-examine.

BARBARA HOYT PERFORMED "THAT ORAL WHATCHMACALLIT"

KANAREK: Is it a fact, Miss Hoyt, that before you went to the Myers Ranch you had orally copulated a man? (Objected to; sustained.)

KANAREK: Did you in fact orally copulate Mr. Flynn?

HOYT: Yes.

KANAREK: Is it a fair statement that the act of oral copulation between people was not unknown to you? (Objected to; sustained.)

KANAREK: Well Miss Hoyt, did you orally copulate anyone else?

HOYT: Yes. For the same reason.

KANAREK: What was that?

HOYT: I was afraid not to.

On re-direct Vincent Bugliosi did not want the jury, distracted by the nature of the testimony, to lose sight of Manson's dominance in a situation that the prosecutor obviously felt was nearly as repugnant to the female members of the jury as was murder; possibly more so. A man who could make a girl do this, Bugliosi clearly implied, could make her do anything.

BUGLIOSI: While you were orally copulating Mr. Flynn did Mr. Manson eventually leave the room?

HOYT: Yes.

BUGLIOSI: When did you stop orally copulating Mr. Flynn? (Irving Kanarek here registered an objection that, as worded, gave the listener pause.) "Object as immaterial, calling for the conclusion on the part of the witness. I would like to inquire on *voir dire* whether she in fact had knowledge of these events."

OLDER: Motion denied.

BUGLIOSI: When did you stop orally copulating Mr. Flynn?

HOYT: When Charlie left.

BUGLIOSI: As soon as Mr. Manson left the room you stopped, is that correct?

HOYT: Yes.

Chapter XXIII

DAY NINETY-NINE

The trial proceedings more and more assumed the characteristics of a theater of the absurd. Events that rarely, if ever, occur in a court of law became commonplace and gave way to situations even more outlandish in their cause and manifestation.

Some of the dialogue had a blackout quality reminiscent of early century vaudeville. Ronald Hughes, cross-examining Danny DeCarlo about the location of an automatic weapon confiscated during a raid on the Spahn Ranch:

HUGHES: Mr. DeCarlo was there a machine gun at the Spahn Ranch?

DECARLO: Yeah.

HUGHES: And where was this machine gun kept?

DECARLO: In the violin case.

One-liners abounded; Irving Kanarek cross-examining a prosecution witness:

KANAREK: Today is October 2, 1970. Would it be a fair statement to say that one year ago today was October 2, 1969?

Or Daye Shinn cross-examining Steven Weiss, the self-possessed young boy who found the .22 caliber murder pistol and reported the discovery to his father.

SHINN: Mr. Weiss, how did you know that the gun was a .22 caliber?

WEISS: My father told me.

SHINN: Your father told you?

WEISS: Yes.

SHINN: (Wrapping up the case) So your father told you it was a .22 caliber gun *after* you found the weapon?

WEISS: (Perplexedly) Yes.

SHINN: I have no further questions, your Honor.

Within a short span of time Irving Kanarek and Vincent Bugliosi were both cited for contempt of court, leaving only Paul Fitzgerald of the original attorneys (Aaron Stovitz had been cited for contempt with the sentence bound over) in a state of virginal advocacy before the court. Judge Older, after repeated warnings, called Kanarek to the bench and came right to the point.

OLDER: Now, Mr. Kanarek, if you are back to your old tactics of using the objection as a tactical trial weapon to interrupt the direct testimony of the witness—the objections you have been making are frivolous. Now, if you keep it up, Mr. Kanarek, I'm going to find you in contempt of court. I want you to understand that very clearly.

The stocky defense attorney apparently did not understand it, resumed his interruptions and was promptly sentenced to two days and three nights in the county jail, from Friday court adjournment to 7:00 A.M. Monday, the most severe sentence meted out by the court thus far.

Vincent Bugliosi continued to show the strain imposed on him because of his increased responsibility and, by implication, the absence of Aaron Stovitz's steadying hand. He began more frequently to engage in loud exchanges with Kanarek despite Older's admonitions to refrain from colloquy between counsel. Finally, after one such shouting-match in which the prosecutor loudly declared, "I'm not going to take it any more. I'm fed up to here," and motioned with his hand over his head, Older asked counsel to approach the bench, found Bugliosi guilty of contempt, and sentenced him to spend one night in jail or to pay a fifty dollar fine. The prosecutor paid up.

This particular day, October 1, was especially eventful, even by Tate/La Bianca standards. Juan Flynn, on whom Barbara Hoyt performed her "Oral whatchamacallit," delivered some testimony that implicated Manson personally as, at very least, an accomplice in the Family murder plans. Manson, Flynn said, told him that, "The only way I'm going to show them niggers how to do it (start a racial war) is to go down and kill a bunch of those motherfucking pigs." Asked what he meant by pigs, Manson had said that, "Pigs were anyone that gave consent to support the system."

Flynn told of talking with Susan Atkins at the Spahn Ranch the night preceding the La Bianca murders. After

telling him that, "We're going to get them fucking pigs," she
got in a car along with Patricia Krenwinkel, Linda Kasabian,
Leslie Van Houten (referred to by Flynn as "The pretty one"
to the defendant's obvious delight), Clem Tufts and Tex
Watson with Charles Manson driving.

The tall, rangy stablehand then told of Manson subsequently approaching him in the ranch kitchen, grabbing him
by the hair, tilting his head back and putting a knife blade
to his throat. "You son-of-a-bitch," Manson told him, "don't
you know I'm the one who's doing all these killings?"

Under cross-examination the part-time motion picture actor
and stunt man stoutly denied that he was on the stand in order
to draw attention to himself and possibly further his show
business career. "I am not here to pompous myself," he told
Irving Kanarek and allowed as how all he wanted to do was
get back to the Spahn Ranch and "shovel some horseshit."
Irritated by defense counsel's harping on the subject, Flynn
blurted out: "It's not the kind of publicity I want, you big
catfish!" to the court's amusement.

That afternoon Manson interrupted his own lawyer's cross-
examination by standing up and breaking into song. "Oh, the
old gray mare ain't what she used to be," he sang in a high,
quavering voice. "The old gray mare ain't what she used to
be. She is a judge now."

Judge Older, his face flushed, ordered the defendant to
stop his outburst.

"Stop what?" Manson asked. "Why don't you stop doing
what you are doing?"

After two more exchanges Older ordered the Family leader
from the courtroom and recessed the court to discuss the
situation in chambers. There, out of the hearing of the press
and his co-defendants, Manson made a most significant state-

ment. He told Judge Older: "I am not after money, I am not after stature. I am not after anything other than just to prove to you that I didn't do anything wrong, even though I may have seen everything that happened and could bring the truth forward to save my face, and to save your face also, because your faces are hanging out!"

Was the ex-con's code of self-survival manifesting itself in Charlie's little speech? Was there a hint of a cop-out? Was he laying the groundwork to make a deal? All these questions may well have raced through Vincent Bugliosi's mind as Judge Older, after some discussion about the defendant's future behavior, ordered the trial to resume in open court with Manson present.

The shaggy-maned, bearded prisoner immediately renewed his disruptive tactics. "I would like everyone to know I'm not represented in this trial," he said. "I do not have a lawyer. I'm not allowed to speak for myself."

The girls, predictably, joined in. "You are just a woman," they chanted at the judge. "You are just a woman, that is all."

The four defendants were removed from the trial, Manson to a holding cell adjacent to the courtroom containing a speaker through which he could hear the proceedings in court, the three girls to a jury room upstairs also wired for sound.

The next day, Friday, October 2, Manson and the girls again spoke up, to bring the orderly procedure to a stop. After repeated warnings the accused murderer had to be removed from the courtroom, forcibly this time, and the girls, too, were led out. Court was then resumed and Juan Flynn was cross-examined without the defendants present, a more restful, though hardly legally desirable, state of affairs.

The following Monday morning, October 5, Judge Older

asked defense counsel into chambers further to discuss the matter.

OLDER: Are you gentlemen able to tell me whether or not your respective clients are willing to come back into the courtroom and conduct themselves properly?

FITZGERALD: Well, I asked my client if she was willing to return. She replied, "Is the judge willing to return to justice?" I am not trying to be equivocal, your Honor.

OLDER: We are not going to keep playing games. As long as we get equivocal answers like that, I am going to bring them back into the courtroom and we will just have to see what develops.

If the same thing develops that happened the other day, they will have to be removed, obviously. . .

Would you explain to me how the trial can be conducted in a setting in which the four defendants are on their feet and either singing or carrying on a monologue?

FITZGERALD: I think, as I read Allen, (Allen vs. Illinois, a case in which the judge barred the defendant from the courtroom for disruptive conduct), when I see what the defendant in Allen did, threatening the judge with his life; where, throughout the opinion, they refer to the conduct of the defendant as outrageous, when they refer to the conduct. . .

OLDER: If it will help any, I will characterize the conduct of these defendants as outrageous. Let there be no mistake about that.

FITZGERALD: I think they were about through, your Honor. I mean, if you would just let them finish, we could continue with the trial.

OLDER: If you look at the record of Friday's proceedings, I let them go on for quite a while.

FITZGERALD: You don't need to be worried about being vindicated by the public. You have already been vindicated.

OLDER: It is not a question of vindication, I assure you. I want the trial to get on, and I don't want to jeopardize any defendant's rights. On the other hand, I am not going to let the defendants jeopardize the people's right to a fair trial, either. So we will just have to take it step by step.

The defendants were then admitted to the courtroom and Sergeant Paul Whitely, a homicide detective with the Los Angeles County Sheriff's Department, testified briefly. Defense counsel declined to cross-examine and Charles Manson spoke up:

MANSON: May I examine him, your Honor?

OLDER: No, you may not.

MANSON: You are going to use this courtroom to kill me.

OLDER: (To witness) You may step down.

MANSON: Are you going to use this courtroom to kill me? Do you want me dead?

OLDER: Mr. Manson!

MANSON: The minute I see you are going to kill me, you know what I am going to do?

OLDER: What are you going to do?

MANSON: You know. You have studied your books. You know who you are talking to.

OLDER: If you don't stop, Mr. Manson—and I order you to stop now—I will have to have you removed as I did the other day.

MANSON: Order me to be quiet while you kill me with your courtroom? Does that make much sense? Am I supposed to lay here and just let you kill me?
I am a human being. I am going to fight for my life, one way or another. You should let me do it with words.

OLDER: If you don't stop, I will have to have you removed.

MANSON: I will have to have *you* removed if you don't stop. I have a little system of my own.

OLDER: (To Bugliosi) Call your next witness.

MANSON: Do you think I'm kidding?

OLDER: Mr. Manson, I'm going to have you removed if you don't stop it immediately.

Manson then vaulted the defense table, heading for Judge Older with a pencil in one hand. A bailiff tackled him from behind, knocked him to the floor in front of the bench and, with the help of two other bailiffs, subdued him and carried him from the courtroom. "In the name of Christian justice," Manson, as he was taken out, told Judge Older, "someone should cut your head off."

The three female defendants then stood and began chanting something that came over phonetically as, "Moem be oro decaio." They kept repeating what Fitzgerald later characterized as a "meaningless phrase" over and over again despite repeated warnings to desist. Finally they, too, were ordered from the courtroom to a lockup where, like Manson, they would be able to listen to the trial proceedings over a sound

MANSON VAULTED THE DEFENSE TABLE

system. The judge then called counsel to the bench for a private conference.

OLDER: I want the record to clearly reflect that Mr. Manson came completely over the counsel table and ended up on the floor directly in front of the bench. The bailiffs in order to get at him, had to take the same route, at least one of them, and there was a violent scuffle when the bailiffs attempted to subdue him, and then he had to be forcibly removed from the courtroom.

I also want the record to reflect again, although I stated it many times to counsel, the defendants may come back into the courtroom at any time they are willing to affirm their willingness to conduct themselves properly, and when you gentlemen can advise me that such is the case they will be immediately returned to the courtroom. Do you have something?

FITZGERALD: Yes. With all due respect to the court, and I sincerely mean that, I wonder if I might ask your Honor a question. Is your Honor able to state with any degree of certainty concerning your state of mind as to the intent of Mr. Manson's coming over the counsel table?

OLDER: He looked like he was coming for me.

FITZGERALD: That is what I was afraid of, and although. . .

OLDER: If he had taken one more step I would have done something to defend myself.

Fitzgerald then moved for a mistrial on the grounds that his client, Patricia Krenwinkel, might be unjustly linked with Manson in his attempt to physically assault Judge Older. His Honor responded:

OLDER: . . .(The three female defendants) are not going to profit from their own wrong, and they are just as culpable as he is, the fact they did not come over the counsel table doesn't mean a thing; they were ready, willing and able to engage in disruptive conduct, and that is what they did, all of them. There isn't the slightest difference in their culpability. As far as I'm concerned there will be no mistrial.

Back in open court the testimony soon resumed its reassuringly erratic path; it was as though Manson's act of overt violence had brought an unwelcome note of realism to proceedings that may be described as mad-hatterish as the weeks stretched into seemingly interminable months. Appropriately Irving Kanarek took us back through the looking glass when

Vincent Bugliosi was questioning Los Angeles Police Homicide Sergeant Manuel Gutierrez, a constant courtroom spectator, about what he observed when Manson first scratched an "X" on his forehead during the trial.

BUGLIOSI: Did you observe an "X" on Mr. Manson's forehead.

GUTIERREZ: I did, sir.

KANAREK: Your Honor I would object on the ground that the prejudicial value far outweighs the probative value. Also, your Honor, on the grounds of violation of freedom of religion. Seriously. Freedom of religion.

OLDER: You had to add "seriously?"

KANAREK: Yes, because I heard someone snicker.

OLDER: Who did you hear snicker?

FITZGERALD: I did.

The objection was overruled.

Chapter XXIV

DAY ONE HUNDRED AND TWELVE

Ronni Howard, the woman to whom Susan Atkins confessed her complicity in the Tate/La Bianca murders while both were dormitory-mates at the Sybil Brand Institute, a Los Angeles women's detention facility, actually testified twice during the trial. Miss Howard, whom Vincent Bugliosi privately conceded, "Really broke the case," when she called the authorities late in December, 1969 to report the conversations, spoke first in Judge Older's chambers to give an unexpurgated version of the talks to defense and prosecution counsel; then she testified in open court with a completely censored description of Miss Atkin's revelations.

The reason for the double standard was simple: Miss Howard, providing she was allowed to testify at all, would be permitted to relate only what the defendant had said about her personal connection with the crime. The witness was to quote only those parts of the conversation where Miss Atkins used "I" in relation to the crimes. Since, as we have seen, it was very much a "We" crime, the safeguard against incriminating the other defendants severely limited the final testimony.

Nonetheless Miss Howard, an early-thirties brunette in good shape despite considerable mileage, was able to establish Susan Atkins as, at very least, the stabber of Sharon Tate. "We were talking about acid trips," the witness recalled before the jury, when "Sadie told me that she was in Sharon Tate's bedroom and that a man was sitting on the bed near her."

When Sharon came into the living room, according to Miss Atkins, "She couldn't believe what was happening." The actress pleaded for the life of her baby but the defendant told her, "I have no feeling for you bitch," and proceeded to stab her. "When you stab a person," Susan Atkins explained to Miss Howard during that fateful conversation in Dormitory 8000 at Sybil Brand, "it's just like having a climax. The more you do it the better you like it." When Sharon Tate screamed, Ronni Howard went on, "She'd stab her; she just kept stabbing her until she stopped screaming." Miss Atkins, Miss Howard recalled, "was very excited," telling her about the murder. "She enjoyed telling me," the witness concluded.

Earlier, in chambers, Miss Howard told of how Miss Atkins discussed her present incarceration as a suspect in the murder of Gary Hinman, for which Robert Beausoleil has since been convicted, with charges still pending against herself, Charles Manson and Bruce Davis.

"I was trying to help her figure out how to defend herself against the Hinman case," the witness told Judge Older and the attorneys. "And she went on to tell me how she and this other girl and this guy were in the house, and they were going to tear the house up and make it look as if a fight had been there and everything, so it would look like somebody had robbed Gary, or something.

"She said she had done just about everything there is to do.

"And I said, 'Oh, really?'

"And she said, 'Oh, yes.'

"And, anyway, that is when she went on to tell me about
—she says 'Well, you know about the Tate murder.'

"I said, 'Yes.'

"She said, 'Well, we are the ones that did it.' "

On being challenged by Ronni Howard as to the truth of
her allegation Susan Atkins began relating details of the
crimes.

"One of the guys (victims) made a run for it," Miss
Atkins recalled, "and I struggled with him and slashed at
him. He grabbed me by the hair and he was too strong for
me and I called for help; everything was such a scramble,
happened so fast. They put a noose around this girl's and

RONNI HOWARD, " . . . REALLY BROKE THE CASE"

guy's necks and they were going to string this guy up to stab him and if he moved too much he would hang himself."

Susan Atkins was intent on convincing Ronni Howard that she was telling the truth. She told of how Sharon Tate pleaded for her unborn baby's life. The defendant said that she stabbed the movie star "in the chest," and that she wanted to take the baby with her. "We would have had to cut it out of her," Miss Atkins explained, but "I went back inside to write 'pig' on the door and when I dipped the towel in her blood I wanted to cut the baby out but everything happened so fast, so quick I just ran out of there."

Ronni Howard, by now half-believing what she was being told, asked Susan Atkins why she had done these things. "We wanted to shock the world," the accused murderess replied. "We were going to make it really gruesome, we were going to take their eyeballs out and squish them against the walls."

Another former inmate of Sybil Brand, Virginia Graham Castro, confirmed Ronni Howard's story by telling of her own conversations with Susan Atkins. In secret testimony Mrs. Castro told how Miss Atkins said she had blood on her hand and she looked at her hand and she took her hand and she put it up to her mouth and she said, "To taste death and yet give life: wow, what a trip!"

It was most trying for the courtroom observer, senses dulled by sixteen weeks of trial, to look at the actual physical figure of the young girl seated at the defense table and make himself believe her capable of such depravity. Yet, given the truth of the matter, one could wonder why the jury had not been permitted to hear the most damning of the testimony. The suggestion that the prejudicial value far outweighed the probative, that the jury would be more shocked than informed, seemed scarcely valid under the circumstances, The slayings *were* bizarre and, to use one of Irving Kanarek's favorite phrases, calling attention to "the state of mind" of one of the perpetrators appeared to be most germane to the proper presentation of the case. "Well, you can't do that," Vince Bugliosi told me later. "It might be considered to be prejudicial to the defendant's right to a fair trial."

It became increasingly difficult, assuming the nature of the crimes in Tate/La Bianca, to grapple with the legal reasoning processes. Paul Fitzgerald was certain that the defendants could not get a fair trial, yet here were his adversaries, the representatives of the very People who would supposedly deny him that right, attempting to water-down the enormity of the crime, to tailor it to the concepts of an organized, law-abiding society so that it would be more palatable to straight, i.e. non-depraved minds.

The temptation to "Let it all hang out," to let the jury see and hear *all* the pertinent testimony (Judge Older had ruled out the coroner's color photographs, for example) so that the crime might be properly fitted into its anti-social niche, can only be resisted, one supposes, on the assumption that uncivilized behavior does not call for a retaliatory, vengeful societal presence. One difference between the People and the Defense, it might be argued, is that the People must hold to an established set of values if only so that the Defense might have some secure base from which to lash out in their frustration.

Fitzgerald, for example, had come full circle. Gone were the eloquent philippics against the court-applied restrictions, against the free dissemination of information. Smiling less and less as the trial progressed, the *de facto* leader of the defense team finally abandoned the buddy-buddy pose so carefully cultivated with the media and, in a rare spontaneous outburst, moved that Judge Older expel reporters John Kendall of the *Los Angeles Times* and William Farr of the *Los Angeles Herald-Examiner* from the courtroom for filing stories about events that occurred in open court but that Fitzgerald felt were inimical to his cause.

The implied irresponsibility in the subsequently denied motions was especially puzzling in the case of Kendall, a meticulous, determinedly objective reporter: Farr, a man of great personal integrity, had several times aroused defense ire by breaking stories in the more free-wheeling *Examiner* that presented the defendants in a less than pleasing light. (One such story involved Family plans to murder a group of celebrities, including Frank Sinatra, Elizabeth Taylor and Richard Burton as part of their Helter Skelter plot. What was not reported was the intention to cut off Burton's penis and mail it to Miss Taylor's ex-husband, Eddie Fisher.)

The confrontation between Fitzgerald and the representatives of the two largest domestic daily newspapers to report the trial at length was symptomatic of the mental and emotional fatigue that infected almost everyone connected with Tate/La Bianca. The defendants, for example, after an appeal by all counsel to Judge Older, were permitted to return to open court without having to promise that they would be on their good behavior: once seated they appeared to have cast open defiance temporarily aside and sat docilely listening to testimony that was, in many ways, the most damning yet presented against Manson personally.

Deputy District Attorney Vincent Bugliosi too had his dreams of Helter Skelter, and he was now prepared to cause those dreams to become a reality. Very early in the case Bugliosi, after interviewing the next four witnesses he would call to the stand, had "bought" the Helter Skelter theory as Manson's motive for initiating both the Tate and La Bianca slayings. Despite the opposition of his colleagues in the district attorney's office who preferred to "Shoot from the hip," that is prosecute the case on its merits without involving a convoluted motive that might possibly boomerang if the jury failed to accept its plausibility, the prosecutor doggedly followed his own instincts and proceeded to put his case together. (These instincts had served him well in the past; of one hundred felony cases tried before a jury, he had lost only one.)

Ironically it was quite possible that Bugliosi believed in Helter Skelter more than did Manson! The defendant, who now appeared beardless with his long hair drawn back from his face and held in place behind his neck by a rubber band, had fashioned what many believed to be an ersatz philosophy involving his own deification and a twentieth century Armageddon assembled from bits and pieces of vaguely understood extracts from the Bible, the Beatles' songs and whatever other portions of disjointed thoughts he might have assimilated; Manson tested his theory on his Family and on straight people who might help him in his musical career; if his audience went for one section of his demented doctrine the wily ex-con emphasized that point without being capable of the rational thinking process required to put the whole thing together, if, indeed, any such potential entity ever existed.

Vincent Bugliosi supplied that organized, reasoning mind. The temperamental, at times tempestuous young prosecutor possessed just the right qualifications to tie in all of Charles Manson's pseudo-philosophical loose ends. One could easily imagine, watching Bugliosi present Manson with the finished, damning product in court, a Becket-like confrontation between them in which good and evil, presented by both in their own terms of reference, would be refreshingly redefined.

Gregg Jacobson, comedian Lou Costello's son-in-law and at one time a talent scout for record producer Terry Melcher, took the stand next as a prosecution witness. Jacobson stated that he believed in Charles Manson's potential as a musical performer. Manson's music, according to the witness, "Made a very unique, strong honest package."

Manson told Jacobson, through the course of many conversations, that he believed there was no such thing as right or wrong and that he personally could do no right or wrong.

Q: (By Bugliosi) He told you that it was not wrong to kill?

A: Yes.

Q: He told you that pain does not exist?

A: Yes.

Q: Did Mr. Manson ever say he was Jesus Christ?

KANAREK: Object. On the grounds that it is a violation of freedom of religion.

(Paul Fitzgerald laughs out loud)

OLDER: Overruled.

A: (By witness) Yes.

Manson then told Jacobson that a war between the blacks and whites was imminent and he called that war Helter Skelter. According to the witness, the defendant underwent a complete change of life-style. He began amassing material things, "Firearms, vehicles, money." He needed these things, he said, "to go to the desert because Helter Skelter was coming."

Jacobson, in some especially damaging testimony, told of seeing Manson after the Tate/La Bianca murders and that he, "Moved just like an animal in a cage. The electricity was coming out of him. His hair was on end and his eyes were wild. He was like a bobcat in a cage." Clearly, the prosecution implied, something of great moment had occurred during the intervening time that brought about, in the witness's words, a "Complete contradiction," in the accused murderer's personality.

Once in the desert, Manson told Jacobson, the Family were going to descend into a "Bottomless pit," by means of a special gold rope, and remain there until the blacks had decimated the whites. Finding themselves incapable of ruling the world, the victors would call upon the Family to take over while they (the blacks) reverted to their natural servant status. Irving Kanarek, on cross-examination, tried to ridicule the entire series of conversations but the witness was adamant in his belief that Charlie wasn't kidding at the time. Kanarek facetiously asked how much such a rope would cost and Jacobson replied, "I think it costs around three dollars a foot." (Such a special climber's rope does exist, a fact very much in keeping with the real-unreal dichotomy that characterized most of the testimony relating to Charles Manson.)

Terry Melcher, actress Doris Day's son and the state's 68th witness, took the stand to testify that, at Jacobson's insistence, he had gone to the Spahn Ranch (levelled, at the time of his testimony, by a Southern California forest fire) to listen to Charlie sing and play. Melcher, a nervous, stylishly "mod" young man who looked as though he hadn't touched a milk shake in years, was unimpressed by the defendant's musical ability but, "was impressed by the whole scene . . . by Charlie's strength and his obvious leadership."

Melcher was followed by Brooks Poston, a soft-spoken, introverted former Family devotee, given to long, reflective pauses on the stand. He said that he had many conversations with Manson during which the defendant had told him that he had to, "Get through your fear of death. Acid can take you through it." Poston, possessed of a retiring personality, said on direct examination that, at both the Spahn and Barker Ranches, he believed absolutely that Charles Manson was Jesus Christ and that he was completely subservient to his will. "I went," the witness told Bugliosi, "to the Barker Ranch because I felt I was supposed to go."

Manson, doodling on a yellow foolscap pad, looked up and remarked aloud: "Because no one else was dumb enough to take care of you." Judge Older admonished him to be quiet and the Family leader, obviously annoyed by the testimony, went back to his doodling.

Irving Kanarek tried to shake Poston's assertion that, "I wanted to be with Charlie because I thought he was Jesus Christ," but the very simplicity of the witness who projected a Mortimer Snerd syndrome, made his statements all the more believable. Kanarek, using a favorite ploy of his, asked Poston to recall *every* conversation he had with Manson, knowing from past experience that he was asking the impossible and hoping to impeach the witness's powers of recollection. Twenty-eight agonizing minutes later, with defense counsel, who had resumed his seat half-way through the recital, staring morosely at the table before him, Poston triumphantly concluded his painstaking recollective.

It was left to Ronald Hughes, however, to seek new levels of rhetoric when, heaving himself to his feet on cross-examination, he confronted a somewhat intimidated Brooks Poston with the following shouted questions:

Q: Did Mr. Manson ever tell you to go get a knife?

A: Yes.

Q: Did he ever ask you to get a change of clothes?

A: Well, I don't . . . wait a minute. Yes, he did.

Q: Did he ever tell you to *kill* anyone?

A: Yes.

Q: Who did he tell you to kill?

A: The sheriff of Shoshone.

Vincent Bugliosi, obviously delighted with defense counsel's interrogation, asked, on redirect, for a more detailed recollection. "He (Manson) said," the witness related, " 'If you're with us you'll take this knife, sneak into the sheriff's house in Shoshone and cut his throat.' "

The next witness, Paul Watkins, a self-possessed twenty year old now living with Poston in Shoshone, a small desert community about sixty-five miles as the buzzard flies from the Barker Ranch on the other side of Death Valley, told of his experiences recruiting young girls for Charles Manson. Charlie, according to Watkins, wanted him to get the girls and bring them to the Family leader before he (Watkins) "Had touched them. That," Watkins continued as Manson grinned approvingly, "was quite a trick," and not too much happened in the way of recruitment. However, one acolyte that Watkins picked up in San Jose, California, Leslie Van Houten, stayed on to the end as a member of the faithful.

Watkins, identifying the defendant's philosophy with a matter-of-fact "Death is Charlie's trip," said that Manson discussed Helter Skelter "constantly." The witness was important for another reason: he was the first ex-Family member to confirm Aaron Stovitz's acid theory expressed earlier in this book. Watkins, who admitted that he first dropped acid when he was sixteen, told of taking between 150 and 200 trips, "about thirty of them" in Charlie's company. "One day we was sittin' around on acid," the witness told Bugliosi, "and Charlie said that blackie never did anything on his own so somebody was going to have to show him how to start Helter Skelter."

Watkins testified on direct examination that Charlie, "Re-experienced dying on the cross during an acid trip," and Paul Fitzgerald cross-examined him about dying on the cross in general. Manson, according to the witness, asked him if he would consent to be crucified on a cross at the Fountain of the World, a minor religious sect with headquarters not far from the Spahn Ranch. Watkins allowed as how he was quite willing to be crucified if Charlie wanted it that way. Studiedly incredulous, Fitzgerald asked him how he planned to go about being crucified. "Well," Watkins replied cheerfully, "I didn't know how I was going to get up on that there cross." He turned in further explanation to Judge Older, "I just figured that Charlie would take care of it." His Honor, after a herculean attempt at maintaining the dignity of the court, broke up.

Irving Kanarek cross-examined about Watkin's LSD experiences with Manson. "We used to talk about how turned-on J.C. was," the witness told him.

Q: (By Kanarek) Did you celebrate Christmas as Mr. Manson's birthday?

A: No.

To which a wag in the press section responded, not too *sotto voce:* "Hell, everyone forgets a birthday now and then."

Chapter XXV

DAY ONE HUNDRED AND TWENTY

Almost everyone connected with Tate/La Bianca had, by now, taken their best shots at Irving Kanarek. The prosecution had shouted at him, his co-counsel had objected to his questions, the judge had cited him for contempt and his client had disowned him. Some members of the press were openly hostile. Stan Atkinson, reporting the trial for KNBC, NBC's Los Angeles television outlet, foiled in an attempt to interview a witness by Kanarek pressing a copy of the court's gag order on him, told the defense attorney to, "Go to hell." Kanarek stood up in court shortly after and complained that he had been "threatened" by the press. Judge Older told him to sit down.

Through it all Manson's attorney, seemingly unaffected by the indignities heaped upon his stocky frame, stood in open court, legs spread wide as though to support the extra burden, mouth slightly agape as he reacted in shocked surprise to the hostility displayed toward him, stolidly facing the next witness.

For there, cross-examining the people's witness, Irving

Kanarek was in his element. An ungrateful world may clobber him with personal invective and censure him for failing to observe the legal proprieties, but in that courtroom with a hostile witness on the stand Kanarek experienced, in the excitement of impending combat, a warm glow of fulfillment that was almost visual in its manifestation. This was his arena where, as we have seen, even the most determined, relaxed witnesses felt the pressure of his questioning. Witnesses, unlike judges, attorneys and reporters, did not talk back; they merely answered questions, no matter how obtuse their form or content. It was, from Kanarek's viewpoint, an ideal confrontation.

They did not answer back, that is, until Wednesday, October 21, when Irving Kanarek took Rudolph Altobelli under cross-examination.

The witness, owner of the Cielo Drive property and friend

RUDOLPH ALTOBELLI UNDER CROSS-EXAMINATION

and landlord to Sharon Tate and, before her, Terry Melcher, projected a suave toughness during his direct examination by Vincent Bugliosi. A manager of professional talent, Altobelli told of meeting Charles Manson in musician Dennis Wilson's home in the summer of 1968 and of listening to a tape recording of Manson's singing and guitar playing.

Altobelli testified that on March 23, 1969, Manson, apparently thinking that Melcher still lived at the Cielo Drive address then inhabited by Sharon Tate, had come to the guest house occupied by Altobelli, looking for the record producer. The defendant had announced, "I am Charles Manson," and Altobelli recognized him from their previous meeting.

The testimony was important, in that it definitely placed Manson at what was later to be the murder scene. Melcher, of course, had vacated the main house and Sharon Tate and Roman Polanski had moved in. Altobelli told Manson that Melcher did not live there and, after a brief conversation during which Manson asked to come back and talk with Altobelli, the defendant left.

Irving Kanarek had scarcely asked his first question when the courtroom observer sensed that this was going to be a somewhat different type of cross-examination. Manson's attorney apparently had tried, unsuccessfully, to gain access to the Cielo Drive residence to conduct an on-the-scene investigation. He asked Altobelli about it:

Q: Do you remember having a conversation with me when I tried to get into your fortress out there on Cielo Drive?

A: I remember your insinuation of threats.

Q: What were my insinuations and threats?

A: That "We will take care of you, Mr. Altobelli," "We

will see about you, Mr. Altobelli," "We will get the court up at your house and have the trial at your house, Mr. Altobelli." "I will see that the judge has the trial at your house."

The defense table joined the court in the general laughter as Kanarek, momentarily at a loss for words, stood frowning in concentration. Someone was tattling on him and he didn't like it one little bit.

Q: Is it your state of mind that it is a threat for a lawyer to want to view the premises where the events that we are talking about in this courtroom purportedly occurred? Do you consider that a threat?

A: I consider it a threat when I refused you, and I said, "If the court gives you permission and tells me that I have to let you on my premises," I said, "it would be perfectly okay." And you told me, "We will see about you, Mr. Altobelli."

Q: I stated that "I will see about you?"

A: Yes. "We will see about you." And you said, "We will get the trial up at your house." And I swear under oath that you said that to me.

The general courtroom atmosphere was now one of amused interest; how much more did the witness have to say and, most importantly, would the defense attorney give him an opportunity to say it? The spectators needn't have worried, as Kanarek continued his usual dogged pursuit of an elusive point.

Q: Do you respect our courts of law, Mr. Altobelli?

A: I think more than you do, Mr. Kanarek.

Q: You do? Would you tell the court and the jury what you told me about our courts of law when I spoke with you?

A: I probably said it was a circus with you in it. That is probably what I said to you.

Q: I see. Now, would you tell us what you said, if anything, concerning our courts of law?

A: You gave me — you told me that Charles Manson had never been up at my house. And I didn't tell you anything one way or the other, whether he was or he wasn't. You were trying to insinuate, to tell me, that he was not, and you wanted to talk to me for fifteen minutes and view the premises. And I told you, "No." I said, "If the court says that you should come up," I said, "It would be perfectly okay."

Another lawyer might have decided that, all things considered, this witness might well be excused, but old habits die hard and Manson's counsel plowed on, intimating that there was something sinister in the fact that Altobelli suggested that he, Kanarek, contact Altobelli's attorney.

Q: Did you tell me to speak with your lawyer concerning the possible visitation to the premises on Cielo Drive when I spoke with you on that Sunday afternoon, and did you not give me the name of a lawyer?

A: I would never do that because I make my own decisions who comes on my premises.

Q: You didn't suggest to me . . .

A: No. *You* told me his name. You said you were a friend of his.

Q: How would I know your lawyer's name if you hadn't told it to me?

A: *I* did not tell *you. You* told me, Mr. Kanarek. You said you had worked on a case with him once before. You said you were friends. And I called him up and I said, "If this is the kind of friends you have, I would change attorneys."

Clearly, it was not Irving Kanarek's day.

•

An interesting conversation took place in chambers that day because it effectively refutes the hyperbole regarding the lack of a fair trial with which defense counsel and the defendants, particularly Charles Manson, constantly regaled the public through press interviews and courtroom rhetoric.

A previous witness, Shakrokh Hatami, a professional photographer and friend of Sharon Tate's, had testified that a man who resembled a police photograph of Charles Manson had approached him at the Cielo Drive residence. Hatami did not know Manson and did not identify the visitor specifically.

The physical lay-out of the courtroom is such that the court clerk, Eugene Darrow, can overhear Manson in the lockup if the defendant speaks loudly. (Remember the four defendants were, at that time, outside the courtroom, listening to the testimony over loudspeakers.) On the basis of a reported conversation overheard by Mr. Darrow, Judge Older called the defendants and their attorneys into chambers.

OLDER: . . . the clerk overheard a conversation yesterday which indicated that Mr. Manson wanted to confront Mr. Hatami. Now, the state of the record at the present time so far as the jury is concerned is that Mr. Hatami has described the person that he saw at the Tate residence about March of 1969. He did not attempt to make any identification of that person. He did not say he resembles Mr. Manson. He did not say it was Mr. Manson.

He did not say it was anyone. He just described a person. Are we agreed on that?

FITZGERALD: Yes.

OLDER: Do you understand, Mr. Manson?

MANSON: I understand what you are saying.

OLDER: All right. Now I think the right to confront a witness is a fundamental right that you may exercise notwithstanding your counsel. However, you should recognize fully at this point that this witness has not identified you and has made no effort to identify you.

Now, if you confront this witness and he makes an identification, in effect you have brought in evidence against yourself that is not now before the jury. Do you understand that?

MANSON: (Incredulously) It is not before the jury now!

OLDER: No, there is nothing before the jury now. This man has not identified you or made an attempt to identify you.

After further discussion it was decided that Charles Manson would not confront Shahrokh Hatami. Comparisons are necessarily odious and especially so when Charles H. Older and Charles M. Manson are concerned; suffice it to say that equal protection under the law assumes a new meaning when one is privy to the jurist's remarkable objectivity in the face of extreme personal provocation. It might be noted, also, that no defense attorney leaked the details of that particular exchange to any member of the press.

Chapter XXVI

DAY ONE HUNDRED AND TWENTY-EIGHT

A brooding, Dostoevskian threat of impending death hovered in the shadows behind the players occupying stage center in Department 104 as the district attorney's office investigated an apparent murder attempt against the life of Barbara Hoyt. It was that way in Tate/LaBianca. The laughter-provoking antics of some of the courtroom principals tended to obscure both the underlying reality of four accused murderers on trial for their lives as well as the possibility that Family members still at liberty might well possess a capacity for irrational violence.

The suspected near homicide was but one of two significant events that, although they occurred outside of Judge Older's courtroom, bore a close relationship to the trial.

Shortly before she was called to testify, Miss Hoyt was visited by two Family members who strongly suggested that it would be in her best interests to absent herself from Los Angeles on the day that she was scheduled to take the stand. The eighteen year old girl accompanied the other two back to the Spahn Ranch (she had been living with her mother and father) and was either coerced or persuaded to believe that her testimony would do the defendants grievous harm.

Using a credit card traded by a male acquaintance in exchange for two female members' sexual services, Miss Hoyt and another Family girl flew to Honolulu, Hawaii. They put up at a luxurious hotel with the intention of finding an apartment for Barbara to live in until the prosecution had rested its case. Five family members, Katherine Shore, Lynne Fromme, Ruth Ann Morehouse, Steve Grogan and Dennis Rice, were subsequently indicted by the Grand Jury for assault with intent to commit murder.

Ruth Ann Morehouse, "Ouisch," was to fly back to the mainland to get expense money while Barbara waited in Hawaii. At the Honolulu airport the Family member suggested they share a hamburger while waiting for the plane. Barbara went to the restaurant cashier to pay for the purchase; when she returned the other girl handed her the hamburger, saying that it was time to board the plane and that they would be unable to share it. The departing girl remarked that, "It would sure be some trip if there was five thousand 'Mikes' (of LSD) on that," — indicating the hamburger — and Barbara agreed that it would.

The plane took off, Barbara ate the hamburger and boarded an airport bus back to the hotel.

She never made it.

She became violently sick to her stomach, got off the bus and began vomiting. Scarcely able to stand, she sought refuge down a side street and slumped, semi-conscious, to the ground. Fortunately she was discovered near the Dole pineapple factory by a social worker who chanced by. Barbara was rushed to the Queen's Medical Center where she was officially received in the Emergency Room on September 9, 1970 at 3:10 P.M. The admitting nurse's report is instructive:

"Patient was found by passer-by. Patient was lying on street at Iwelei Road on 'Acid trip.' Patient says to call Mr. Bugliosi and tell him 'I won't be able to testify today in the Sharon Tate case.' Pupils dilated. Very loose associations. Said she had 10 tabs of acid in a hamburger, that a 'friend' put it in without telling her. Says her 'trip' is fine. Inappropriate affect at times but mostly appropriate considering her euphoria."

Barbara was given Valium intravenously to help bring her down from her "High," and transferred to the psychiatric clinic for further observation. Dr. Alice P. Rieckelman, a staff psychiatrist, noted her condition.

Skin: Strongly acidic body odor.

Physical Impression: Normal, healthy female coming down from an LSD trip.

Psychiatric Impression: Recovering from acute psychotic hallucinating episode following use of LSD.

Dr. Rieckelman, who took a personal interest in Barbara, later observed, "If in fact, ten LSD pills were ingested by her, then accidental death from misperception of surroundings could easily occur."

There is little doubt that, at the time, the Queen's hospital staff were aware that they were dealing with a potentially violent situation. Barbara was forbidden phone, mail or visiting privileges and her clothes, including a pocket knife and a sewing kit, were taken away from her. Only on the arrival of her mother, Mrs. William Hoyt, from the mainland was she released.

The point, of course, is that Dr. Rieckelman's "accidental death" takes on an entirely new connotation if the LSD was administered with malicious intent.

It would seem most probable that Barbara Hoyt was poisoned by some external agent. Arsenic, for example, must be taken in small doses to be lethal. Its effect is cumulative. Taken in large doses it provokes a reaction very similar to that of Barbara Hoyt's. Whether or not a sufficiently large quantity of LSD, say five thousand micrograms or ten tabs, would be equally toxic is as yet unproven pharmacologically.

One thing seems certain, had it not been for the senseless attempt on Barbara Hoyt's life, the prosecution could well have been deprived of important testimony. Barbara's loyalty to the memory of her relationship to the Family vanished in that Honolulu hospital and she became a willing People's witness.

As the Honolulu investigation continued, Charles "Tex" Watson, finally extradited from Texas after months of delaying litigation, was committed to Atascadero State Hospital under the provisions of Section 1368 of the California Penal Code, as "presently insane."

Tex, by all accounts and confessions, accused leader of both the Tate and La Bianca murder excursions, had begun to exhibit the first symptoms of what would later be diagnosed by three court-appointed psychiatrists as "A severe psychotic depression, and/or schizophrenic reaction, catatonic type," when it seemed that his last appeal against extradition would be denied by Texas courts.

He sat in his Texas cell, according to one account, "staring vacantly into space, refusing to talk to anyone, with a transistor radio pressed to his ear."

Carl George, enterprising news reporter and commentator for CBS's Los Angeles television station KNXT, flew to Dallas, Texas with a camera and sound crew to drive to McKinney and accompany Watson on his extradition trip back to

Los Angeles. George got some footage but little else on the flight home. "Watson sat on the plane like a department store mannequin," the newscaster told me. "He was a cardboard man."

George, after scooping the entire Los Angeles press corps, (One rival station, waiting for the plane at L.A. International Airport with "live" cameras, very nearly interviewed him as a member of the official party), got only two "No comments" from Watson. The newsman was vaguely disturbed by the atmosphere in McKinney. "Sheriff Tom Montgomery (who had known Watson for most of the young man's life) was quite emotional about his leaving," he recalled. "I felt as though I was attending a funeral at which the deceased walked to the grave."

Although down to 120 from his normal 160 pounds, Watson was very much alive when he appeared in Judge George H. Dell's court in Los Angeles for his formal arraignment. Staring straight ahead, smiling for no apparent reason, the Family member refused to acknowledge the court's presence or reply to any questions. Thoughtful observers noted, however, that when Judge Dell, describing Watson for the record, remarked somewhat cynically that he "would not attempt to characterize the expression on his face," the twenty-four year old suspect broke into a broad smile quite different from his usual vacuous grins. The judge's remark obviously had penetrated; could the smile have been an involuntary relaxation of a carefully played game designed to suggest insanity?

The dramatic events of the next few weeks seemed to indicate that Watson was playing no game but was, in fact, losing his capacity for rational behavior. His weight dropped to 118 pounds as he refused to eat; Dr. Marcus Crahan, one of three original examining physchiatrists, issued a hurried supplemental report on October 29, describing the suspect's rapidly deteriorating condition.

" . . . It is felt necessary to render this supplemental report," Dr. Crahan informed Sam Bubrick, Watson's court-appointed attorney, "because Mr. Watson in the last week has become listless, flaccid, he makes no movements, his lips are pursed, it is impossible to spoon feed him, and we are starting to feed him by nasal tube. He is virtually vegetative, has to be shaved, bathed. His weight dropped from 118 pounds to 110 in one week.

"He is rapidly reverting to a fetal state, and is undergoing an involutional state which could be rapidly fatal."

Watson had also begun to masturbate compulsively, a symptom in keeping with the medical diagnosis and one which, coupled with his failure to ingest nourishment, was contributing to his physical deterioration. He was, in fact, manifesting all the symptoms of the *Ganser syndrome,* a condition named after its discoverer, German psychiatrist Sigbert Ganser, in which "A pattern of psychopathological behavior (is) found in prisoners and others who consciously seek to give misleading information regarding their mental state."

The syndrome, supposedly triggered by extreme apprehension, is endemic to prisoners on a penitentiary "Death Row." One of the most famous Ganser cases involved one Erwin M. (Machine Gun) Walker, sentenced to death at San Quentin in the fatal shooting of a peace officer. As Walker's time neared (that was back in the days when condemned prisoners were being executed) he became more and more withdrawn until, one morning, his guards found him loping around his cell on all fours, sniffing suspiciously at the bars. For all intents and purposes Machine Gun had become a dog. And you can't very well execute a dog for a man's crime.

Psychologists and psychiatrists gave him every conceivable test in an attempt to break down what they believed to be a conscious charade. Nothing worked. "Finally," J. Miller Leavy recalls, "they took him off the row and put him in the hospital. Immediately he began reverting to normal behavior. He got well, they put him back in the death house and down he went again on all fours." The veteran prosecutor chuckled. "It was no use. Every time they took him back to the hospital he stood up and became human. Back on death row he went dog again."

They never did execute Machine Gun. As this is written he is serving a life sentence and petitioning the courts for a new trial.

Recovery, once the immediate stress is removed, is a characteristic of Ganser's syndrome and Charles "Tex" Watson ran true to form. Transported to the Atascadero maximum security facility for the criminally insane, Tex began to perk up and take an interest in his surroundings. "Remember," Aaron Stovitz pointed out, "all he has to do is become capable of being aware that he is in a court of law and that proceedings are being taken against him. My guess would be that within ninety days the doctors at Atascadero will find him sufficiently competent to stand trial." Stovitz shrugged. "What happens after that, no one can say."

Despite the extreme symptoms in Tex Watson's case — Los Angeles jail deputies refused to be held responsible for his survival should he have been ordered into court before his commitment to Atascadero — there was a by no means unanimous agreement as to the legitimacy of his condition. Rumors that two psychiatrists regularly visited him in his McKinney, Texas cell, not to examine him but to coach him as to how to simulate Ganser's syndrome, persisted. A McKinney turnkey, in his cups, reportedly told Los Angeles investigators that he had personally witnessed such instruction.

The generally overlooked importance of Watson's condition in relation to Tate/La Bianca, aside from the obvious Family tie-in, was the fact that Manson, when apprised of his ex-follower's condition, offered "to straighten him out in twenty minutes," if granted the opportunity.

It would have been an interesting confrontation. Had Charlie been able to render Tex sane, a powerful argument could have been made by the People that the leader's hold on his subjects was even more binding than previously had been suggested. If, and this is more likely, Charlie failed to "heal" Tex but merely wanted to see how he was making out, it may well have been that an epidemic of Ganser's syndrome might have broken out in Department 104 among all four defendants. Charlie, all through his pretrial hearings had kept the schizophrenic option open by occasionally lapsing into extremely neurotic, if not pre-psychotic, behavior. He once jumped up in Judge Keene's court, for example, and threw copies of the United States and California constitutions into a wastebasket directly in front of the bench. He was in turn moody and extroverted, sullen and loquacious; it was as though he didn't know how to play it, what manner to adopt that would best extricate himself from his appalling predicament.

Now, with the prosecution calling Dianne Lake, its last important witness, Manson sparked rumors of an impending strategy switch. He appeared in court on Monday, November 2, clean shaven with his hair trimmed much shorter than normal and combed back on either side of his head in a ducktail style reminiscent of early Rory Calhoun. Was Charlie going "establishment" preparatory to taking the witness stand? Or

MANSON THROWS CONSTITUTION IN WASTEBASKET

was he attempting to look as "straight" as possible pending a rumored three girl defendant confession that would exonerate him completely?

Speculation as to defense tactics was rampant as Miss Lake, an apple-cheeked, pretty young lady of seventeen, told of a conversation with Leslie Van Houten at Willow Springs,

DIANNE LAKE, TURNED ON AT THIRTEEN

a minor oasis in the Panamint Range near Death Valley, when both were Family members. The defendant told Dianne that she had stabbed someone who was already dead, that she hadn't wanted to do it at first but that, once started, she found the experience not unpleasant. Leslie Van Houten also told the witness that she had wiped off some fingerprints and that the incident had occurred near Griffith Park, the area in which the La Biancas lived.

This was the first, direct testimony against Miss Van Houten other than that of Linda Kasabian. It was, by its very content, much more damaging; Ronald Hughes elected to cross-examine.

Dianne had testified that a man who had given Leslie a ride from the Griffith Park area the night of the La Bianca murders had returned to the Spahn Ranch to look for her and that the defendant had hidden under a sheet on a mattress in a back room. Hughes successfully established that Dianne was not certain of either the time that Leslie came back the morning after the killings or the time that the man came looking for her. Having impeached the witness's memory, if not her veracity, the bearded, corpulent defense attorney embarked on a line of questioning that was, at very least, puzzling to the layman.

Q: What did Leslie do when she came in that morning?

A: She sat down.

Q: What else was she doing, if anything?

A: She was counting money.

Q: Did she do anything else in that period besides count money?

A: She built a fire.

Q: Did she do anything else?

A: I believe she started burning things.

Q: Well, did you see Leslie put anything into that fire?

A: Yes.

Q: What?

A: A rope.

Q: Anything else?

A: Some credit cards.

Q: Did she have anything else with her?

A: Yes.

Q: What else did she have with her?

A: A purse.

Q: She burned that?

A: Yes.

Q: Did you ask Leslie about the money?

A: Yes.

Q: What did she say?

A: It wasn't stolen.

Q: She burnt a rope and a credit card, what else did she burn?

A: Her own clothes.

Q: Her own clothes?

A: Yes.

Q: Did they say Leslie on them?

A: No.

Q: How do you know they were Leslie's clothes?

A: She had them on.

Q: She took them off to burn them?

A: Yes.

It was difficult to comprehend Hughes's purpose in eliciting damaging information that had not been brought out on direct examination and, had he not inquired, probably would never have been heard by the jury. Had Hughes been a *prosecuting* attorney the interrogation would have made sense. (Bugliosi, in his redirect examination, delightedly took Dianne back through all of the above testimony to be certain that no juror had missed its significance.)

Another possibility suggested itself. If Ronald Hughes had been representing Charles Manson rather than Leslie Van Houten, his cross-examination was subject to an entirely different interpretation. Miss Van Houten, if Dianne Lake was to be believed, had strongly implicated herself in the La Bianca murders, something that no prosecution witness had been able to do. Even Linda Kasabian had been able to testify only to the fact that Leslie had accompanied Tex Watson and Patricia Krenwinkel up a driveway in the direction of the La Bianca house.

Now, under Hughes's persistent examination (he cross-examined no less than three times) Dianne Lake repeatedly was asked to describe the money that Leslie Van Houten was counting the morning after the La Bianca murders. A typical exchange between Hughes and Miss Lake:

Q: Were you given a sack of change?

A: No.

Q: But you helped count the sack of change, is that right?

A: Yes.

Q: And it had about eight dollars worth of change in it, is that correct?

A: Yes.

Hughes then would ask about the presence of foreign coins in the sack (Dianne recalled some Canadian nickels), going into great detail about the possible inclusion of gold pieces, Canadian silver dollars and the type of coins that a collector might have been expected to possess. For Leno La Bianca was a coin collector and it seemed that Hughes was trying to establish his client in possession of some part of just such a collection.

If a robbery motive for the La Bianca slayings could be established, a courtroom observer speculated, it would dilute the effect of Vincent Bugliosi's carefully developed Helter Skelter theory and, by implication, assign Charles Manson a lesser role in the murder conspiracy. Yet Hughes was Leslie Van Houten's attorney of record . . . but further speculation as to the motives of the defense principals only prompts disquieting, uncharitable thoughts. This is a murder trial, not a game. Attempting to ascertain another's state of mind, as Irving Kanarek repeatedly learned, is a thankless, often fruitless enterprise.

As a prosecution witness, Dianne Lake testified with something less than impeccable credentials. A hippie through her formative years, (her father, a scraggily bearded, fiftyish, would-be artist, had turned her on to LSD when she was thirteen), Dianne had joined the Family when she was fourteen and, by her own admission had participated willingly in the sexual and drug-oriented activities that such a membership suggested.

When she was picked up in the desert raids that netted the other Family members, Dianne was interrogated at some length by Inyo County Assistant District Attorney Buck Gibbons, then committed to Patton State Hospital because of a "drug induced acute schizophrenia." After several months at Patton she was released to the custody of Inyo County District Attorney's Investigator Jack M. Gardner, became his ward and, living as a member of his quite conventional family, rehabilitated herself. "I started out as a hippie," she told me, "and never knew any other life. This is a wonderful, new experience for me."

However, no matter how remarkable her adjustment to society, the fact that she lied first to Buck Gibbons and then to an Inyo County Grand Jury (this time under oath) was brought out by each of the defense attorneys in an attempt to impeach her present testimony. If, the defense suggested, this girl lied under oath once about her name, age and whereabouts at the time of the murders, why should the jury believe her now?

Yet, although she was no Linda Kasabian, Dianne Lake did project a strong sense of telling the truth when she spoke of her conversation with Leslie Van Houten. She had also heard Patricia Krenwinkel describe how the defendant had dragged Abigail Folger from the bedroom to the living room of the Tate residence on the night of those murders.

During Miss Lake's testimony, the defendants, as they did constantly throughout the trial, doodled on legal-sized yellow pads. Apparently Miss Krenwinkel left her pad behind during the noon recess and Sergeant Manuel Gutierrez, noting that the defendant had written "Healter Skelter" on her pad

LA BIANCA REFRIGERATOR

(the identical misspelling with which the words were written in blood on the La Bianca refrigerator), brought the pad to the prosecution's attention. Vincent Bugliosi requested that the court order Miss Krenwinkel to submit an exemplar of her printing and handwriting so that it might be compared by an expert or experts to the blood writing at the La Bianca home.

After Dianne Lake had completed her testimony Judge

Older asked Patricia Krenwinkel for the exemplars. "On the advice of my counsel (Paul Fitzgerald)," the defendant told the court, "I respectfully refuse." After this minor, though potentially damning exchange, Vincent Bugliosi rose and, at 4:29 P.M., on Monday, November 16, 1970, one hundred and forty-six days after the trial began, announced simply that, "The people of the State of California rest their case."

Judge Older set Thursday, November 19, as the day for the defense to begin presentation of its case, and adjourned the court.

Chapter XXVII

DAY ONE HUNDRED AND FIFTY-EIGHT

On Thursday, November 19, when Paul Fitzgerald, after a Section 1118 defense motion to dismiss all counts had been argued and denied, stood up and matter-of-factly informed the court that, "The defense rests," this writer experienced a feeling of profound relief.

It was an emotion shared, in my opinion, by the majority of those present in Department 104. Charles Manson would later state on the witness stand: "I would like to get this over with as soon as possible, and I'm sure everyone else would like to get it over with, too."

Two to three months had been cut from the trial length by the defense's decision to offer no defense. It was a decision that, although not without precedent, was considered highly unorthodox in a case of this seriousness and complexity. Usually such a position is taken when the defense feels that the People's case is so thin that no further action is needed or when the defense position is so weak that any further action will do more harm than good. In Tate/La Bianca it might be assumed that a third reason guided Fitzgerald, Shinn,

Kanarek and Hughes in their decision: a final attempt to get enough error into the record so that the jury's verdict would be reversed on appeal.

As soon as Fitzgerald had dropped his no-defense bombshell but before his co-counsel had time to complete their concurring statements, Patricia Krenwinkel, dressed as were the other girl defendants in a modishly styled pantsuit, stood up and told Judge Older that she wished to testify. Susan Atkins and Leslie Van Houten quickly joined in her request. The defense counsel just as quickly indicated at a conference at the bench that they were unalterably opposed to the three defendants testifying before a jury. Their clients would, it was strongly implied, confess to the crimes and hold Charlie innocent of complicity or blame. Vincent Bugliosi thought so too, and in a rare declaration of unanimity joined in opposing such testimony.

Judge Older called all defendants and counsel into his chambers for a private hearing and soon made it known how *he* felt about the situation.

OLDER: I want the record to be perfectly clear that I have analyzed the situation very carefully. I have had a chance to observe all of you in action now for a long time, and I am convinced that this little gambit, and I don't say that in a light manner, but I think it is a gambit, was a carefully planned maneuver, trial maneuver . . .

MANSON: You would not call it inadequate, would you?

OLDER: . . . to put the court on the horns of a dilemma. As I say, I don't think the court is on the horns of a dilemma. I think there is a way out. I think that way out may well entail the fact that at least three attorneys in this case failed miserably in their attorney duties un-

der the law as attorneys, but if that is the only way
out, I intend to take it.

But I want the record to be perfectly clear that the
way in which it happened this morning, and without any
warning, the four attorneys for the defendants stand
up in open court and announce that they rest, following which immediately three of the defendants rise in
unison and say that they want to testify.

It had all the earmarks of a very well rehearsed performance.

A performance, one suspects, produced, written and choreo-
graphed by Paul Fitzgerald.

Whatever its origins, the "gambit" did present Judge
Older with a number of problems. He left no doubt that he
believed that the defendants had an inalienable right to testify,
their counsels' advice notwithstanding. And he was faced
with, in the light of five trial months during which it appeared
frequently that all four defense counsel were representing
only Charles Manson, a nauseating display of for-the-record
self-righteousness. Lawyers for the three female defendants
let it be known that, if their clients were permitted to testify
in a manner that incriminated themselves, they would take no
part in the proceedings. Each refused to ask his client to take
the stand, even for the purpose of a narrative form of testimony. They wanted Older to call those girls to the stand so
that the record would be made. Ronald Hughes said it for
them all in chambers:

HUGHES: I believe that it is clear that this court has, on the
one hand, wanted the defendants to hurtle themselves
out the window, but has always demanded that someone
be there to push them as they go. Your Honor, I refuse
to take part in any proceedings where I am forced to

push a client out the window. I believe, your Honor — I
do not know the questions — but I believe that we
are going to have today judicial confessions before this
court, and I will refuse to take any part in helping the
court make those confessions or have these confessions
come forth.

I believe that the position that the court has put
counsel and put the defendants in absolutely interferes
with the attorney-client relationship. It interferes with
the Sixth Amendment right to effective counsel.

Vincent Bugliosi didn't want the three girls getting up and
letting Charlie off the hook. Yet Judge Older held firm to his
position that the defendants must "exercise their constitutional
right to testify," if they so chose. A further stumbling block
was provided by the Aranda-Bruton court decisions which
state that an accomplice may testify only to his or her own
involvement in a crime. How, both defense and prosecution
attorneys argued, could a female defendant testifying in
open court before a jury, be expected to carefully tailor her
story so as to not implicate any of the others?

Judge Older's solution was to ask that each defendant testify out of the hearing of the jury so that anything legally inadmissible could be expunged from their statements. It was,
his Honor admitted, a unique situation and one that, so far
as he knew, had no precedent in law. As he had predicted in
his first meeting with all counsel in chambers on June 15,
1970, Tate/La Bianca would "make law," but he was probably finding the gestation process more painful than he had
anticipated.

How could anyone successfully "expunge" an alleged murderess's testimony given on the stand in front of a jury? Fortunately or unfortunately — only time and the appellate pro-

cess would tell which — Judge Older never had to face up to that eventuality. Whether meeting the situation or, as it turned out, being relieved of that necessity was more desirable from a legal standpoint remains to be seen. Here is what happened when Judge Older, with no jury present, asked Susan Atkins if she would testify out of the jury's hearing:

ATKINS: I would respectfully refuse to do that. If it cannot be done in front of the jury first, there is no sense in doing it. It is for the jury. It is for the jury's ears. They are the ones that hold my life in their hands.

OLDER: Well, that is true. But this procedure would simply permit inadmissible matter to be deleted from your statement to be made to the jury. You don't have an absolute right to get up and say anything you like.

ATKINS: In effect, what you are telling me is that the truth, in certain respects to this case, can be inadmissible. I say anything and everything that has to do with this case must be spoken and must be spoken in the light of truth.

OLDER: And I am offering you that opportunity to testify.

ATKINS: Before the jury.

OLDER: Well, if you are not willing to testify outside of the presence of the jury, you may very well not have a right to testify at all. You are being offered that right.

Susan Atkins, Patricia Krenwinkel and Leslie Van Houten all refused to testify out of the presence of the jury. Despite the fact that Judge Older later pointedly offered each female defendant an opportunity to testify in front of the jury without any prior appearance on the stand and each refused, the impression was created *at the time* that testimony before the jury could only follow testimony away from it. Speculation as to what effect, if any, this might have had on the course of the trial became academic when Charles Manson, over Irving Kanarek's apoplectic objections, offered to testify then and there, without the jury present.

Manson was duly sworn. His rambling, disjointed one hour and twenty-minute narrative presented the listener with an accurate, though perhaps unintentional, delineation of a not unintelligent but dissociated individual attempting to grope his way through a maze of half-conceived ideas without bringing about his own destruction.

He was, by turn, humble: "I never went to school, so I never growed up in the respect to learn to read and write too good, so I have stayed in jail and I have stayed stupid, and I have stayed a child . . . " and arrogant: "If I could get angry at you I would try to kill every one of you. If that's guilt I accept it."

Most interestingly, he twice came close to laying all the murders off on the girl defendants, who he referred to as his "children."

"These children that come at you with knives," he said, "they are your children. You taught them. I didn't teach them. These children, everything they have done, they have done for love of their brother."

And again: "Yes, these children there were finding themselves. Whatever they did, if they did whatever they did, or whatever they did is up to them. They will have to explain to you that. I'm just explaining to you what I am explaining to you."

As to the murders: "I have killed no one and I have ordered no one to be killed. I don't place myself in the seat of judgment. I may have implied on several occasions that I may have been Jesus Christ, but I haven't decided yet who I am or what I am. I was given a name and a number and I was put in a cell, and I have lived in a cell with a name and a number.

"I don't know who I am.

"I am whoever you make me, but what you want is a fiend; you want a sadistic fiend because that is what you are."

About Linda Kasabian: "You set this woman up there to testify against me. And she tells you a sad story, how she has only taken every narcotic that it is possible to take. She has only stolen, lied, cheated and done everything you have got there in the book.

"But it is okay. She is telling the truth now. She is telling the truth now. She wouldn't have any ulterior motive like immunity for seven counts of murder. And then, comical as it may seem, you look at me and you say 'You threatened to kill the person if they snitch.'

"Well, that is the law where I am from. Where I am from, if you snitch, you leave yourself open to be killed."

Charlie's voice took on an edge as he talked about killing people who snitch. But with that same instinct that had guided him through many a lesser tight spot he sensed that he was coming on up-tight and got off the subject. He talked of Helter Skelter:

"Like Helter Skelter is a nightclub. Helter Skelter means confusion, literally. It doesn't mean any war with anyone. It doesn't mean that those people are going to kill other people. It only means what it means.

"Helter Skelter is confusion. Confusion is coming down fast. If you can't see the confusion coming around you fast, you can call it what you wish. It is not my conspiracy. It is not my music. I hear what it relates. It says, 'Rise,' it says, 'Kill.' Why blame it on me? I didn't write the music."

He addressed himself to the evidence. "The rope, the gun, the clothes. It was really convenient that Mr. Baggott (King Baggott, television cameraman) found those clothes. I imagine he got a little taste of money for that. I imagine that it just so happens, out of all that territory up there, Mulholland Drive, he just turned the corner and pop, he happens to see those clothes. Isn't that marvellous?

"And the bloodstains. Well they are not exactly bloodstains, they are Benzidine reaction." (A Benzidine test is a standard test to determine the presence of blood.) "What is a Benzidine reaction? We got into semantics. It is not a bloodstain. It is not a bloodstain. It is not a bloodstain. I call it a Benzidine reaction. That is somewhere in another courtroom."

About the Bottomless Pit: "I found a hole in the desert that goes down into a river that runs north underground, and I call it a Bottomless Pit because where could a river be going north underground?"

About truth: "Now the girls were talking about testifying. If the girls come up here to testify and they said anything good about me, you would have to reverse it and say that it was bad. You would have to say, 'Well, he put the girls up to saying that. He put the girls to not telling the truth.'

"Then you say the truth is as I am saying it, but then when it is gone, tomorrow it is gone, it changes, it's another day and it is a new truth, as it constantly moves thousands of miles an hour through space.

"Hippie cult leader, actually, hippie cult leader, that is your words. I am a dumb country boy who never grew up. I went to jail when I was eight years old and I got out when I was thirty-two. I have never adjusted to your free world. I am still that stupid, corn-picking country boy that I have always been.

"If you tend to compliment a contradiction about yourself, you can live in that confusion. To me it's all simple right here, right now, and each of us knew what we did, and I know what I did, and I know what I'm going to do, and what you do is up to you.

"You see, you can send me to the penitentiary; it's not a big thing. I've been there all my life anyway. What about your children, just a few, there is many, many more coming in the same direction; they are running in the streets and they are coming right at you."

●

The gospel according to Charles Manson. He refused to repeat it in front of the jury possibly because he feared Vincent Bugliosi's cross-examination. The girls, offered another opportunity by Judge Older to testify before the jury, declined. There was a sense of finality in the courtroom when Judge Older, after consultation with all counsel, set Monday, November 30, for discussion of jury instructions and the prosecution's opening argument. The defense would give its final argument and Vincent Bugliosi would have the last word with his final summation. The case would then go to the jury. It was all coming to an end, at last. "We'll have a verdict by Christmas," a reporter noted. "Nothing can happen now."

As happened so frequently in Tate/La Bianca, the reporter was wrong.

Chapter XXVIII

DAY ONE HUNDRED AND SIXTY-NINE

Ronald Hughes failed to appear in court today, Monday, November 30.

In any other murder trial this fact alone would have caused a minor sensation. Headlines would have announced the unprecedented, unexplained absence of an attorney defending a client on two counts of murder and one of conspiracy, and, at very least, a statewide search would have been instituted.

In Department 104 that morning the obese, balding attorney's absence was duly noted for the record, the judge and attorneys proceeded to informally discuss the court's forthcoming instructions to the jury, and the press, over a mid-morning cup of coffee, wondered what Ron was up to this time. Twice before, on October 30 Leslie Van Houten's attorney-of-record had caused a delay in the trial, once because of his arrest on an outstanding traffic warrant and the second time when his delapidated car was stopped on the freeway and declared unsafe by the California Highway Patrol. Judge Older had let it be known that a third delay would bring swift judicial retribution.

News that Hughes had spent the weekend in Sespe Hot Springs, a hippie-frequented natural spa set in rugged terrain in neighboring Ventura County, merely heightened everyone's sense of anticipation. A heavy rainfall had inundated much of Los Angeles and Ventura Counties during the preceding three days, isolating the Sespe area. A report that the defense attorney had refused transportation out of Sespe on Saturday and was last seen clad in shorts, tennis shoes and a T-shirt — a bush-league Falstaff sitting in a hot spring with rain pouring over him — confirmed the severity of his ultimate punishment.

Meantime, counsel and Judge Older thrashed out what special instructions would finally be given by the court to the jury before they began their deliberations as to the guilt or innocence of the defendants. Decisions would be made subject to ratification by the missing attorney on his return.

Jury instruction is an extremely important part of the trial process; it is here that appellate courts very often find grounds for reversal and it is here that "pure law," as opposed to court-room theatrics and trial tactics, holds sway. Largely over-looked by the public and lying in a limbo between the drama of the closing arguments and the anticipation of a verdict, jury instruction is treated with the utmost seriousness by all counsel and by the presiding judge. Quite often the defense lawyer's hope for successful appeal and the subsequent evaluation by his peers of the presiding jurist's performance are decided in chambers prior to the beginning of closing arguments.

Each side, defense and prosecution, brings in a set of in-structions, supported by legal precedent, that it would like the judge to read to the jury. The instructions may be given as requested, given as modified, refused or withdrawn. In addi-tion to deciding upon the appropriateness of counsels' pro-posed instructions, the court may issue some of its own "On court's motion," if it feels that the salient facts of the case have not been sufficiently delineated by either side. This is essentially a bargaining process with each side asking for the maximum and hoping for decisions favorable to their position by a jurist conscious of the weight both the jury and the appellate courts will give to his final determinations.

In Tate/La Bianca the selection of final instructions took on an added importance when Judge Older ruled that Linda Kasabian was an accomplice to all seven murders as a matter of law. This meant that her testimony must be corroborated to have legal status as evidence of guilt. The prosecution attempted to have the instructions so worded as to minimize the significance of the need for corroboration. The defense attempted to create confusion by noting the number of individual exceptions that had been made during the trial when the jury had been admonished to exclude one or more of the defendants from consideration in evidence relating to one or more of the crimes. For example: "This evidence shall apply to Charles Manson and only to Charles Manson;" or: "This testimony is not to be considered against defendant Leslie Van Houten."

As the debate over jury instruction carried over into the first week of December (no business was conducted in open court during this period), the inescapable fact that Ronald Hughes was missing began to dawn, with all its serious implications, on the minds of the trial participants. The most pressing problem, of course, involved the physical well-being of the defense attorney himself. A two hundred and fifty pound man simply does not disappear in an area that was accessible first to helicopter, then to intensive ground search. Yet Hughes did just that.

Driven to Sespe by a teen-age boy and his girl friend who

later took a polygraph test to substantiate their story, the attorney turned down their offer of a drive back to Los Angeles after it became apparent that the rain would cause a flood condition in the vicinity of the hot springs. (The boy and girl later had to abandon their panel truck in the mud and walk out some twenty miles even at that.)

Normally Hughes would go to Sespe, stay overnight then return next day, rarely, if ever, remaining at the springs longer than that. On this occasion, long after some stranded campers had been evacuated from the Los Padres National Forest and the Ventura County Sheriff's department had conducted extensive air and ground searches, no trace of the lawyer could be found. As the sheriff gradually shifted the emphasis from a search for a missing person to that of a "body search," Judge Older appointed Attorney Maxwell Keith as co-counsel for Leslie Van Houten and, over her vehement objections, set him to reading the pertinent parts of the more than eighteen thousand pages of trial transcript.

Denying defense motions for a mistrial and a severance of Leslie Van Houten's case, the jurist granted Keith a two week continuance to either prepare a final argument on behalf of Miss Van Houten or to reopen the defense case. Keith elected to argue after his motion for a mistrial had been denied and, on Monday, December 21, the Tate/La Bianca trial returned to open court.

What happened to Ronald Hughes? Speculation ran from the somewhat paranoic theory that the Family had caused his demise on the mistaken assumption that a mistrial for all defendants would result, to the more reasonable postulation that the portly Hughes, unsteady of gait even on firm, level flooring may have lost his balance and been struck by one or more of the large boulders that tumbled down the canyon walls in a torrent of mud and brush. Perhaps he sought shelter in a natural cave or crevice and, badly injured, succumbed from exposure in the below freezing nighttime temperatures that followed the heavy downpour.

Whatever his fate, as of this writing, early January, 1971, it is both an oversimplification and a truism to report that Ronald Hughes has disappeared. Barring his deliberately absenting himself, an almost unthinkable act that would result in his first trial being his last as a licensed California attorney, not to mention a lengthy jail term for his contempt of court, it can only be assumed that he suffered an accidental death. The bodies of seven Boy Scouts, lost in the same area a year previously, have yet to be recovered. Ronald Hughes, in presumed death as in life, continued to perplex and bemuse the participants in Tate/La Bianca.

Chapter XXIX

DAY ONE HUNDRED AND NINETY

The morning that Vincent Bugliosi was scheduled to begin his opening arguments the defendants began a series of disruptive actions that was to find them, the next day, barred from the courtroom for the duration of the guilt phase of the trial. Miss Van Houten rose to express her displeasure at Maxwell Keith's appointment. "I have nothing to do with Ronald Hughes's disappearance," she told Judge Older. "I'm beginning to wonder what *you* did with him." Amid expressions of agreement from the other defendants and demands that they be allowed to put on a defense, his honor told her to sit down.

"*You* stand up," Miss Van Houten shot back, escalating the confrontation.

Manson's "Hey, you look at me when I'm talking to you," to Judge Older resulted first in the Family leader, then his three disciples, being forcibly ejected from the courtroom. Miss Van Houten tarnished her little-girl image by turning on an approaching female bailiff, cursing at her and punching her on the shoulder.

After the unruly demonstrations were repeated that afternoon and again the next morning, Judge Older called a private meeting of counsel in chambers.

OLDER: It is perfectly clear that it was a calculated performance by the three of them (Manson had not returned to open court) to interrupt the proceedings, and they will not be brought back into this courtroom again during the remainder of the guilt phase of the trial.

With the four defendants listening out-of-court through a speaker system, Bugliosi began his argument of smilingly suggesting that the jurors take notes because, "Even I can't remember all the details of this trial." Then he proceeded, in three and a half fact-filled days, to disprove that disclaimer. The senior prosecutor, speaking for the most part with a quiet, even-toned projection, appeared to remember *everything* connected with the case. As he summarized the evidence and testimony, he recalled names, dates and exact times in an impressive display of meticulosity. Scarcely glancing at the thick sheaf of handwritten yellow foolscap notes on the lectern in front of him, the prosecutor projected a self-confidence that was made all the more credible by his ability to restructure out-of-sequence testimony into a comprehensive, logical recitation of the events leading up to the murders.

"Let's face it," Bugliosi told me one day after court, "I'm no genius. But I do my homework."

Indeed he did. In a calm, self-assured manner that contrasted sharply with three of the defense presentations to follow, the prosecutor reminded the jury that the vicarious liability rule of conspiracy made Charles Manson guilty of all seven murders and that either the defendants were guilty of "willful, deliberate, premeditated first degree murder or they are not guilty at all."

He interspersed his recital with sarcasm: (Referring to testimony that Patricia Krenwinkel had stated that her hands hurt because her knife kept hitting bone structure during the stabbings) "That little sweetheart. Her hands hurt. Poor little, sweet innocent Patricia Krenwinkel. Her hands hurt." And a try at humor: "Charlie Manson had a captive audience in the Family, just like I have now. You may not like what I'm saying but you've got to listen." He smiled and some of the jurors smiled back.

After noting that motive may be considered as evidence of guilt (much juror note-taking here) Bugliosi reiterated the defendants' alleged three main motives for the slayings.

First, "Charles Manson's hatred of human beings and his lust and passion for violent death." When Bugliosi said "lust and passion" the words took on an infinitely more shocking thrust; Bugliosi's "lust" was another man's "motherfucker," a word which, when he was called upon to repeat it while recapping testimony, he managed to break down into a reverently pronounced "mother" and a primly spelled out "f-u-c-k-e-r." The prosecutor had a great sense of theatre and was very much at home stage center in Department 104.

The second motive was, "Manson's extreme anti-establishment hatred."

And the third motive, the "Principal" motive, was Charlie's, and now Bugliosi's beloved Helter Skelter.

Helter Skelter, the prosecutor reminded the jury, was "Charlie's religion. It represented war between the black and the white man." After summarizing the Helter Skelter theory in some detail Bugliosi suggested that "Instead of Helter Skelter (written in blood at the La Bianca residence) the killers could have written 'Charles Manson.' "

Time and again the prosecutor hammered away at the concept of Manson as a Family leader. "Manson controlled their sex life," he said at one point, dropping his voice deferentially as he explained, "the most intimate of human experiences."

"Manson thought he would get off by not killing anyone," Bugliosi speculated. "Well," he said as his voice took on a menacing tone, "it's not that easy." He pursed his lips and turned to stare toward the door behind which the defendant paced his holding-cell, listening. "It's not that easy," the deputy district attorney repeated more loudly this time, carrying the word directly to the prisoner. "The law of conspiracy," he continued, "has trapped these murderers even as the killers trapped their victims."

"The fact," Bugliosi told the still attentive jury, "that Charles 'Tex' Watson's fingerprint established him at the scene is evidence against his co-conspirators." Several of the jurors began writing on their notepads and the prosecutor, as teacher would to pupil, repeated that sentence more slowly and with greater emphasis. Someone who knew Vincent Bugliosi quite well might speculate that he was saying to himself: *That's it. Get it all down. Get it all written down so it won't bounce out of your little rubber heads the first time you tilt your necks. That's a good jury.* But that is fantasy in its most pristine form and may be permitted only rarely, even to someone who has followed Tate/La Bianca these many months.

There was little doubt that Vincent Bugliosi considered Charles Manson his prime target, the callous manipulator of other peoples' lives. In response to testimony that Manson loved animals, the prosecutor drew an intriguing analogy. Adolf Hitler liked animals, too. "While his ovens were spitting out fire and operating at optimum capacity," Bugliosi declared, his voice rising in indignation, "at Auschwitz, Buchenwald, Treblinka and Belsen, the horrible smell of burning human flesh pervading the stark countryside for miles, Adolph Hitler, ensconced in the green, rarified, serene atmosphere of Berchtesgaden high in the Bavarian Alps, was very solicitous over the health of his dog Blondi and even, historians say, the health of the pets belonging to Hitler's sycophantic, slavish coterie of bootlickers, Goering, Goebbels and Himmler."

In case anyone didn't get the message, the prosecutor, visibly aroused now, threw cliché to the winds as he called for a first degree murder conviction for both the three female members of "A closely knit band of vagabond, mindless robots," and "The dictatorial master of a tribe of bootlicking slaves."

When Paul Fitzgerald, dark stress circles under his eyes, rose to make the first defense closing argument he wryly observed that the defendants were obviously now charged with, at most, second degree murder because "Mindless robots cannot be guilty of first degree murder," and the premeditation implicit in that charge.

There were many in the courtroom who felt that Fitzgerald should have stopped right there, thanked the jury and sat down. In the first place he was making argument for a nonexistent defense. In order to be at all effective he had to adopt what, for want of a better term, might be called a negative interrogatory posture aimed at tearing down the credibility of the prosecution's case. That credibility could not be challenged in a positive manner by citing the contradictory testimony of defense witnesses. It had to be attacked negatively using a "You don't really believe that?" approach.

A poised, prepared Fitzgerald might have taken some of the steam out of the prosecution's carefully documented case. The attorney who stood up and addressed the court on Monday, December 28 at 11:05 A.M. bore little resemblance to the public defender who dramatically resigned from that office to defend Patricia Krenwinkel privately. Fitzgerald who, even if he had nothing to say, could always be counted on to say it with eloquent grace, began awkwardly by apologizing, "Without my client's authorization," for her courtroom behavior. Worse, he began misstating the facts.

"You are," he told the jury, "the first jury in the history of California to be sequestered." That is simply not true. As far back as 1936 a jury was sequestered trying the so-called "White Flame" case in which Paul Wright was found not guilty of murder by reason of insanity. The most recent example, of course, was the Sirhan jury.

In attempting to impeach Linda Kasabian's testimony he spoke of "Five knives and a gun," in the car driven by Tex Watson, when the testimony referred to only three knives. He had Mrs. Kasabian throwing the gun from the car after the crimes were committed when there was no testimony to that supposed act. "Manson and two girls," according to the defense attorney, walked up the driveway to the La Bianca residence; the testimony clearly indicated that Manson alone went up that driveway.

These discrepancies, all through Fitzgerald's argument, may have been deliberate in order to confuse the jury or they may have been unintentional which, in a man of Fitzgerald's demonstrated intelligence, may be an even more damning supposition.

He lionized Harry S. Truman as his "Ideal juror," referred to the Tate residence as being located "Where the moguls of the entertainment industry resided," and equated Helter Skelter with Mau Mau terrorism, in a rambling, disjointed narrative that seemed to go nowhere and have little purpose.

"Maybe," the defense attorney said at one point, "a better lawyer than I could have examined these witnesses and made some sense out of what went on." It was the kind of self-defeating statement that the other Paul Fitzgerald would never have permitted himself.

The lanky, tousle-haired attorney, Sir Galahad unhorsed, resorted to dubious tactics in his scatter-gun search for something of substance on which to base his plea. He questioned, for example, why the jury had not been permitted to hear all of Diane Lake's conversation with Leslie Van Houten at Willow Springs, implying that the prosecution had deliberately omitted portions that might have been favorable to Patricia Krenwinkel. Fitzgerald knew full well that other portions of that damaging testimony had been excised as a matter of law because it pertained to events not admissible in the present trial.

Patricia Krenwinkel's attorney, conceding that "People are dead as the result of a criminal agency," continued to toss red herrings into the already polluted waters of the defense's case. He mentioned the eyeglasses found at the Tate home whose presence has never been explained, pointing out that they were found near two steamer trunks on which samples of Jay Sebring's blood had been located. Was it possible, he asked the jury, that Sebring died defending the trunks? Later he would have Sebring hung from a living room rafter when, in fact, it was Sharon Tate who, according to Coroner Noguchi, was briefly suspended. Why, the attorney wondered, hadn't the killers washed at the house instead of further on down the road? He was disturbed, too, by the inefficiency of the killers (as, allegedly, was Manson on August 9), speculating that bodies lying around both inside and outside of the house showed poor planning.

Describing Linda Kasabian as a "Hippie Ma Barker," Fitzgerald cautioned the jury to consider only the witnesses' answers to the attorney's questions, stressing that the answers and the manner in which they were given alone constituted pertinent information as to the guilt or innocence of the defendants. He ended his presentation with an emotional self reassurance that the jury, of which privately he was contemptuous, would do the right thing and acquit the defendants.

Daye Shinn argued for approximately one hour and a half. He was on too long.

Irving Kanarek began an incredible eight day exercise in legal circumlocution by stressing that the jury not be misled into listening only to the answers given by the prosecution witnesses. It was the *questions,* for the most part leading and suggestive, that the jury must view with the utmost suspicion. "They were on a 'Linda-Vince' relationship," the stocky attorney asserted, explaining the alleged close collaboration between the senior prosecutor and his most important witness.

"Whether I am a nice guy or not a nice guy is not important," Kanarek said at the beginning of his argument. There were those in the courtroom who might dispute that assumption. The behavior of the jury, for example, during his seemingly interminable discourse proved to be instructive. Their attention began wandering during the third day of Kanarek; they stared into space, looked at the spectators and otherwise seemed preoccupied with their own thoughts.

At times, however, the jurors' attention was sharply focused on Manson's attorney, in situations where he was not being a nice guy. "The fact," he said on one such occasion, "that Mr. Frykowski has passed away does not corroborate Linda Kasabian's testimony." He then held up an 8½ by 11 color print of Frykowski's battered and bloody corpse, stepped to the railing separating him from the jury and carefully displayed it so that every juror would have a good, close look. Some female jurors averted their eyes and the men appeared to be uncomfortable.

Kanarek began repeating the performance with every one of the People's exhibits portraying the seven murder victims. Remarking that since the prosecution had introduced the pictures for their shock value they might as well take a good look at them now, he held the pictures up and continued to show them even after it was obvious to most courtroom observers that the jury, who would have access to them later in any case, had had quite enough of that particular demonstration.

Why did Kanarek do it? What did he gain by thrusting ghastly photographs of stabbed, shot and beaten bodies in front of a jury sitting in judgment of his client? Was he satisfying some inner emotional need or did he hope that the jury would feel that Charles Manson could not possibly have been a party to such savagery?

But if not Charlie, who? Very simple: Tex Watson.

Far from being a robot sent out by Manson to lead a band of murderers, Watson, "A personable boy," was described by Kanarek as a leader, acting on his own. Referring to a much circulated picture of Watson that portrayed him as a grinning hippie idiot, the defense attorney said that anyone looking at that photograph could see that Mr. Watson had at least a couple of years of college. Vincent Bugliosi laughed out loud as did Paul Fitzgerald and many of the spectators. Kanarek solemnly observed that the prosecutor's laugh was another trick to throw the jury off the real issues; what he failed to note was that Judge Older, too, had smiled at the remark.

If the situation had not been so basically serious—if four people's lives had not been at stake—Kanarek, who described the trial proceedings as the equivalent of "The circus of ancient Rome," would have proved himself an able ringmaster.

Linda Kasabian, at the Tate murder scene, could have, according to Manson's counsel, saved Frykowski's life if she had chosen. "All she had to do," Kanarek pointed out, "was remonstrate with another person." She could say something like "Hey there, what's going on? Stop it." After positing the theory that Mrs. Kasabian went into the Tate house to protect her lover, Tex Watson, and that her whole story was a pack of lies destined to shield Watson, the attorney asked "Did you feel that Linda Kasabian had the credibility of Dr. Noguchi?"

While the listener was probing the relevance of that comparison, Kanarek attacked Mrs. Kasabian as a negligent mother who permitted her daughter Tanya to be cared for by the Family at the Spahn Ranch instead of having her remain with her father and Charles Melton, then living in a van. How could Linda Kasabian, Kanarek indignantly demanded, "take Tanya out of a home atmosphere, no matter what it was like in that truck?"

Holding up the La Bianca death pictures Kanarek asked: "Is President Nixon responsible for My Lai? Is Mr. Manson responsible for La Bianca?" He compared his client to Thomas Jefferson saying that both had the same "Qualities of dissent."

In between non sequiturs Kanarek began sprinkling-in a

number of references outside the scope of the evidence, to which Vincent Bugliosi increasingly objected. Judge Older, in addition to sustaining the prosecutor's objections, began taking Kanarek to task on his own. The defense attorney, for example, would slip in a statement that "The court will instruct the jury that the conspiracy took place during those two days." (Presumably August 9 and 10.) Judge Older admonished him: "That is not an accurate statement, Mr. Kanarek."

Each time Kanarek would frown his puzzlement at the strange behavior of his supposed oppressors, adjust his stance to accommodate the extra burden, and plow on. He appeared inpervious to any interruption, no matter how germane, from whatever source. Once, when he was making the point that Manson's conversation with Juan Flynn in which he said "Don't you know I'm the one responsible for all those killings," was not a confession to the Tate murders, his client spoke up loudly through a small slatted window in the lock-up. "It's not a confession to any murder," he shouted in the jury's hearing. "Why don't you sit down, Irving? You're just making things worse." Kanarek smiled and reached for a new set of pictures.

Always back to the pictures. This time the coroner's pictures of the victims' bodies. "Now we come to an unpleasant aspect," he said, introducing what John Kendall described in the *Los Angeles Times* as a "freshet of horror," into the courtroom. It began to appear that the relationship between Irving Kanarek and those photographs had taken on an identity all its own, far removed from the trial itself. He picked them up, shuffled through them, looked at them for many seconds, showed them to the jury with agonizing slowness and set them face up on the counsel table to await his future pleasure. The photographs intrigued the defense attorney; he seemed loathe to set them aside.

Kanarek's capacity for factual obfuscation was matched only by his ability to draw an inept analogy. Referring to the uncommunicative Tex Watson as the true commander of the murder band, Manson's attorney reminded the jury that "Salazar of Portugal" was also a silent, despotic leader.

"They put conspiracy in there to confuse you," Kanarek, referring to the prosecution, later told the jurors, then went on to suggest that the jury was too ignorant to grasp the nature of the charges against his client. After invoking the constitutional provision for freedom of religion on behalf of Manson, "A man can be a church inside his own body," Kanarek, after repeated private urging by Judge Older, neared the end of his argument. He reached, once again, for the pictures.

The "Various, and sundry and horrible wounds," the defense counsel declared, holding up the photographs, were the result of "a personal vendetta." Tex Watson, coming from Texas, "Didn't like black people," and, by inference, inflicted "personal wounds," on the bodies of six of the seven victims, presumably to start his own version of Helter Skelter. Kanarek kept referring to the stab wounds as "personal" wounds, "Made by the person himself or herself," as opposed, one supposes, to impersonal wounds made in a more objective manner. If one stayed with him long enough—the courtroom was virtually empty during the last three days of his argument —one grasped the idea that he was differentiating between Charles Manson ordering the killings and Tex Watson personally carrying out the murders. At least that was the only near-rational explanation that could be deduced from Irving Kanarek's marathon exercise in tedium when, doggedly implying that the best was yet to come, he reluctantly terminated his closing argument on Friday, January 8, 1971.

Chapter XXX

DAY TWO HUNDRED AND ELEVEN

A strange thing happened in Department 104 at ten o'clock on the morning of January 11, 1971: a defense attorney began making sense.

Maxwell Keith, forty-six year old court appointed replacement for Ronald Hughes, dressed in a double-breasted establishment gray pin-stripe, his head cocked at a perpetually quizzical cant, began arguing his client's case. Using the low-key, scholarly approach that is his courtroom trademark, Keith acknowledged that he was arguing from the transcript and that he had not been able personally to judge the demeanor of any of the prosecution witnesses. "We're all going to assume," he began, "for the sake of argument that what they (the prosecution) said is essentially true," then proceeded to subject the People's case to an unprecedented critical analysis.

First, he went after Linda Kasabian. "His honor is going to tell you," he said to the jury, "that you must view her testimony with distrust." After pointing out that drug abuse had a bearing on both her character and testimony — "We know

MAXWELL KEITH: AN IRONY OF CLASSIC DIMENSIONS

of people who have gone completely around the bend as a result of the use of drugs," Keith said that there was something "sinister" about the prosecution's star witness. He used the word conversationally, as though his discovery disturbed him and he would like the jury's help in straightening out the matter.

Mrs. Kasabian's sex life, drug habits and nomadic existence aside, Keith found "more sinister" the fact that she "always landed on her feet," that no matter in what difficult situation she found herself, Linda "always got what Linda wanted." Describing her as "Wily, opportunistic and frightfully resilient," a description that noticeably piqued the jury's interest, Keith noted that "There is no stronger human drive than self-preservation."

Recalling Mrs. Kasabian's description of herself as "A little girl lost in the forest," the soft-spoken, articulate attorney paraphrased Winston Churchill with a "Some forest!" observation that, while it seemed to sail serenely above the jurors' level of intellectual awareness, drew an appreciative smile from Judge Older. Clearly, here was a man to be reckoned with, an advocate capable of addressing himself to the issues at hand. One could only speculate with more than passing interest as to what might have happened if he had been able to confront Linda Kasabian in open court.

Keith then addressed himself to Diane Lake's testimony. "The case," he said, "against Leslie Van Houten is thread-thin. It rests solely on the testimony of this little girl." (Keith conveniently forgot that Juan Flynn, in addition to Linda Kasabian, had implicated his client.) He paused, looked at the jury, leaned over the lectern and announced gravely: "She's a *drug addict*. A mentally ill person." He shook his head and added, more in sorrow than in anger, "You're not in good shape when you're a schizophrenic.

"A conviction based on her testimony is indefensible," Keith continued, "it's frightening." Once again he leaned toward the jury, hesitated as though searching for words to convey the extent of his dismay. *"Don't do it,"* he said imploringly. He was very effective.

Vincent Bugliosi, "a brilliant man," according to Maxwell Keith, would not have propounded the "Mindless robot" theory if there had not been something to it; "He's always got something on his mind," Keith added, nodding toward the seated prosecutor. "Vincent Bugliosi isn't going to argue something to you that isn't reasonable, ladies and gentlemen," he added, impressing on the jury the supposed absence of premeditation.

It soon became clear that Keith, alone among the defense attorneys, was defending his client, not Charles Manson, and that he was attempting to shift the blame for the murders onto the Family leader's shoulders.

"Somebody," Keith supposed, "had the intent (to commit the murders.) Is it so far fetched," he asked, "to find that there was something in the nature of a transferred intent in this case?"

Keith left no doubt as to where he thought the intent had originated. "I think," he argued, "the relationship between Charles Manson and the Family . . . there's something mystical, occult about it. They all thought Manson was God."

After pointing out that Leslie Van Houten thought that she was going out on a creepy-crawly mission on the night of August 10, Keith told the jurors that they would be instructed by the court that any evidence of oral admissions or confessions ought to be viewed with caution, and that "most of us can't remember what was said yesterday and relate it with any accuracy." The defense attorney characterized first degree murder and conspiracy as "Thinking man's crimes," and told the jury that, on the basis of the prosecution's case, they must acquit Leslie Van Houten of the crimes with which she was charged.

"Max Keith did a good job," Vincent Bugliosi told me

later. "Despite the fact that he came into the case during its final stages he was by far the most effective of the four defense attorneys." The trial deputy does not offer praise lightly and his opinion was shared by most of the people present during the trial's closing arguments.

Which brings up an interesting point. Maxwell Keith, as a court appointed attorney, was the only defense lawyer being paid by the People of the State of California. The usual fee for services performed under similar circumstances is between $350 and $400 per day. In a case of the magnitude of Tate/La Bianca, it would not be unreasonable to assume that the fee was raised substantially by Judge Older, who has sole jurisdiction. (Since the fee is a private matter between judge and attorney, exact figures are very difficult to come by.)

We now are faced with an irony of classic dimensions. The only defense attorney to effectively represent his client *over that client's objections* is being paid something on the order of $500 per day by the very People who are prosecuting her for first degree murder! And Paul Fitzgerald can still step out into the corridor outside of Department 104, fling his arms wide in despair as he casts his eyes heavenward in supplication and declare: "There's just no way they can get a fair trial."

One can only conclude that the very presence in court of three of the defense attorneys assured the validity of Fitzgerald's assumption.

Vincent T. Bugliosi had been doing a slow burn during the defense's final arguments. In the case of the senior prosecutor the effect of the internal combustion is cumulative and, in this instance, was fueled in great part by Irving Kanarek. Bugliosi, essentially a moral individual, could not understand how Kanarek, in good faith, could imply that the prosecution had conspired with the witness to frame Charles Manson. The mere suggestion of such an impropriety enraged the youthful prosecutor and when Kanarek hammered it home in an increasingly personal attack, Bugliosi, in the jargon of the space age, appeared to be close to blast-off.

When Kanarek, in defiance of all legal propriety, began objecting to the prosecutor's summation, final ignition was achieved. "Am I," the prosecutor asked the jury, "suffering from an intellectual hernia or is Mr. Kanarek?"

Kanarek, according to Bugliosi, "wrote his own scenario of the case, based on Irving's fertile world of *Alice In Wonderland*. Either he has an allergy to the evidence or he was present at some other trial." Perhaps that was the answer, Bugliosi suggested; "Irving sneaked back every night when the courtroom was deserted and, with the goblins, put on his own trial using puppets and marionettes."

While Manson's attorney sat sideways to the defense table, his scowling face buried in the thick fingers of his cupped left hand, Bugliosi continued to apply the needle. He accused Kanarek of "demeaning the dignity of this trial. He told you," Bugliosi continued, obviously having difficulty containing himself, "that the Los Angeles Police Department, the Sheriff's Department and the District Attorney's office got together in in the backroom of Joe's place to frame Charles Manson."

Bugliosi turned to face Kanarek. "He accused the police and prosecution of subornation of perjury," Bugliosi declared, his voice rising to a shout. "There are absolutely no depths to which Irving Kanarek will not descend in order to assure an acquittal."

Maxwell Keith objected and Judge Older asked counsel to approach the bench. Irving Kanarek, out of the hearing of the jury and press, asked for a mistrial.

OLDER: The motion is denied. And I admonish you, Mr. Bugliosi, that is not a proper statement to make.

An interesting situation now presented itself. Earlier in Bugliosi's final summation Judge Older had called Kanarek to the bench on several occasions, the last time to warn him that one more outburst on his part would result in his being held in contempt of court. News of this ultimatum leaked to the press who watched with some fascination to see how long Irving could restrain himself under Bugliosi's blistering attack.

The prosecutor, after pointing out some twenty instances of factual error in Paul Fitzgerald's argument, dismissed the effectiveness of Patricia Krenwinkel's attorney-of-record: "Paul Fitzgerald," Bugliosi said, "made statements that just floated around lazily in the atmosphere." Fitzgerald, ungracious in defeat, took his shoes off and turned his back on the court in a boorish display that even some female press members, known to be partial to his cause, found difficult to justify.

Bugliosi defended his "Robot" statements by pointing out that he had used it as "an obvious figure of speech," meaning "Someone who is slavishly obedient to someone else." After complimenting Maxwell Keith on his argument the prosecutor pointed out that Keith "had raised such a smoke screen that Mayor Yorty should have called a smog alert." Then he once again directed his attention to Irving Kanarek and his client, Charles Manson.

"It was your client, Mr. Kanarek," Bugliosi loudly declared, turning and pointing to the chunky attorney, "who ordered the commission of these horrible murders." The Family, the prosecutor said, "were not suffering from any diminished mental capacity, they suffered from a diminished heart and a diminished soul.

"I'm not going to be like Mr. Kanarek and show you all these pictures," Bugliosi began, picking them up from the counsel table and approaching the jury. Reminding the jurors of the "Unbelievable orgy of murder," in which the accused had participated, the prosecutor, beginning with "Beautiful, honey-blonde Sharon Tate," flipped through the murder pictures of all seven victims.

Although he felt that "The ingestion of LSD has no relevance in this case," pointing out that its use "has crossed and penetrated all social and economic classes," Bugliosi, "because the sickening, nauseating issue" had been brought up by Irving Kanarek and the other attorneys with regard to Linda Kasabian, felt compelled to discuss it. Irving Kanarek jumped to his feet.

KANAREK: May we include marijuana, your honor?

OLDER: Sit down and refrain from such comments. You're interrupting the argument.

Judge Older then called counsel to the bench, found Irving Kanarek in contempt of court and, at a later brief hearing, fined him $100 or two days in the county jail. Kanarek paid the fine.

With Kanarek out of his system, Vincent Bugliosi spent one and a half days of closely reasoned, at times brilliant argument summarizing the entire case with a forcefulness and precision that left little doubt as to the guilt of the four defendants. The jury paid him the supreme compliment, after more than six months of trial, of taking notes. Recapitulating the circumstances surrounding each defendant's participation in each crime, the prosecutor bared the flimsiness of the defense position by an application of incisive logic to the trial evidence.

Throwing "A penetrating spotlight on those two dark nights of murder," the prosecutor gave the lie to Charles Manson's supposed indifference to death. "Charlie," Bugliosi said, "knows that a violent death and to be brutally murdered is the ultimate wrong. Or he wouldn't be fighting for his life now." Citing two hundred and thirty eight places in the trial transcript confirming Manson's "total dominance over the members of his Family," the deputy district attorney equated Manson's concept of love with that of murder.

"Charles Manson," Bugliosi told the jury, "is on trial because he is a cold blooded, diabolical murderer. As sure as I'm standing here, as sure as night follows day, these defendants are guilty." He paused, then carefully enunciating each name, he said "Sharon Tate, Abigail Folger, Jay Sebring, Voityck Frykowski, Steven Parent, Leno La Bianca, Rosemary La Bianca are not here in this courtroom now." Bugliosi paused again, moistened his lips then shouted the plea: *"But from their graves they cry out for justice!"*

With the reminder that "The People of the State of California are the plaintiffs in this case. I have every confidence that you will not let them down," at 11:50 on the morning of Friday, January 15, 1971, 215 days after the trial began, Vincent T. Bugliosi ended the prosecution's case.

After lunch Judge Older read his instructions to the jury, swore in the five male and three female bailiffs charged with the care of the jurors, then, at twenty minutes past three, said "You may now escort the jury to the jury room."

It should come as no surprise to followers of Tate/La Bianca that the jury, in their first official action, elected as their foreman, juror Herman C. Tubick, a mortician.

Chapter XXXI

A SUMMATION

How does a Charles Manson happen? What gives him this seemingly incredible dominance over members of a Family who meekly follow his most demanding emotional and physical dictates even, one supposes, through the death chamber door? True, his was a shoddy fiefdom, but the character of his subjects does not make him any less a lord or, as he would have it, a Christ-Devil incarnate.

How, for example, do we explain Leslie Van Houten? Ira Reiner, her first attorney, correctly assessing the relatively meager case against her, began pointedly divorcing her from the other defendants. But Reiner had to go. Charlie so ordered and Charlie also declared Ronald Hughes as Reiner's successor. Hughes, his lack of experience aside, adopted an attitude that could be interpreted as at best sycophantic and at worst duplicitous by emphasizing that his nominal client had common cause with Charles Manson, that her defense was, by implication, tied in with his own.

Leslie Van Houten sat in court and listened unprotestingly

as she was inextricably drawn into the murder conspiracy of the other three.

How do we explain Sandra Good who, all through the trial, daily squatted or knelt on the sidewalk at the corner of the Hall of Justice bounded by Temple and Broadway Streets waiting, as she told me, for her "Father," incarcerated nine stories above, to be set free?

Twenty-nine years old, with a *petite,* not unpretty face, Sandy was a charter Family member.

"I married Charlie in 1967," she explained. "We've been together ever since."

Presumably she uses the term "married" in a religious, acolyte-God relationship; she has become a bride of Christ, her father, although her filial duties by all accounts transcended the spiritual. Sandy, blue eyes and impish smile notwithstanding, seems to have attracted violence during her adult life. A male friend purporting to be her husband registered as Joel Dean Pugh at the Talgarth Hotel on Talgarth Road in London, England and was found dead in his room on December 3, 1969 under suspicious circumstances. According to London Metropolitan Police pathologist Richard Pearce, the death was violent. Pearce, in his confidential report, described the death scene:

"The body is thin, there are bruises on the forehead and left shin. There are incised wounds in either side of the neck (three inches long) parallel to the sterno-mastoid muscles and extending deeply to the muscle; the external jugular veins are divided. Trial cuts are present. There are a number of slashes of both wrists in the long axis of the forearms and a superficial cut across the front of the left elbow."

Despite the assertion that, "There was no wound not capable of being self-inflicted," it is known that a male mem-

ber of the Family was in England at that time and that Joel
Dean Pugh had been out of favor with Manson because of
the influence that Pugh exerted on Sandy.

Back in 1967 Sandy received a monthly allowance check
from her father, George Good. She regularly turned the money
over to Charlie but apparently it wasn't enough; Charlie
visited Good on at least three occasions and threatened violence if the allowance was not increased. Good, because of his
fear of the Family leader, reportedly changed his place of
residence and ceased all communication with his daughter.

Sandy, together with Gypsy (Katherine Share), and
Squeaky (Lynne Fromme), kept a constant vigil on the sidewalk outside of the Hall of Justice. Regularly renewing the
"X's" scratched on their foreheads in emulation of Charlie's
courtroom theatrics (although he had long since abandoned
that ploy), they slept at night in a panel truck loaned by a
Family sympathizer and parked on Temple Street.

The often asked question as to the nature of the Family
leader's influence over the women outside, an influence that
supposedly extends through prison walls and defies a waning
that might be expected because of the diminished personal
contact, is put, it seems to this writer, in the wrong context.
Repeated talks with the female members, in addition to the
tenacity implicit in their vigil and their frequent jail visits to
see Charlie, leave me with a strong impression that, with
Sandy and Gypsy especially, motivation is communicated in
at least equal measure from the women to Charlie.

Gypsy, for example, eight months pregnant as the trial
drew to a close when she and Squeaky were arrested for the
attempt on Barbara Hoyt's life, is a person of immense "cool."
On one law enforcement sweep through the high desert looking for fugitive Family member Bruce Davis (later arraigned

as a participant in both the Gary Hinman and "Shorty" Shea murders) members of the patrol were startled to see Gypsy lying on her back on a rock in the middle of nowhere, sunbathing in the nude. I was in the four-wheel drive vehicle that detached itself from the main column to question her. She leisurely pulled on a pair of jeans and a blouse as we approached and acted as spokeswoman for herself and two bearded men who sat near her.

There, in the wilds of the Panamint, a few miles from the Barker Ranch where Charlie was first arrested on the arson charge, the dark haired, twenty-nine year old Family member disdainfully parried the lawmen's questions. Other than the police vehicles there was no transportation in sight, no visible means of life support, no human habitation for miles around, yet Gypsy, as she pointed out, was doing nothing wrong; she strongly suggested that the police leave her alone; after a few superficial questions directed to her companions, they did.

Sometimes referred to as "the female Charlie," Gypsy, in the street sense, is "tough," as are Sandy and Squeaky. If a comparison could be made between the three female defendants in Tate/La Bianca and the three who squatted outside awaiting their deliverance, one might easily conclude that the dumb ones got caught. The knowledgeable observer could not easily imagine Sandy or Gypsy blindly following a "Tex" Watson on Charlie's orders. Significantly none of the kneeling three are known to have been involved in either the Tate or La Bianca slayings, although one of them is under suspicion in the "Shorty" Shea murder. The former Spahn Ranchhand, according to authorities, was tortured, killed and dismembered by Manson, Davis and Clem Tufts, the sleepy sentinel with the sawed-off shotgun captured during the Barker Ranch raid.

Manson, now under indictment for the Hinman and Shea

murders, in addition to the seven Tate/La Bianca slayings, would probably—allowing for pretrial motions and other delays—spend two more years in prison even if found innocent of all charges! He also has a "hold" on him by Inyo County where, Inyo District Attorney Frank Fowles told me, he would be "vigorously prosecuted" for Grand Theft, Auto; and Arson.

"Wisest men," the poet Milton wrote, "have erred, and by bad women been deceived." It is arguable that Charles Manson, demonstrably not the wisest of men, may be finding himself the victim of his own proselytism. He began something with the Family that took on a momentum all its own; it rode past him carrying him with it into the bottomless pit of first degree murder. Members of his Family went out to do his bidding and when they returned, blood-spattered and triumphant, the leader may well have known that fate, in the guise of the emotional and mental "Confusion" that he later alluded to so frequently, had inflicted the ultimate indignity on his sparse, pale frame: it had made him an accused murderer.

His rambling statement under oath while it may, at one time, have impressed the review board of the Federal Reformatory at Chillicothe, Ohio where he was imprisoned, did not seem effective in the Superior Court of the County of Los Angeles. Manson did manage to spread his "Confusion," however unwittingly, to the very jury who were trying him and, indirectly, to now senior prosecutor Vincent Bugliosi.

Reports that the jury were getting on one another's nerves, while hardly surprising in view of their long sequestration, took on an ominous note when it became known that one juror was keeping a detailed journal supposedly with a view to publishing it later in book form and that, to help his story

INSIDE THE JURY ROOM

along, he was deliberately provoking his co-jurors into mutually recriminatory situations.

"A fellow like that," Bugliosi told me after his closing argument, "could hang the jury (cast the one dissenting vote to make the mandatory unanimous verdict impossible) just to further his own ends." It was difficult, I suggested, to comprehend that kind of irresponsibility assuming, of course, that the juror thought the defendants guilty.

"You never know," the youthful prosecutor, as pale as the prisoners after more than eight months in the courtroom, replied. "The man who hung the Tate/La Bianca jury might feel that he had a great selling point. He may have something going against society and this is his great chance to get even."

Bugliosi shook his head worriedly. "It's kind of an unbelievable situation, isn't it?" He answered his own question as he stared at the walls of his fifth floor office. "After all this time . . . unbelievable."

While waiting for the jury to bring in a verdict I drove thirty-five miles to Santa Ana, California to ask Dr. Everett L. Shostrom, whose Institute of Therapeutic Psychology is

AARON STOVITZ: "MANSON HAS FORFEITED HIS RIGHT TO LIVE."

rapidly gaining an international reputation as the focal point of a uniquely avant garde school of Dependence-Independence-Interdependence theory of psychotherapy, his opinion of Manson's relationship to the Family.

"I think it's obvious," Dr. Shostrom told me, "that Charles Manson initiated a manipulative technique over the female members especially, and that it culminated in an interdependence that probably still exists."

I asked him if it might be a case of his theory being proven in a freak situation gone bad.

"Undoubtedly Manson responded to the need for interdependence," the Institute founder agreed. "It was both his strength and the instrument of his ultimate downfall."

Aaron Stovitz put it more simply back at the Hall of Justice with the jury still out.

"Manson is evil," the Head of Trials said simply. "Anyone who could set up the Hinman thing, know and reflect on what he had done, then set up the Tate murders, once again know and reflect on what he had done, then arrange the La Bianca killings is inherently evil. He has forfeited his right to life. He should die. And, unless justice is blinder than even I sometimes believe, he will die."

●

On Monday, January 25, in the emotion-charged atmosphere of a crowded Department 104, the prisoners took their places at the defense table after being excluded from the courtroom for over a month. The girls wore their prison issue shapeless blue denim dresses but Manson, his beard neatly

trimmed down to a vandyke for the occasion, sported mod
trousers and a white shirt with a kerchief tied at his throat.

Judge Older asked foreman Herman C. Tubick if the jury,
which had deliberated seven days, had reached a verdict.
Tubick, a gray-haired man of sober mien, replied that they
had; Older then asked him to give "All the forms to the bailiff." Tubick did so, the bailiff handed them up to the judge
who proceeded, count by count, to read through the twenty-
seven sheets of paper. Although the process took less than

THE VERDICT

three minutes, time appeared to stretch interminably in the hushed courtroom.

Finally Judge Older, after neatly squaring the small sheaf of paper, passed it to clerk Eugene Darrow, ordering him, with what appeared to be a trace of resignation in his voice, to "Read the verdicts."

Darrow, visibly nervous, began with "We the jury in the above suited action (killing of Abigail Folger) find the defendant, Charles Manson guilty of the crime of murder in violation of penal code 187, a felony, and we further find it to be murder of the first degree," and continued to read through each charge against each defendant in each of the murders. The conclusions were exactly the same except in the counts of conspiracy to commit murder: the four defendants were found guilty but no degree was fixed.

Among the defendants only Leslie Van Houten, brushing her fingers repeatedly across her face before the verdicts were read, betrayed any suggestion of apprehension; after the reading she quickly joined her co-conspirators in a seemingly blasé, even flighty reaction to hearing herself convicted of the crimes.

Manson alone spoke out after the clerk had finished, saying to the jury: "You're all guilty"; and to the judge: "We weren't allowed to put on a defense, old man. And you won't forget it for a long time."

Irving Kanarek rose to make a motion and Judge Older, after curtly telling him to put it in writing, adjourned the court. It was all over.

INDEX

Acid, 8-10, 29, 72, 122, 177,
195, 208, 346, 354, 356,
366
See Narcotics, LSD,
Marijuana
Adamson, Allan, 317
Altobelli, Rudolph, 110, 358-
62
Atascadero State Hospital,
367, 370
Atkins, Susan Denice, 3, 5, 32,
37, 43, 48, 53, 92-93, 126,
143, 149, 154, 156, 158-
60, 169-73, 194, 305, 318-
21, 330, 336-37, 345-48,
382, 385
Atkinson, Stan, 357

Ballarat, 15, 20
Barker Ranch, 4, 11, 15, 24-
26, 33, 316, 354-55
Beatles, The, 141, 351
Beausoleil, Gayle, 12
Beausoleil, Robert (Cupid),
12-13, 36, 43, 64, 95-97,
138, 346

Bottomless Pit, 353, 388
Branden, Nathaniel, 105-6,
176
Bubrick, Sam, 369
Bugliosi, Vincent, 8, 39, 41,
46-48, 65, 73-75, 91-93,
95-100, 109-17, 127-75,
202-3, 255, 303-5, 323-31,
335-36, 349-52, 379, 382,
395-99, 405, 411-16,
421-23
Burton, Richard, 350
Busch, Joseph P., 322

Caballero, Richard, 43
California Highway Patrol, 4,
15-16, 25, 37, 390
Castro, Virginia Graham, 348
Chapman, Winnifred, 108-10,
306
Costello, Lou, 352
Cox, Dennis, 12-13
Crahan, Marcus, 368-69
Crockett, Paul, 15
Crowley, Father, 18
Curtis, Merril H., 36-37

Darrow, Eugene, 362
Davis, Bruce, 346, 419
Day, Doris, 353
Death Valley, 1, 4, 12-13, 16,
    18-19, 21, 24, 355
De Carlo, Danny, 160, 326-30
Dell, George H., 44-45, 55-57
    368

Emmer, June, 123, 213-26

Family, The, 4, 7, 16, 21-27,
    30-35, 55-88, 87, 101-2,
    116, 129-30, 138-39, 146,
    187-88, 190, 194, 267-68,
    279-81, 318, 327, 336,
    364-65, 367, 371, 377
Farr, William, 350
Fisher, Eddie, 350
Fitzgerald, Paul, 5-9, 40-44,
    75-76, 110, 115-16, 118-
    24, 150, 176-89, 201-12,
    229-30, 278, 298-99, 302,
    318-19, 335, 339-40, 343-
    44, 349, 380-83, 399-402,
    414
Flynn, John Lee, (Juan Flynn)
    22, 330-33, 336-37
Folger, Abigail Anne, 3, 93,
    102, 149, 306, 308, 378
Fowles, Frank H., 16, 22-23,
    34, 36, 421
Fromme, Lynne, (Squeaky),
    194, 268-69, 365, 419
Frykowski, Voityk, 93, 102,
    149, 264, 306-8

Ganser Syndrome, 369-71
Gardner, Jack M., 378
Garretson, William, 102, 110-
    16
George, Carl, 367-68
Gibbons, Buck, 16, 36, 378

Goler Wash, 15-16, 22, 24
Good, Sandy, (Sandra Pugh),
    33, 57, 171, 194-95, 418-19
Grogan, Stephen Dennis (Clem
    Tufts) 21-23, 27, 160, 163,
    169-73, 297-98, 337, 365
Guenther, Charles C., 36
Gutierrez, Manuel, 344, 378

Hailey, Ray, 4, 18, 20-21, 23,
    25
Hatami, Shakrokh, 362-63
Hathcock, Dick, 295
Helter Skelter, 97-98, 142-43,
    350-56, 377-78, 387, 397
Hinman, Gary, 13, 36, 43, 64,
    95, 346
Hippies, 2, 12-13, 15-17, 32,
    35-37, 100-1, 216, 378,
    388, 391
Hitler, Adolf, 399
Hollopeter, Charles, 31-32, 65
Howard, Ronni, 345-48
Hoyt, Barbara, 330-33, 364-
    67
Hughes, Ronald, 39, 83-89,
    99, 110, 130-31, 143-44,
    153-54, 166-68, 228, 236,
    278-84, 290-96, 304, 334,
    354-55, 374-77, 383-84,
    390-91, 393-94
Hurlbut, Howard M., 16, 20-
    21, 24

Independence, Calif., 2, 32-37
Institute of Therapeutic
    Psychology, 423
Inyo County, 2, 29, 33, 37
    District Attorney of, 16
    Sheriff of, 12-13, 34, 36-37

Jacobson, Gregg, 352-53
Jesus Christ, 6, 15, 19, 24, 29,
  95, 99, 104, 210, 282, 354,
  386
Jury,
  Choosing of, 60-61
  Dissension in, 421-22
  Foreman of, 416
  Instruction of, 391-92
  Voir dire of, 247-49

Kanarek, Irving, 40, 47-48,
  62-72, 92-93, 98, 117-18,
  123-29, 132-37, 141, 150-
  52, 160-62, 168, 212-18,
  233-34, 241-52, 255-67,
  270-73, 284, 286-90, 300-
  4, 306-7, 323, 328-29, 331-
  32, 335-36, 353-54, 356-
  62, 402-7, 412-15
Kasabian, Linda, 3, 87, 95,
  117-89, 201-11, 231-33,
  241-44, 255-67, 270-73,
  278-84, 287-88, 290-92,
  297-300, 304, 337,387,
  392, 400, 408-10
Katsuyama, David A., 308
Katz, Burton, 64
Kay, Stephen R., 39, 323
Keene, William B., 5, 40-44,
  51-52, 56, 371
Keith, Maxwell, 39, 393, 408-
  12, 414
Kendall, John, 350, 405
Krenwinkel, Patricia, 3, 5, 9,
  27, 34, 41, 43, 48, 92-93,
  99, 109, 143, 149-50, 154,
  156, 163, 165-66, 169, 174,
  337, 378-80, 382, 397

La Bianca, Leno, 5, 92-93, 98,
  166, 308, 374, 377
Lake, Dianne, 371-79, 410
Leavy, J. Miller, 89, 326, 370

London Metropolitan Police,
  418
Los Angeles County, 51
  District Attorney of, 301,
    322
  Jail, 250, 254, 275-76, 319
  Public Defender, 40, 43-44,
    58, 84
  Sheriff of, 13, 36-37, 100,
    146, 276, 413
  Superior Court, 3, 41, 120
Los Angeles Herald-Examiner,
  52, 350
Los Angeles Police Depart-
  ment, 4-5, 16, 19, 37, 82,
  166, 267, 306, 316, 413
Los Angeles Times, 238,
  244-46, 350, 405
LSD, 7-8, 11, 27, 32-33, 118,
  121, 173-74, 176-83, 195-
  99, 215, 271, 356, 365-67,
  377, 415
  See Narcotics, Acid,
    Marijuana
Lutesinger, Kathleen, 24

McCaron, Margaret, 319
Maddox, Kathleen, 314
Manson, Charles, 3-6, 8-11,
  16, 19-27, 29-34, 55-58,
  66-67, 71-72, 91-92, 97-99,
  103-7, 133-35, 140-47,
  162-66, 169-74, 190-92,
  198-99, 229-30, 239-41,
  244-45, 273-77, 314-18,
  327-33, 330-33, 336-38,
  351-56, 361-63, 386-89,
  395, 396-98, 417-24
Marijuana, (Pot), (Grass),
  29, 290, 306, 316, 318, 415
  See Narcotics, LSD, Acid
Melcher, Terry, 353, 359
Miner, John, 64
Montgomery, Tom, 368

Morehouse, Ruth, (Ouisch), 330, 365
Musich, Donald A., 39, 323
Myers Ranch, 4, 26

Narcotics, 306, 316
  abuse of, 11
  and hallucinations, 181-83, 232
  use of, 4, 253, 291
  See Acid, LSD, Marijuana
Neiswender, Mary, 256
Nixon, Richard M., 229-31, 237-39, 245-49, 254, 289, 404
Noguchi, Thomas T., 306-14, 318
Nolan, Bijou, 44

Older, Charles H., 39, 41, 45, 47-54, 61-62, 67-72, 75, 83-84, 89-93, 100, 106-9, 115-18, 122-31, 136-37, 141, 143-44, 152-54, 161-62, 167-68, 198-99, 203, 212-13, 226, 240-41, 257, 270-74, 279, 286-90, 292-96, 302-4, 319-21, 335-44, 349-50, 356, 362-63, 382-85, 391-93, 395-96, 405, 412, 413-15
Olmstead, S., 318

Panamint Range, 1-2, 12-20, 24, 29, 33, 35, 38, 373, 420
Parent, Steven, 93, 113, 258
Parent, Wilfred E., 102-3
Patton State Hospital, 378
Pigs, (Piggies), 26, 98, 170, 328, 336-37, 348
Polanski, Roman, 359
Poston, Brooks, 15, 317, 354-55

Powell, Richard, 1, 12-13, 15-16
President of the United States (See *Nixon, Richard M.*)
Pugh, Joel Dean, 418-19
Pursell, James, 15-16, 24

Queen's Medical Center, 365

Reagan, Ronald, 20, 45
Reiner, Ira K., 39, 53-54, 77-83, 86-87, 278-79
Rice, Dennis, 365
Rieckelman, Alice P., 366

Schram, Stephanie, 26
Scientology, Church of, 318
Sebring, Jay, 93, 100-2, 308-13, 401
Seldeen, Richard, 300
Sespe Hot Springs, 391, 392
Sex, 10, 15, 135, 176, 188-89, 201, 204, 268-69, 317, 328, 378
  and love, 279, 284
  and orgasm, 346
  intercourse, 132-33, 205, 262-63
  oral, 331-33
  orgy, 136, 138, 140, 297
Share, Katherine, (Gypsy), 128, 182-83, 186, 203, 365, 419-20
Shea, "Shorty", 317, 420
Shinn, Daye, 39, 53, 89, 106-7, 162, 227, 231-35, 249-52, 320, 335, 402
Shoshone
  Sheriff of, 355
Shostrom, Everett L., 423-24
Sinatra, Frank, 350

Spahn Ranch, 17, 22, 128-29, 141, 143, 155, 159, 173-74, 187, 203, 255-56, 268, 297, 305, 317-18, 330, 334, 336-37, 353, 365, 374

Stovitz, Aaron, 3-5, 9-11, 31, 41, 44, 47, 50-51, 54-58, 67, 70-71, 76-77, 82-84, 88-89, 99, 102-3, 144, 151, 160, 192-93, 218-26, 233, 242-44, 270, 286-90, 294-95, 321-26, 336, 356, 370, 424

Swartz, John Harold, Jr., 305

Sybil Brand Institute, 345-48

Tate, Paul J., 100-2

Tate, Sharon, 5, 93, 100, 216, 257, 259-60, 308-14, 330, 346-48, 359

Taylor, Elizabeth, 350

Truman, Harry S., 401

Ungerleider, Thomas, 195-98, 200

Van Houten, Leslie, 48, 52-53, 82-87, 92-93, 163-66, 278, 337, 355, 372-78, 382, 393, 395, 417

Voir dire, 30, 51, 56, 62, 66-67, 75, 78, 83, 92, 248

Walker, Erwin M. (Machine Gun), 369-70

Watkins, Paul, 317, 355-56

Watson, Charles "Tex", 3, 93, 109, 143, 147-49, 156, 158-61, 163, 165, 169, 205, 207, 255, 262, 297-98, 307, 337, 367-71, 398, 403-6

Weber, Rudolf, 305

Weiss, Steven, 335

Whiteley, Paul J., 36, 340

Willow Springs, 24, 372

Winnedumah Hotel, 35

Younger, Evelle J., 3, 41, 65-66, 79, 239, 289